Muckraking
and
Objectivity

Recent Titles in
Contributions to the Study of Mass Media and Communications

Muckraking and Objectivity

JOURNALISM'S COLLIDING TRADITIONS

Robert Miraldi

Contributions to the Study of Mass Media and Communications, Number 18

Bernard K. Johnpoll, Series Editor

GREENWOOD PRESS
New York • Westport, Connecticut • London

Annenberg Reserve
PN
4888
E8
m57
1990

Library of Congress Cataloging-in-Publication Data

Miraldi, Robert.
  Muckraking and objectivity : journalism's colliding traditions /
Robert Miraldi.
    p. cm. — (Contributions to the study of mass media and
communications, ISSN 0732–4456 ; no. 18)
  Includes bibliographical references.
  ISBN 0–313–27298–0 (lib. bdg. : alk. paper)
  1. Journalistic ethics—United States.   2. Journalism—United
States—Objectivity.   3. Journalism—United States—Political
aspects.   I. Title.   II. Series.
PN4888.E8M57   1990
174'.9097—dc20   89–26010

British Library Cataloguing in Publication Data is available.

Library of Congress Catalog Card Number: 89–26010
ISBN: 0–313–27298–0
ISSN: 0732–4456

First published in 1990

Greenwood Press, Inc.
88 Post Road West, Westport, Connecticut 06881

Printed in the United States of America

The paper used in this book complies with the
Permanent Paper Standard issued by the National
Information Standards Organization (Z39.48–1984).

10 9 8 7 6 5 4 3 2

Copyright Acknowledgment

The author wishes to thank the Association for Education in Journalism and Mass
Communication for allowing the publication of Chapter 5, parts of which appeared
previously in Robert Miraldi, "Objectivity and the New Muckraking: John L. Hess and
the Nursing Home Scandal," *Journalism Monographs* No. 115 in August 1989.

To Edith and Rocco, who cared,
and Mary Beth, who listened.

Contents

Acknowledgments

Various colleagues, professional acquaintances, librarians, and friends helped in the research and writing of this book. I am especially grateful to the library staff at the Sojourner Truth Library at the State University of New York's College at New Paltz, as well as librarians at Ulster Community College, New York University, Columbia University, and Vassar College. Among the people who aided my work, with encouragement, discussion, readings, and recommendations, were Howard Good, Joseph McKerns, Richard Katims, Carley Bogarad, Paul Baker, Martin Gottlieb, Gerald Sorin, and Lawrence Miraldi. Many thanks to Lynn Wheeler for her careful copyediting of the manuscript. I am particularly grateful to the College at New Paltz and its academic vice president, William W. Vasse, for two research grants I was awarded. My two children, Sara Elspeth and Robert Michael, made me laugh throughout the writing of this book. And my wife, Mary Beth Pfeiffer, not only read manuscripts and listened to me as I endlessly worked through every idea, but made me believe that I could complete this work and that it was indeed important.

1

The Muckrakers: Heroes or Villains?

Tappen Park consists of a small rectangular greensward, a cluster of benches, and maybe two dozen old oak trees which surround brick paths. It is barely a park. Located in the heart of a commercial district known as Stapleton, a small town on the eastern shore of Staten Island, one of New York City's five boroughs, this village has thrived ever since Cornelius Vanderbilt plied his ferryboat off its deep port. A park visitor today can see tankers entering New York Harbor, cruising under the Verrazano-Narrows Bridge. The Manhattan skyline beckons to the north.

In the mid-1960s Tappen Park became known to locals as "Needle Park" because Staten Island's North Shore heroin addicts would gather under the trees, drink wine, hang out, shoot dope, and scare off the shoppers who had come to the quaint stores that surround the park. Since all of New York City was in the grip of a heroin epidemic, Tappen Park was not alone as a drug haven. Many of the city's parks had become shooting galleries, and clinics to treat drug addicts were just in their infancy.

One of the treatments for heroin that became popular—and controversial—was methadone, a synthetic opiate that stops the craving for heroin and allows addicts to lead normal lives. An addict could go to a publicly funded clinic, take methadone, and be back off to work, home, or play. Sometimes an addict could take home a few days' supply of methadone and not have to return daily to the clinic. Thousands of heroin addicts were maintained on methadone, while thousands more waited for admission. Sometimes the ex-heroin addict, street-smart from years of surviving on guile and burglaries, would sell his methadone on the street. Since methadone also gets people high, there was a thriving black market. "Methadone diversion" was how drug treatment officials and police described the illegal street sales that began to take place.[1]

In 1979 I was a newspaper reporter. A source had told me that in Stapleton, where a clinic had been operating in an old storefront, methadone was being diverted from clients to junkies, right on the street, in broad daylight. For years merchants and shoppers had complained that this methadone clinic was inappropriately located in a business district. If methadone diversion was taking place, it confirmed their complaint and certainly was a public scandal—and an important news story. I wanted to document the illegal sales.

Sales were brisk on Friday morning, I was told by my source, for that was when many clients received their take-home, weekend supply of methadone. It was a spring day when I went to Stapleton to investigate. I wore an old dungaree jacket, faded blue jean pants, a red flannel shirt, and old work boots. I needed a shave and my hair, which was long, made me look not unlike many of those who were huddling that day at the park. I was 29 years old, young enough to fit in.

With the tabloid New York *Daily News* tucked under my arm, I sat on a ledge near the entrance to the methadone clinic, a short distance from a New York City off-track betting parlor. Pedestrian traffic on the sidewalk was heavy, with bettors and clinic clients mingling. After ten minutes, a man in his mid-twenties approached me. He was a thin, wiry, black man, his eyes deep set and hollow. A few of his front teeth were missing. He nodded and asked me a question: "You looking to score?" "Might be," I replied. "I got it," he said. "Methadone . . . get you good and high for the day . . . twenty bucks." "Right here?" I asked. "Drink it now," he said, "cause I gotta return the bottle."

The man was a methadone user; he had just gotten his supply, and he was offering to sell it to me. I was taken aback, by the swiftness of the offer and about how casual he was. I didn't know how to respond. Frankly, I was scared. I hadn't talked to my editors about what to do if I was offered a buy; I had barely briefed my editors, in fact, about what I was setting out to do. I hadn't thought out this venture very carefully.

If I make a buy, I break the law. But I also get a marvelous story, the smoking gun, so to speak, the documentation of the diversion that everyone suspected was taking place. The story would embarrass the police and get the clinic into trouble. Possibly the story would force the clinic to stop take-home methadone, arguably a bad policy to begin with, but it would also anger the local community to the point where it might force the clinic to close, leaving nearly 600 clients with no local treatment.

Methadone, after all, had taken hundreds of people off the streets and made them productive, or, at the very least, stopped them from stealing to get their dope money. I wasn't sure I wanted to be responsible for the closing of the clinic, but I was sure that the police were not doing their job and needed to be embarrassed. I was equally sure that the diversion was out of hand and not being dealt with by the clinic.

Where were the cops anyway, I wondered, while all this dealing was taking place? Maybe they were watching the whole encounter. Maybe the seller was a cop setting me up. A stroll down the street later showed me that the police were indeed in the area, with a foot patrol on the other side of the park and police vehicles riding past the clinic at regular intervals. But they were in the wrong place for sure. Claude Brown once wrote in his book on growing up in Harlem, *Manchild in the Promised Land*, that he could never understand how, as an eight-year-old, he knew all the dope dealers and prostitutes while the police, a few yards away, didn't. It was that way in Stapleton. I found the diversion in 10 minutes, but the police never found it.

As thoughts about the police and about whether I should break the law raced through my head, the man with the methadone pressed me for an answer. I looked closely at his face and an eerie feeling came to me. I knew this man. Many years before, more than a decade earlier, I had been in a Staten Island junior high school with him. We were in a school play together. I recalled that backstage one afternoon, showing off for some girls, we had wrestled on a mat, trying to show who was strongest. He wrestled me down that day and then let me up with a gentle smile. Now, a decade later, he knew me only as a potential customer. What a great angle, I thought, a personal element to the story: two kids take different paths, and wind up on the street facing each other over a drug deal. But could I name him? Wouldn't that get him arrested? Would he be thrown out of the methadone program? Might he retaliate? Moreover, what about my employer, the *Staten Island Advance*, a daily newspaper, circulation 80,000, owned by the Newhouse family? Its management preferred to follow the unwritten code of "objective" journalism: reporters stayed out of the stories they covered, even if their past intertwined with the facts they gathered. There would be time to answer—although not resolve—all those questions.

For now, I had to decide on the buy. I asked more questions, but then I declined the offer, more out of fear than journalistic principle. The dealer just shrugged and moved down the fence. To my shock again, he walked up to another young man seated nearby and made the same offer. I overheard it and observed the purchase being made. The young man drank the methadone while I watched. The two of them walked off, both high. I had a story right there, but I stayed around for more. I moved to the front of the clinic, where I sat on a bench in Tappen Park and watched more clients come and go. Some entered cars and drove off. Other clients sought buyers, however, and I was able to document more sales. I ran around a corner to follow one man as he met a woman on a street corner after making a telephone call. I watched him hand over a bottle, and I watched again as the contents were swallowed, quickly, furtively. By late morning I had watched methadone diversion take place three times on a sunny spring morning near "Needle Park."

By late afternoon, I was ready to begin putting together a story. Over the next few days, I located a congressional study of nationwide patterns of diversion. I called drug treatment and law enforcement officials and then made the most difficult telephone call, to the officials who ran the treatment center in Stapleton. They were chagrined, although not surprised. They asked if I had names, and I said I had one but would decline to reveal it to them or the public. If I had, they said, the person would be asked to leave the clinic. They were cooperative and wanted to know how I would write the story. I wanted to know how I would write the story. It was sensational stuff, but the question for me as reporter was how to capture the essence of what had happened, the drama of the diversion, how casual it all was, and yet not miss the larger context of the importance of methadone as a treatment option, albeit one with serious flaws. I felt an obligation to the community on one hand—this was a bad place for a clinic—and to the clients on the other— they needed treatment somewhere, in their community. I felt obligated to be balanced.

I quickly rejected the idea of becoming personally involved in the story by telling my connection to the dealer. My own reluctance to emerge as a focal point of the story killed that idea, especially since my personal connection was less important than the lawbreaking. Perhaps that was foolish because, when I eventually did write the story, I chose the journalistic cliche of referring to myself on a few occasions as "the man" who was offered drugs. This was not much different from the approach of Gay Talese, who, when he tried to get an interview with Joe DiMaggio, wrote of "the man" to whom DiMaggio would not speak. Talese was the man. Dan Wakefield once scoffed at his early years as a journalist when he, too, hid between the lines of his stories. When he emerged finally, he said he felt like "the Shadow unmasked."[2] I was not Gay Talese or Dan Wakefield, of course. I was a small-town reporter, somewhat ambitious for a headline, with some sort of a social conscience—but I was also struggling with questions that were not easily answered, or even being asked in the newsroom. What was my function as a reporter? What should be the role of the journalist in this tale of methadone diversion?

I chose to rake muck.

My story began with a re-creation of the drug deal offer, with dialogue, and some colorful touches about how the participants looked, dressed, and acted. I re-created three incidents of methadone diversion, somewhat like a short story unfolding. Then, using interviews, statistics, and government documents, I discussed the problem of diversion in New York City. My story was an exposé of an illegal activity, and it received page one coverage. As a result of the story, the community was angered, the police were embarrassed and also angered, and the clinic was under considerable pressure to close, although it never did. The story provoked a heated debate in the Staten Island community, one that had been simmering for quite some time, and it set off anew a discussion on whether taxpayer money should be used to maintain addicts on a drug. The police for their part stepped up surveillance, and the clinic cut back on take-home supplies and began to patrol the area in front of its storefront.[3]

This was not muckraking journalism on the scale of Carl Bernstein and Bob Woodward of Watergate fame, but the story makes for a useful beginning, an introduction to a genre of American journalism that has been constructive and controversial ever since a band of turn-of-the-century reporters used exposé to attack the flaws in American society. Ninety years ago, muckraking journalists pried into the dark corners of America, both spurred by and spurring a reform movement that was coming to dominate the nation. Writing in mass circulation magazines during America's Progressive Era, roughly between the years 1900 and 1915, the muckrakers exposed many of the excesses of industrialism, the thievery of politics, and the squalid injustices of urban life. The reporters emerged from the scandals as legendary figures who are still studied by grammar school students as the champions of the people. The muckrakers included well-known journalists such as Upton Sinclair, Ida Tarbell, and Lincoln Steffens. Others, such as David Graham Phillips, Will Irwin, and Samuel Hopkins Adams, are less well known today, but they had considerable fame during the Progressive Era. The magazines for which they wrote became household favorites: *McClure's, Collier's, Cosmopolitan, Everybody's.* The combined circulation of the magazines that muckraked approached three million a month. By the time the muckrakers had finished their decade or so of writing, they had helped create, for better or worse, a new regulatory state and an enlarged centralized government, and they had permanently added a new weapon to the journalist's story arsenal: the muckraking exposé.[4]

When this generation of Progressive Era muckrakers gradually moved from journalism to other forms of writing and other ways to earn a living, the flame of muckraking flickered. Some of the nation's small liberal magazines continued to champion reform causes and to expose misdeeds in political and corporate corners, but muckraking became more the exception for many years than the rule.[5] Not until waves of rebellion engulfed America in the 1960s, much like in the Progressive Era, did an accepted muckraking movement reappear. The more formal title, investigative reporter, replaced muckraker. The reporter again became a well-known public figure, a modern American hero. Names such as I. F. Stone, Jack Anderson, Fred Cook, and Seymour Hersh and magazines such as *Ramparts*, *The Nation*, *Life*, and *Mother Jones* became associated with an enterprising, adversarial form of journalism—muckraking.[6]

CLASHING POINTS OF VIEW

From Lincoln Steffens in 1902 to Seymour Hersh in 1988, muckraking journalism has been on the cutting edge of liberalism and reform, a force with both wonderful potential and clear limits.[7] I have chosen to write about muckraking journalism to raise basic questions about the role and function of the press in America. What should a journalist be? This issue of purpose is paramount because all else in reporting is determined by it. Once I understand my purpose as a reporter, once I know what my role should be, I can decide what to write about, whom to write for, and what perspective or point of view to adopt. The point of view of muckraking—an adversarial, critical, outsider's point of view—is far afield from the one that dominates the conventional press, that is, the objective or neutral point of view. The objective journalist is simply an observer, who follows events, describes occurrences, provides background, and perhaps lends some perspective. But he or she is not an active partner in shaping events or re-forming society. The journalist is a neutral technician who, in the end, is an unknowing partner in the maintenance of the status quo. The activist tradition of muckraking collides head-on with objectivity, this fetish of the mainstream press.

The ideal of reporter objectivity or neutrality is called into question and challenged by muckraking. When a reporter crusades on an issue and decides to expose what he sees as evil, he sheds the objective stance. Implicit in the decision to write an exposé is the belief that something needs to be done about the problem or person being exposed. This, of course, represents a point of view. To muckrake in order to effect change brings to a head the larger questions of purpose and effect. Is the reporter the mere recorder of events as they occur, the objective observer, or is the journalist supposed to take a stand, to become passionately involved in a form of engage journalism? Once involved, can the press seriously claim to be independent since its crusading may align it with forces of the political left or right? Or is the true purpose of the press to be a constant adversary and critic, a muckraking activist who keeps both masses and elites in pursuit of a better society? This book explores those questions with muckraking—past and present—as its focus.

When I wrote my story on methadone diversion, I didn't think of myself as a muckraker. Neither, of course, did Lincoln Steffens, the prototypical muckraking writer. "I did not intend to be a muckraker; I did not know I was one till President Roosevelt picked the name," Steffens said in his autobiography. Ray Stannard Baker, one of the premier muckrakers who wrote about railroads and race relations, said that soon after Roosevelt made a 1906 speech attacking these muckraking writers who looked down not up, a friend greeted him with, "Hello, Muckraker." He wasn't sure he liked the title, nor did Ida Tarbell, a careful and exhaustive researcher who wrote about John D. Rockerfeller's corrupt oil empire. "To my chagrin," she wrote, "I found myself included in a new school, that of muckraking." Muckraking, they quickly realized, had a clear double meaning as a term of approbation—"a name of odium," Baker said—and a badge of honor.[8]

I learned this lesson while working as a reporter during the 1970s. I went once to visit the owner of a nursing home. A scandal in New York State had involved many nursing homes in criminal investigations, and I was speaking with this owner about allegations concerning his 500-bed facility which was located not far from Tappen Park. I kept asking questions about the owner's payroll and he kept changing the topic. Finally, he stood up, took off his black suit jacket, and rolled up his sleeve. On his arm there was a stamp from the days when the owner had been in a Nazi concentration camp. It had nothing to do with my questions or the criminal investigation. He said, "See. Persecution." I was silent. He rolled down the sleeve and turned away, muttering: "You don't care. You're nothing but a muck raker." He said it as two words, not one, and his tone made it clear that he was not giving a compliment. I felt as if he had just cursed me. A few years later, while I was writing stories about the Willowbrook State School, a scandal-ridden, state-run institution on Staten Island where 6,000 retarded people had lived in appalling conditions, I called a source, an attorney, to ask questions. "What," she asked me, "is your little muckraking mind up to today?" My little muckraking mind! I didn't know if I had been insulted. Was it a compliment to be called a muckraker?

In the months before I left daily journalism to become a journalism professor, I received an award from a parents group for reporting on the Willowbrook State School. They gave me a plaque at a luncheon at which the person introducing me, a New York City television reporter, called me "a respected muckraking reporter." Finally, the title was a compliment, and the parents applauded. But applause for muckrakers often comes late and sometimes not at all. My reporting on Willowbrook regularly brought complaints from workers and parents that I focused on the bad things, that I was dragging down the morale of the workers, and that I was a destructive force. This was the same complaint that

Vice President Spiro Agnew made in 1969 about the American media: Why only the bad news?[9] When Edward R. Murrow dramatically exposed the plight of migrant farm workers in America in 1960, a case I discuss in detail in chapter 4, he was venomously attacked as a propagandist and liar. The messenger was blamed for the message. Things have not changed since Theodore Roosevelt's description of the turn-of-the-century investigative reporters which was meant to disparage their reporting. The muckrakers were letting in the sewer gas as well as the light, Roosevelt charged.[10]

Indeed, muckraking has always gotten mixed reviews. "To be sure, there are those today who do not love muckraking," writes Louis Filler, the movement's preeminent historian. Muckraking has two reputations, as Filler notes, "of significant exposure without fear or favor, on one side, and of shabby and malicious rumor-mongering, on the other." Filler has portrayed the muckrakers as "crusaders for American liberalism" while historian Gabriel Kolko attacks the muckrakers as a "puerile" band of self-interested profiteers who played into the hands of conservatives.[11] Journalism, of course, is itself a dual institution. Muckraker Will Irwin tartly pegged journalism in 1911. Downstairs in the newsroom, he wrote, journalists are risking life and limb to bring "truth" to the people. Meanwhile, upstairs, the sellers of advertising are promising favors to any merchant who can foot the bill for an advertisement and thus compromising the news pages. A simplistic view, no doubt; more real perhaps in 1911 than today, but symbolic of the dual news/business nature of journalism. Ida Tarbell noted the business "forces working against the type of journalism in which we believed. We were classified as muckrakers, and [yet] the school had been so commercialized that the public was beginning to suspect it. . . . [Muckraking] has lost the passion for facts in a passion for subscription."[12]

That the press relies on commerce for support (as Tarbell bemoaned) but acts also as a critic of commerce is an integral part of the story of muckraking journalism. As I discuss in chapter 3, the legend of the decline of muckraking is that it faded in the years before World War I when the profiteers turned their wrath on the muckraking magazines. With J. P. Morgan at the helm of a conspiracy, so legend has it, finance created one more trust—the magazine trust—to silence its critics. Even if true, this conspiracy theory leaves out the various other factors that contributed to the decline of muckraking; and, more important, it is irreconcilable with the fact that the muckrakers were, after all, a rather conservative bunch. I use the word conservative guardedly, with a lower-case "c," for sure. The muckrakers were liberals—they did seek changes of various sorts and in various degrees—but, with minor exceptions, they wanted to conserve capitalism and private incentive. In their desire to reform the existing system of state-capital relations, the muckrakers helped stabilize the American democracy at a point when it was volatile, and they helped bring about the modern regulatory state.[13]

Why, then, would the business community be hostile? The answer is simple: the defenders of the status quo always rebel at any suggestions that a system treating them well, that is, enabling them to make profits, should be altered. The muckrakers' piercing of the behind-the-scenes relationships between capital and government, and of the methods of business that had helped bring the "trusts" or monopolies into power, clearly augered for changes that might threaten profits. Some feared that those changes might result in socialism, and that was a change too far to the political left. The muckrakers, except perhaps for Upton Sinclair and Charles Edward Russell, did not wish to see socialism come to America. In fact, they were not too sure what they wanted to see come to America; they had no grand plan for change, and certainly they didn't want a revolution. Nonetheless, they were the focus of angry attacks, as the messenger with bad news often is.[14]

The muckrakers were, in the end, reporter-reformers who liked to tell stories, albeit stories with a social significance. Overlooked in most studies of journalism is the concept of the "story." When I saw the drug deals go down in Stapleton, I thought about the great "story" that I would have. In 1980, Bob Woodward was city editor of the *Washington Post* when the plight of an eight-year-old heroin addict, Jimmy, was concocted by reporter Janet Cooke. Woodward told a colleague just after he learned of the alleged existence of Jimmy: "You'll be interested in this. One of our reporters has just come up with one hell of a story about an 8-year-old heroin addict." A "hell of a story."[15] Journalists are storytellers first, and social scientists and analysts second, if at all. Reporters are taught to look for stories, to tell people's stories, and to let the public decide what those stories mean. At times, the stories are written less for the facts they contain than for the enjoyment they can bring. The turn-of-the-century muckrakers, many of whom hoped to become novelists, were adept at telling stories. Their exposés, serialized each month in national magazines, had soap-opera qualities. Charles Edward Russell told the story, for example, of a young man who was thrown into a prison, condemned to hard labor and horrible conditions. A child entered prison for a minor offense and exited a hardened criminal. Penal reform was the obvious moral of the story. Russell didn't have to offer the solution—it was obvious from the story. Facts coincided with entertainment, a blending of information and story ideals that will be discussed in chapter 2, which describes the writing of the muckrakers.[16]

The stories that the muckrakers told captured and stirred the reform imagination in Progressive Era America. Reaching for the first time a large middle-class audience, respectable magazines offered the public not only interesting facts, but a new hero—the activist-journalist-reformer. Unabashedly, the muckrakers could shed any pretense of objectivity. Russell, for example, would eventually call his autobiography the "recollections of a side-line reformer."[17] The leap from journalist to reformer, of course, raises troubling questions. Ever since America's pre-Revolutionary days when some publications carried the tag line "published by authority," the press in America had struggled to win its independence from government and political parties. In the years after the Civil War, the press essentially established that independence and developed a new role as an outsider and as the tribunal of the people. By taking the people's side, the press became a partisan of a different sort. Although once, in its early years, the press had been the mouthpiece of political parties and an information guide for commerce, by the 1870s it has begun to shift sides. In the "new journalism" exemplified by Joseph Pulitzer's New York *World*, the press spoke for the teeming masses and began to champion the people's causes.[18] This was the beginning of new forms of journalism. Crusading, the mounting of campaigns to alter social conditions, was one of the forms. Crusading's closest relative was muckraking, the exposure of those people and institutions that were threatening the people's rights. The point here is simply that muckraking is a point of view: to decide to expose and crusade is a decision that the status quo needs altering. The next logical step for a reporter would be to ally himself with the forces that will bring about solutions to the conditions that he has just exposed. Independence, objectivity, and neutrality call for holding the middle ground between competing factions and solutions; muckraking and crusading, activist choices, call for a partisan view. Objectivity observes; muckraking intrudes.

WHICH SHOULD BE THE CHOICE OF THE JOURNALIST?

Back to Staten Island, Stapleton, and the methadone story for a moment. When I went to the streets to see if methadone was being diverted and sold illegally, I was looking for a story. The potential story overcame all ideology . . . for the moment. I had studied journalism in graduate school, I read closely the conventional press, I knew what my colleagues were allowed to write in their stories, and I knew essentially that the rules of objectivity didn't allow reporter opinion to creep—at least not obviously—into a story. And at this point I had no strong opinions about methadone. All I knew was that I had found an instance of lawbreaking and a great story. Others would have to determine what it meant. I was going to rake the muck—let in the light—and let the muck fall where it may. My function was to tell this story to the public, to the police, and to the clinic's administrators. I had what sociolgist Michael Schudson has called a "simple and noble vision" of journalism as the force that would inform rational, participating citizens.[19] By exposing the wrongs, I was ensuring that some changes would take place, an optimistic assumption that the turn-of-the-century muckrakers generally shared.[20] I knew that eventually I wanted some reforms to occur. But first, I wanted the story to be told . . . in a dramatic way because this would grab a headline, draw attention, and provoke the debate.

During the few seconds when the man who wanted to sell me methadone was waiting for my reply, did thoughts of ideology and function flash through my head? Possibly, but not likely. The question about my function was lost in the muddle of an instantaneous decision, pushed out of focus by the perceived pressure for a good story, and deemed irrelevant in a newsroom where the daily operation of a business was more important. Only many years later was the question of function asked. Is muckraking what the press should be all about? Should the press' point of view be one of attacking its institutions and probing its dark corners? Should the press be an active partner in efforts to reform society? If so, how far does the reporter carry the effort, to what lengths should the reporter go to make change happen? If the reporter becomes a reformer, why should those who disagree with reform trust the reporter's facts? Is not the reporter simply a propagandist for a cause, and not the independent voice that the press has struggled to become?

These are very basic questions about the purpose and function of journalism in a society, questions I especially explore in Chapter 5 when I describe the work of a reporter for the New York *Times* who championed reform of the nursing home industry. In 1974, John L. Hess discovered pervasive mistreatment of patients and financial irregularities in New York's nursing homes. In order to force the government to respond, he worked closely with a state commission to reveal the powers who, behind the scenes, were responsible for the corruption. Finally, after many months, he led a discussion of solutions. Objectivity, in the last days of the crusade, however, stymied him from advocating the kind of solution that he and others favored. Despite months of activist reporting, his perogatives were limited by the professional standard of objectivity imposed on reporters. Hess could present his "facts," but not his opinions. Does a journalist function best when he eliminates his "values" and presents only the "facts," tells what has happened, without passing judgment, without attempting to make the "facts" show a solution? With trepidation, I must say no. Let me relate a story which further introduces the dilemma of function.

Geraldo Rivera: Good Guy or Bad Guy?

Nationally known newsman Geraldo Rivera is a controversial figure in journalism. His syndicated television show, "Geraldo," begun in 1988, is a news entertainment program that is part of an increasing genre of talk-news-entertainment that often trivializes important social issues.[21] However, Rivera got his start in television on a moral plane and muckraking note. With a law degree in hand, Rivera took a job with WABC television in New York City in 1970, a time when television news, attempting to reach new audiences, began to highlight ethnic reporters. Rivera, whose mother is Jewish and father Puerto Rican, was a dashing Hispanic, "the beautiful ethnic," one headline declared. Today, television critic Ron Powers writes, "[T]here are countless clones of Rivera on TV news staffs around the country: soft-haired, mustachioed, handsome devils with Latino surnames, all smoldering with ill-contained outrage on behalf of the downtrodden common man."[22]

Ambitious, Rivera looked for a big story. Across the bay from Manhattan on Staten Island, the story he was seeking was brewing in the Willowbrook State School, the institution where 6,000 retarded people were crammed into a facility meant to house 1,500. Robert Kennedy, when he visited in 1965, called it a "snake pit." The full shame of Willowbrook began to reach the public in 1971 when Jane Kurtin, a reporter for Staten Island's daily newspaper, the *Advance*, began to snoop around the red-brick, barracks-like buildings. She found people dying because no doctors were available. "The animals at the Staten Island Zoo have more space and get better care than the children at Willowbrook," she wrote. She found teenagers, deformed and untreated, lying in their own feces; and she found disease rampant. "This place is like the Congo," a doctor told her. "We have sickness here that you just don't find anymore in the civilized world."[23] Outrage among Staten Island legislators followed Kurtin's stories, but there was little real movement toward meaningful change. Then Rivera entered the picture. After a doctor at Willowbrook told Rivera of conditions there, he took a camera crew from Manhattan to Staten Island. They snuck onto the 380-acre wooded grounds of Willowbrook and made a five-minute film at a residence hall. "It was the worst thing I've ever seen in my life," Rivera said. "The horrible smell of the place staggered me."[24] His cameras captured much of it on film; groaning, wretched-looking people lying naked on concrete floors.

After filming, Rivera and his crew regrouped at a local diner. They knew that to go on the air, to meet the rules of balance prescribed by objective journalism, they would need a response from the facility's administrators. WABC's producer would demand a response. Rivera's crew went back to speak with Willowbrook's director, "another old-line bureaucrat," according to Rivera. The visit was just a "token gesture," because, Rivera later decided, there really was no "other side" to the Willowbrook story. The plight of the retarded was all that mattered in what he called this "dynamite story." It took only a five-minute visit to one building for Rivera to decide that the Willowbrook story had only one side. It was a decision he generally stuck with throughout the next month. "We're going back to Willowbrook . . . again. And look at those horrible wards . . . again. And show them to you again and again and again. Until somebody changes them, " Rivera declared on the air.[25] He would reform conditions. Outraged, the public, seemingly, loved the spectacle. ABC's Nielson ratings in New York City soared to double that of its competitors. When Rivera broadcast a special program on Willowbrook on February 2, 2.5 million people tuned in, one of the highest rated local news shows ever. The broadcast was a one-sided attack on the state of New York. Rivera said, "We haven't given the people who run the New York program equal time to give their side of the story. Perhaps the governor can defend or explain away the budget cuts [and] the filthy dehumanizing conditions we found . . . but they won't do it on this program." Rivera concluded: "We have to change the way we care for our mentally retarded. We ask for change. We demand change." This was not objective journalism; Rivera stood on the side of reform, not balance (and perhaps not on the side of fairness either).[26]

In 1988, sixteen years after Geraldo Rivera turned Willowbrook from a local story into a national disgrace, New York State closed the doors of the institution. Its residents were dispersed into small, home-like facilities throughout the state, and New York spent millions to accomplish the change. It took a precedent-setting lawsuit by the American Civil Liberties Union to complete what Kurtin and Rivera had begun, but it was accomplished.[27] The change Rivera demanded occurred.

Nonetheless, Rivera's rejection of objective journalism is problematic, a rejection, in one sense, of what the press had sought for so many years—a fact-oriented, impartial perspective, independent of state power, of advertisers, and of any special interest, one that allowed competing versions of the "truth" to appear before a rational, choosing public. The press would supply the public—and the decision-making elites— with the knowledge needed to make public policy decisions. However, having access to competing versions of the "truth," not just the newsman's version, is a vital part of what the public needs. Rivera presented only one version; yet, the dilemma is that he was most effective in promoting a heightened public sense of scandal and in bringing change. Objectivity might have failed the 6,000 residents of Willowbrook State School; one-sided, angry, muckraking exposé did not.

Objectivity Defined

Balance is only one, perhaps small, part of the concept of objectivity. It entails much more, in theory and practice. I will use two words often throughout this book: objectivity and muckraking. They both need clarification. Objectivity—this "unfortunately dim silhouette of journalism's foremost practice," as one author has called it —is the fuel that fires journalism's engine, an ideal and an ideology.[28] It is the way a reporter approaches his sources, his material, and his public; it is the hidden frame of reference around which the American press organizes its existence; it is an unwritten guide book that is passed on, unquestioningly, from one generation of journalists to another. To some it is a god and to others a devil. Some journalists embrace it and others damn it.

Jack Newfield, a long-time investigative reporter with the *Village Voice* and now the New York *Daily News*, views objectivity as the establishment's way of hiding its misdeeds. "Certain facts are not morally neutral," Newfield has written. Journalists, he says, need to be committed in their bones, not to being neutral, but to bringing change. Wes Gallagher, the former managing editor of the Associated Press, takes the opposite view. He urges reporters to stay above the fray, to be neutral observers, "to be cool, clear and objective . . . objective, not activist as desired by some. There are enough activist voices now without journalists adding theirs and destroying public confidence in the profession."[29] Quite obviously, these are different interpretations about the function of the journalist which mirror a long-standing dispute and debate in journalism, pitting proponents of a professionalized, objective, restrained, and technically efficient journalism against those advocating a socially responsible and activist brand of reporting.[30] This raises the question of whether the journalist should be an observer of or a participant in the social process. I am interested in the interaction of these two approaches to journalism: objectivity, which might better be called observer neutrality, and muckraking, an activist and reform-oriented school of journalism. Oddly enough, although the muckraking writers have been studied for years by historians, no one has analyzed the muckrakers' mode of writing and looked at how the developing notion of objectivity impacted on their journalism between 1900 to 1915. That is the task of the next chapter.

Ever since late in the 1970s, when journalists and scholars concluded that the press failed in its coverage of both the witch-hunting Senator Joseph McCarthy and the divisive Vietnam War because of the limitations imposed by objectivity, there has been a growing literature and argument over the concept.[31] Doubts about the efficacy of objective journalism have led to difficult questions—and very different answers. The neutrality/advocacy question is only one. What forces in American culture have led journalism to seek a neutral stance? What has spurred its evolution? When did it begin? What limits does it impose on reporters? Does the public lose or benefit, in the long and short run, from a neutral press? Would a partisan, subjective press better serve the public's need for unfettered debate? The questions can be asked more easily than answers can be found. If there is any agreement on objectivity, it is this: to conceive of even the ideal of objectivity as the lack of bias is to misconceive it. Muckraker Will Irwin recognized the objectivity myth many years ago when he wrote: "There is no colorless newspaper; though a few approximate it; every news report has some point of view, expresses some mission of God or of the Devil."[32] To believe that bias can be excluded from news accounts written by human beings, concurs *Washington Post* reporter Lou Cannon, "perpetuates the most damaging bias of American journalism." His comments are similar to those expressed many years earlier by communications scholar George Gerbner who wrote, "[A]ll news is views ... there is no fundamentally non-ideological, apolitical, non-partisan, news gathering and reporting system."[33] Explains John Hersey, who has written both fiction and non-fiction, "The minute a writer offers nine hundred ninety-nine out of one thousand facts, the worm of bias has begun to wriggle."[34] Edmund Lambeth states the obvious: "No news account can be totally free of subjectivity." Objectivity is a scientific ideal, but "it does not describe what a truthful journalist achieves," adds Michael Novak.[35]

If journalistic objectivity does not represent bias-free reportage, as the layperson might expect, what then is it? This question, too, poses difficulties because, as one author points out, "journalism has always had a shifting set of ethical principles ... which have had widely different meanings at different times and places."[36] The meaning of objectivity has evolved over the decades and, even today, it has different meanings from publication to publication. However, whether it is couched in words like "fairness," "accuracy," or "impartiality," or in phrases like "separating fact from comment," there is some uniform agreement on the principles of objectivity. Let me go from the theoretical underpinnings of the concept to some of its specific attributes.

The theoretical rationale for the notion of objectivity is that readers and listeners can best make up their minds about public policy issues when they are given verifiable "facts." These facts are delivered by independent, neutral observers—reporters—who provide for the reader competing versions of the "truth"; in short, a "marketplace" where ideas do battle. This marketplace will contain not only "ideas," but also facts, statistics, opinions, impressions, and a whole range of diverse visions of society. The diversity will encompass both public policy issues and lifestyle questions, the political and personal. But the observer who delivers the components of the marketplace will not give an opinion about which versions are to be embraced. The citizen makes that choice. Reporters may marshall evidence for both sides of the competing claims, and they will need to make value judgments about which sources can provide the most reliable version of the facts, but reporters do not, at least overtly, determine which version of truth is correct. The observer does not intrude in the story but maintains a distanced, usually third-person, point of view or perspective. Other people are actors in the story, but the reporter is not, again, at least not obviously. Furthermore, what the reporter must do to compile the facts—that is, to gather the news—is not a part of the story the reader sees in print or hears on the air.

This notion that facts and a reporter's values are separable, that an observer can be "objective" in collection and presentation of facts, manifests itself in certain journalistic conventions. Sociologist Gaye Tuchman, who has observed how reporters in a newsroom work, found that in order to achieve objectivity, reporters have developed certain "strategic rituals," certain things they do and places they go to compile stories that will withstand the profession's unwritten tests of objectivity.[37] Some of the attributes of this ritual that she and others have identified are as follows. First, an objective story has balance. Geraldo Rivera notwithstanding, there is always the "other side," the need for a "presentation of conflicting possibilities." The reporter can assume that certain facts do not need to be countered (for example, there are 50 states in the United States), but the general approach in reporting is to allow the reader to choose between alternate versions and multiple facts. Second, a reporter needs to provide supporting evidence to back up the various accounts or sides that result from an event or occur when public policy is debated. The best, most objective evidence would come from an official document, perhaps a government report, or from a public event, say, a government agency meeting or a public speech. Equally acceptable would be an interview with a public official or a spokesman for a generally recognized or legitimate group or business. Deciding which documents to choose, which meetings to attend, and which spokesman to interview gives a reporter much subjective leeway. Nonetheless, journalistic objectivity accepts this flexibility.

In citing evidence in a news story, reporters must make clear that someone else is responsible for the facts, words, or opinions. A third characteristic of objectivity then follows: close attribution of all material. Someone else will always be speaking, not the reporter. The attribution may be in the form of direct statements, indicated by quotation marks, or it may simply be a few words indicating the source. Hence, "the police" say a man stole the car, not the reporter. A fourth attribute comes with what is known as a "newspeg"—an event or occurrence (perhaps a City Council meeting, an arrest, a press conference, or a murder trial) on which a reporter can peg a story. Since a reporter must be a neutral observer, the newspeg, and not the activism of the reporter, brings the story into existence. A final attribute, the haziest of the ritual, relates to the structuring and organization of news stories. Objective news stories are, according to the age-old journalistic tradition, organized in an inverted pyramid—the most important information first and the least important last. This order allows the reader to get the most important facts first and allows the editor to delete, if need be, the least important information at the bottom. The most important aspect of this formula is that the lead, the beginning paragraph or paragraphs, calls for a judgment about which of the facts is the most important, a judgment that, on its face, would seem quite subjective. News professionals commonly invoke time-honored definitions of news to defend their choices of leads, but this attribute is probably the least defensible, and the most difficult to describe. Nonetheless, when describing why a certain story is "objective," a reporter will note that it meets a certain accepted formula.

Not all writing in newspapers or magazines is formulaic, of course, and not all of it can be termed objective. Even though objectivity is the dominant characteristic of the mainstream American media, even the casual reader will realize that not all journalistic content is objective in the ritualistic sense just discussed. One will find values or opinions on the news pages—in, for example, editorials or in the writing of columnists. At times, a reporter's opinion may be found in stories that have been clearly labeled "analysis" or "commentary." Additionally, reporters are increasingly allowed leeway in providing perspective and interpretation as a regular part of an objective story (even this must be closely associated with the facts at hand). Alongside news stories can be found feature or human interest stories which often allow for reporter's impressions and call for literary style. Here, too, however, facts are still sacred and although the rules of objectivity may be loosened, they are not by any means suspended.

MUCKRAKING: A SEARCH FOR DEFINITION

I was a student at Boston University in 1974 at the height of journalism's craze for investigative reporting. Bob Woodward and Carl Bernstein were gaining laurels for exposing presidential corruption, and newspapers were establishing teams of investigative reporters to duplicate such feats. A student in a journalism class told one of my professors, James Shen, that he wanted to become an investigative reporter. "All reporting," Dr. Shen replied, in what has become by now a journalism school cliche, "is investigative." Dr. Shen was correct in that even a press release should be investigated to verify facts, to get more information, to see what was not included. But investigative reporting or muckraking is, in general, different from other kinds of objective reporting.

"The work of investigation, like muckraking," note two scholars, "furnishes a careful, accurate, inevitably non-neutral account and analysis

in words and images of a set of events, ideas, circumstances, or persons."
Muckraking, these scholars add, "denounces or praises specific individuals, conditions, or values, and exhorts its audience, explicitly or by
tone, to take action or to support specific remedies."[38] Muckraking stories are not commentaries on another reporter's facts; they are not anal-
yses of policy; they are not "soft," impressionistic, or literary; and they
are not explicit advocacy pieces. They are compilations of documented
fact that lead to an indictment—of individuals or institutions. When
Benjamin Orange Flower protested social conditions in his magazine,
The Arena, circa 1900, he may have supported what the muckrakers' facts
showed, but his editorial protest was not muckraking. When in the 1960s
I. F. Stone's Weekly denounced military expenditures as too large, this
was not muckraking, but when his facts meticulously exposed government lying in the Gulf of Tonkin incident in 1964, that was muckraking.
Angry rhetoric, even if progressive, is not muckraking; detailed factual
exposure is.

Similarly, one must rule out fiction as muckraking journalism, even
if the fiction, like Upton Sinclair's *The Jungle*, exposes a social problem.
Some fiction will have a muckraking tone, but journalism is not fiction.
I agree with John Hersey who points out that "there is one sacred rule
of journalism. The writer must not invent."[39] This is not to say that there
was not a close relationship during the Progressive Era between literature and journalism, one that must be studied in any look at the journalist's point of view. It is also not to say that there may not be a
muckraking brand of literature, one that deserves scrutiny on its own
for its contribution to social progress. It is only to say that in this book
muckraking will be defined as journalism, not literature.

In this book I have included examples of muckraking in newspapers
and magazines and on television. I believe the concept of objectivity is
essentially the same for magazine writers and television reporters as it
is for newspaper reporters. Different media do provide more leeway for
reporter opinion or creativity; however, the guiding principles of objectivity remain firmly in place across the spectrum of the conventional
commercial press. The news magazine, for example, often assumes that
a writer has a preexisting body of knowledge about a subject and he
might be allowed, therefore, to write with more authority, perhaps
omitting at times attribution. At times the magazine writer can draw
conclusions that a newspaper account might not allow, probably because
of the extra time that a magazine writer might have in which to prepare
an article. However, the essential rules of objectivity, that is, the techniques that must be utilized to move certain facts past wary editors, are
the same, especially for the investigative magazine article.

As for television, two factors impact on the objectivity rules. The first
is a legal constraint: the Federal Communication Commission's fairness

doctrine mandates that a balanced point of view by followed in stories, that various sides be given relative equal weight. This legalizes an objectivity rule. On the other hand, because of the amount of time often allowed a broadcaster, some reliance on documents is forsaken and some leeway for the reporter to condense, conclude, and tie his report together in a story formula slightly alters the eventual presentation. Again, however, the basic sense of applying the objectivity rituals remains in place. What a reporter says on the air may not indicate that the objectivity rules have been applied, but I believe that behind the scenes and in the fact-gathering process, they are the same for the broadcaster as for the print journalist.

If this book were to be made into a movie, it might be called "Lincoln Steffens Meets Bob Woodward," because between these two covers the two muckraking eras of American journalism meet, two traditions collide: the ardent exposer crashes into the neutral technician. I begin at the turn of the century, follow the muckrakers through their glory days, and then chronicle their decline in the years before World War I. I pick up muckraking again in 1959, when the press—in print and on television—championed the cause of migrant farm workers. My next episode deals with the 1974 muckraking crusade of John L. Hess, a reporter who exposed the worst nursing home scandal in the nation's history. The chapters are connected by the simple fact that they all deal with muckraking reporting and the principles of objective journalism. Each chapter raises different questions, issues, and dilemmas for American journalism. The central question, however, is this: what is the purpose of the reporter in American democracy? Both the turn-of-the-century and the contemporary muckrakers help shed light on that question.

NOTES

1. On New York's heroin epidemic, see D. C. Desjarlais and C. Uppal, "Heroin Activity in New York City, 1970–78," *American Journal of Drug and Alcohol Abuse* 7 (1981): 335–46. The methadone controversy is discussed in Carl D. Chambers and Leon Brill, eds., *Methadone: Experience and Issues* (New York, 1973).

2. Gary Talese, "The Silent Season of a Hero," in *Fame and Obscurity* (New York, 1970), 77–98. Dan Wakefield, *Between the Lines: A Reporter's Personal Journey through Public Events* (Boston, 1956), 1–22.

3. Robert Miraldi, "Friday Mornings: Drug Deals on a Stapleton Street," *Staten Island Advance*, 6 May 1979, pp. 1, 14; "Lack of Control Makes Street Sales Easy; Clinics' Take-home Policies Help Methadone Trade Prosper," *Staten Island Advance*, 7 May 1979, p. 1.

4. There have been various accounts of the muckraking movement. The most reliable is Louis Filler, *The Muckrakers* (University Park, Pa., 1976), published originally in 1939 as *Crusaders for American Liberalism*. See also, however, C. C. Regier, *The Era of the Muckrakers* (Chapel Hill, N.C., 1932) and Richard Hofstadter,

The Age of Reform (New York, 1955), 185–212. A good summary of the views and interpretations of muckraking is Harry H. Stein, "American Muckrakers and Muckraking: The 50-Year Scholarship," *Journalism Quarterly* 56 (Spring 1979): 9–17.

5. Muckraking in the years between its post–World War I decline and the 1960s revival is discussed by Carey McWilliams, "The Continuing Tradition of Reform Journalism," in *Muckraking: Past, Present and Future*, eds. John M. Harrison and Harry H. Stein. (University Park, Pa., 1973), 118–34.

6. On contemporary muckraking, see the mostly anecdotal account of Leonard Downie, *The New Muckrakers* (New York, 1976). A candid and revealing look at I. F. Stone is given in the documentary film directed by Jerry Brucker, *I. F. Stone's Weekly*. See also Jack Anderson, *Confessions of a Muckraker* (New York, 1979) and Fred J. Cook, *Maverick: Fifty Years of Investigative Reporting* (New York, 1984).

7. The muckrakers are closely identified with liberalism and the popular will by Louis Filler and C. C. Regier and in David Mark Chalmers, *The Social and Political Ideas of the Muckrakers* (New York, 1964).

8. *The Autobiography of Lincoln Steffens* (New York, 1931), 357; Ray Stannard Baker, *American Chronicle: The Autobiography of Ray Stannard Baker* (New York, 1945), 201; Ida Tarbell, *All in a Day's Work* (New York, 1939), 241.

9. William Porter, *Assault on the Media* (Ann Arbor, Mich., 1976), 42–43, 46–48, 262–65.

10. Roosevelt first made his criticism in private. See, for example, his letter to Ray Stannard Baker, January 9, 1906, in Baker, *American Chronicle*, p. 357. He also made a celebrated public speech on April 14, 1906, which is reprinted in *The Muckrakers*, eds. Arthur Weinberg and Lila Weinberg (New York, 1961), 58–65.

11. Louis Filler, "The Muckrakers and Middle America," in *Muckraking: Past, Present, and Future*, eds. John M. Harrison and Harry H. Stein, 25; Filler, *The Muckrakers*; Gabriel Kolko, *The Triumph of Conservatism* (Glencoe, Ill., 1963), 160, 111.

12. Will Irwin, "The Unhealthy Alliance," in *The American Newspaper*, eds. Clifford F. Weigle and David G. Clark (Ames, Iowa, 1969), 34. These articles appeared originally in *Collier's*, January–July 1911. Tarbell, *All in a Day's Work*, 298.

13. Kolko views muckraking and progressive reform during the era as conservative and reinforcing of the status quo, Filler labels the muckrakers as generally moderate, and Chalmers discusses their role in the emergence of the regulatory state in *The Muckrake Years* (New York, 1974).

14. Various authors discuss the political affiliations and ideologies of the muckrakers. See Judson A. Grenier, "The Origins and Nature of Progressive Muckraking" (Ph.D. diss., University of California, Los Angeles, 1965); and David Mark Chalmers, "The Social and Political Philosophy of the Muckrakers" (Ph.D. diss., University of Rochester, 1955).

15. Norman Isaacs, *The Mismanaged Gates* (New York, 1988), 66. Robert Darnton talks about "Writing News and Telling Stories" in *Daedalus* 104 (1975): 175–94.

16. Charles Edward Russell, "A Burglar in the Making," *Everybody's* (June 1908): 753–60.

17. Charles Edward Russell, *Bare Hands and Stone Walls/Some Recollections of a Side-Line Reformer* (New York, 1933).

18. Frank Luther Mott, *American Journalism* (New York, 1941), 15. The "new journalism" of the 1870s is discussed in Edwin Emery and Michael Emery, *The Press and America* (Englewood Cliffs, N.J., 1984), 253–78.

19. Michael Schudson, "Making Journalism Safe for Democracy," *The Quill* (November 1984): 24.

20. Baker said of the muckrakers, "We were not hopeless, we were not cynical"; *American Chronicle*, p. 226. *Everybody's* editors commented, "A muck-raker is not a pessimist, but a working optimist"; "With Everybody's Publishers" (April 1912); 575. Chalmers commented that the muckrakers "were not prophets of gloom. All believed that the evils could be corrected," *Social and Political Ideas*, 109.

21. Rivera's television talk show is discussed in Alex Jones, "Geraldo Gambles on Talk," *New York Times*, 6 September 1987, pp. 21, 23.

22. Ron Powers, *The Newscasters* (New York, 1977), 183.

23. Jane Kurtin, "Parents Protest Cutbacks at State School," *Staten Island Advance*, 15 November 1971, p. 4. Kurtin wrote at least fourteen other stories about Willowbrook throughout November and December.

24. Geraldo Rivera, *Willowbrook: A Report on How It Is and Why It Doesn't Have to Be That Way* (New York, 1972), 23, 3.

25. Rivera, *Willowbrook*, 33, 26, 38.

26. Rivera, *Willowbrook*, 114–15. I began to work as a reporter with the *Staten Island Advance* about a year after Rivera broadcast his Willowbrook exposés. The director of Willowbrook, Dr. Miodrag Ristich, told me in an interview that, of the dozens of reporters who wrote stories about the state center, Rivera was the only one who he felt was unfair and untrustworthy. See Robert Miraldi "Press OK Except for One," *Staten Island Advance*, 8 December 1974, p. 15.

27. A detailed account of the Willowbrook problem and solution can be found in David J. Rothman and Sheila M. Rothman, *The Willowbrook Wars* (New York, 1986).

28. Dan Schiller, *Objectivity and the News* (Philadelphia, 1981), 8.

29. Jack Newfield, "Is There a New Journalism?" in *The Reporter As Artist*, ed. Ronald Weber (New York, 1974), 299–304. Wes Gallagher makes this statement in the documentary film, *I. F. Stone's Weekly*.

30. This dispute over journalistic function is acknowledged by journalists. See John W. C. Johnstone, Edward K. Slawski, and William W. Bowman, *The News People: A Sociological Portrait of American Journalists and Their Work* (Urbana, Ill., 1976), 114.

31. On Vietnam, for example, see James Aronson, *The Press and the Cold War* (Boston, 1973); and Daniel Hallin, *The Uncensored War: The Media and Vietnam* (New York, 1986). On McCarthy, see Edwin Bayley, *Joe McCarthy and the Press* (New York, 1982).

32. Will Irwin, "The Power of the Press," in *The American Newspaper*, p. 17.

33. Lou Cannon, *Reporting: An Inside View* (Sacramento, Calif., 1977), 45;

George Gerbner, "Ideological Perspectives and Political Tendencies in News Reporting," *Journalism Quarterly* 41 (Spring 1964): 508, 495.

34. John Hersey, "The Legend on License," *Yale Review* 70 (Autumn 1980): 2.

35. Edmund Lambeth, *Committed Journalism: An Ethic for the Press* (Bloomington, Ind., 1986), 73; Michael Novak, "Off the Mark," *MORE* (October 1974): 7.

36. Anthony Smith, *Goodbye Gutenberg* (New York, 1980), 159.

37. Any discussion of journalistic objectivity begins with the seminal work of Gaye Tuchman. See "Objectivity as Strategic Ritual: An Examination of Newsmen's Notions of Objectivity," *American Journal of Sociology* 77, 4 (January 1972), 660–79. She included some of her findings in *Making News: A Study in the Construction of Reality* (New York, 1978). Complementing Tuchman, and equally important, is Michael Schudson, *Discovering the News* (New York, 1978). A good historical perspective on objectivity is lent by Mitchell Stephens, *A History of News: From the Drum to the Satellite* (New York, 1988), 252–70. Less satisfactory on objectivity is Lance Bennett, *News: The Politics of Illusion* (New York, 1983), 78–92.

38. Harrison and Stein, "Muckraking Journalism in Twentieth-Century America," *Muckraking*, 14.

39. Hersey, "The Legend on License," 2.

2

The Muckrakers: Storytelling and Reforming

DAVID GRAHAM PHILLIPS—A BORN REPORTER

David Graham Phillips had the looks of a matinee idol: he was tall, handsome, and square-jawed. He parted his dark hair severely in the middle, and he wore tailor-made suits with high-button collars. Each day he tucked a chrysanthemum high on his lapel. As a bachelor in 1890s New York City, he was much in demand on the social circuit, and, since he was a gifted writer who had the young legs needed to get the facts off the city's streets, Phillips was equally in demand as a newsman. This kid from Indiana could hustle, think, and write; he was a born reporter.[1]

After an education at Princeton and a newspaper apprenticeship in Cincinnati, Ohio, Phillips had come to the big city to tackle journalism in 1890. He began under Charles A. Dana, the sage of Park Row, who tutored Phillips in the New York *Sun*'s decrepit Manhattan building where so many other young writers had mastered the Dana-style human interest story. In 1892, as his reputation grew in newspaper circles, Phillips became the beneficiary of a circulation war between Dana and newcomer Joseph Pulitzer.[2] For a hefty raise in pay, the young man who aspired to write novels was lured to the New York *World*, soon to be the largest circulation newspaper in America.

Phillips wasted no time in winning the immediate favor of the eccentric genius Pulitzer. He wrote a twelve-part, thirty-five thousand-word series of articles that lambasted the United States Attorney General Richard

Olney for failing to prosecute and break up the monopolies that were dominating American industry. The Whiskey Trust . . . the Sugar Trust . . . the Cotton Trust. Day after day, Phillips sketched the histories of the "bands of robber barons" who comprised an "unholy alliance of bandits who prey unmolested upon the people." Asserting that prices were being raised, that small businesses were being squeezed out of the market, and that politics were being corrupted, Phillips demanded that the "trusts" must be "smashed." Each day he ended his unsigned articles with a rhetorical flourish: "Such Mr. Olney are the facts. And here, sir, is the law." In italics, Phillips then quoted a relevant portion of the Sherman Anti-Trust Act of 1890.[3] There was no pretense of objectivity here—facts, yes, about the trusts; but these articles, splashed on page one, combined editorial advocacy with muckraking zeal. A decade before he became a member of the exposé movement, David Graham Phillips was muckraking.

So pleased was Pulitzer that he offered an immediate reward to Phillips—a coveted spot as London correspondent. Phillips went to Europe where his "beats" and daily coverage won plaudits back in New York, but the reward he wanted most—a byline—was denied by Pulitzer. Phillips quit and sailed back to New York. Pulitzer met Phillips at the dock, however, and pleaded with him to stay at the newspaper, and Phillips agreed. At first, he was unhappy covering the news again, until his city editor, Charles Edward Russell, a future muckraker himself, assigned Phillips to work only on human interest stories. Freed from the demands of rigid factuality, Phillips, only twenty-six-years old, soon became a writer whose feature articles were widely praised and imitated.[4] Whether recreating morbid scenes in a hospital death ward, sketching political candidates seeking presidential office, or racing to the scene of a war, Phillips showed a literary flair that foreshadowed his novelistic intentions. In only a few years, Phillips had become a legend on Park Row.[5]

In 1896, after four years of writing about New York City, Phillips moved to the top floor of the twenty-storied, domed *World*—the editorial writers' office. Here, he became a key part of what Pulitzer considered his education force, the page-four boys who were to forsake the thunder, stunts, and self-promotion, i.e., yellow journalism, of the news pages for sober insight into American life.[6] Phillips became a blatant advocate on behalf of Progressive causes. There were whispers at the *World* that Pulitzer, in declining health, was grooming Phillips as his editorial heir. They sailed to Europe together on Pulitzer's yacht, they exchanged affectionate letters, and Pulitzer sought and received Phillips' private advice on the future direction of his newspapers. Despite the intimacy, by the turn of the century, fiction was bursting from Phillips' pen. The man who had once declared, "I'd rather be a reporter than President," found the world of imagination more attractive than the world of fact. Phillips prepared to leave journalism. Using a pseudonym, Phillips wrote his first novel in 1901, a newspaper memoir in which he created a power-hungry publisher, who resembled Pulitzer, and Pulitzer's rival, William Randolph Hearst.[7] With mixed emotions, Phillips left the New York *World* to become a free lance who would write novels, essays, journalism, and an odd type of story that blended fiction and nonfiction.

FROM JOURNALISM TO FICTION

For the most part, Phillips became slavishly devoted to fiction. Wrapped in a plush nightcoat and standing at a desk he called his "black pulpit," Phillips wrote nightly from dark to dawn. His byline began to appear frequently in the new, inexpensive mass-circulation magazines—especially the *Saturday Evening Post*—as he turned out an astonishing number of novels and some journalism. By 1906, when he ended his journalism career, he had written sixty-seven magazine articles. By 1911, the year he was assassinated, Phillips had written twenty-three novels, many of which, popular and timely, were front-page headlines turned into fiction.[8] His 1903 roman-à-clef, *The Master Rogue*, typical of his seven muckraking-style novels, was about a tycoon who, privately, so loved money that he threw away all morals and laws but publicly was a humble, pious philanthropist. Was this John D. Rockefeller?[9] When Wall Street financier Thomas Lawson's *Frenzied Finance* (1904) exposed real-life, back-room corporate manipulations, Phillips brought the story to fiction with Matt Blacklock, the people's hero, who battled "the interests." Phillips' most successful novel, *The Plum Tree* (1905), was a tantalizing collection of familiar politicos, all of whom were corrupt, with hands outstretched, looking for fruit off the political plum tree.[10] At the same time that Phillips' novels were being serialized in popular magazines, he wrote nonfiction. In what was ostensibly journalism, he blended composite characters and fictional dialogue with facts to argue on behalf of reform causes. This "faction," a blending of fiction and fact, was popular but problematic also for the reader who was getting from Phillips and other muckrakers both fictional and factual versions of the world at the same time.[11] Could Phillips' facts be believed when they were the same as those he wrote in fiction?

At this driven pace of two novels a year, Phillips seemingly had little time to undertake projects that would divert him from fiction. Then, in 1905, Hearst, who had purchased *Cosmopolitan* magazine, asked Phillips to write an attack on the U.S. Senate for placing the needs of the "trusts" over the needs of the "people." The purpose would be to mount a campaign for direct election of senators to replace the existing method whereby state legislatures chose the Senate members. Popular election would enhance Hearst's own chance of election, should he seek a Senate seat, but it would also assuage the growing Progressive clamor for accountability to the people. At first, Phillips refused the offer; his other writing would not allow it. "What I want the world to know me for is a novelist," he declared.[12] But Hearst's editors were persistent. They offered him a large amount of money plus the help of two assistants; Phillips took the offer. What resulted from March to November of 1906 was a harsh, shrill series of articles, a frontal attack on a body of public men who had been bought off by business: "The Treason of the Senate" was *The Plum Tree* come to life, but it was also an exposé tinged with venom. Phillips wrote profiles of eighteen senators—some of the biggest names in public life, the leaders of both parties who were pictured as fronts for an industrial machine which owned the Senate and controlled the senators. For months, *Cosmopolitan*'s circulation soared —450,000 by May, double its 1905 average—until the presses could not produce enough copies.[13]

TR's Attack and Phillips' Death

The "Treason" articles were either a high or a low point for this movement of journalistic exposé that had started in the popular periodicals soon after the turn of the century. First, there had been Ida Tarbell on Rockefeller's oil monopoly; then Lincoln Steffens on political corruption; Samuel Hopkins Adams on dangerous medicines; Ray Stannard Baker on railroad profiteers; Lawson, financier turned exposer, on Wall Street manipulations; and Russell on "the greatest trust in the world," the beef monopoly.[14] When the "Treason" articles began appearing in 1906, the same year as Upton Sinclair's widely read novel, *The Jungle*, the movement seemed to reach a climax with these two bitter attacks on capitalism and the political establishment.

At first, Phillips was heartened by the favorable initial public reaction to the "Treason" articles, but criticism mounted as the series continued, and Phillips was forced to respond: "These articles have been attacked, but their facts—the facts of the treason of the Senate, taken from the records—have not been attacked. Abuse is not refutation; it is confession." In private, however, Phillips was distressed. He was used to being lionized for his work; the criticism wounded him deeply. He told his friend, Sen. Albert Beveridge, "I don't mind telling you that I would even make some sacrifices in order to carry this thing to some sort of decent finish."[15] Phillips wanted publication to end quickly.

At the White House, a roar was welling up from Theodore Roosevelt. The president was angry that elected officials should have to put up with such an uncharacteristically blunt pillory as Phillips', and he was also fearful that the muckrakers' rhetoric might be, as he wrote to a friend, "building up a revolutionary feeling." In April, Roosevelt decided to respond publicly with a counterattack—on the "Man with the Muckrake, who could look no way but downward" on "the wild preachers of unrest and discontent."[16] In a much-publicized speech, Roosevelt said he feared the "mudslingers" would drive the best men out of public life, that they would make the public despair, and that they would derail serious efforts being made to bring about reform. Behind closed doors, Roosevelt said the mudslingers he had in mind were named Phillips and Sinclair. Phillips, he wrote, was a "dirty, foul-mouthed blackguard," an opinion he later revised when he met the fine-flanneled dandy in a private meeting.[17]

Phillips took the criticism to heart. In fact, he was so "cut up" by the attacks, his friend Russell recalled, that when the articles ended he vowed never again to write nonfiction, a vow he kept. But he had already given birth to the word muckraking. "Muck-rakers we were thereafter," wrote Russell about this band of investigative reporters who were now in for serious scrutiny and serious criticism.[18] For the next five years, Phillips feverishly wrote only from his imagination until a crazed gunman, aggrieved by one of Phillips' biting novels, shot and killed him on a New York City street. The news swept over the city and was flashed throughout the country: Phillips was dead . . . but not before he had left behind a remarkable body of work, in fiction and fact.[19] Perhaps the most important legacy of David Graham Phillips, at least to journalism, was that the harsh reaction to his "Treason of the Senate" series helped define the limits of conventional journalism at a time when professional responsibility was only emerging, a time when journalism was groping and in transition. Phillips' journalism had gone too far, the establishment had struck back, and now the parameters of journalistic inquiry were made clearer. Neutrality was safer than passion.

THE TYPICAL MUCKRAKER

David Graham Phillips was a typical progressive reformer and a typical muckraking journalist, two good reasons to start this chapter with his story. His social and professional backgrounds match up closely to the dozen or so other young men who became the heart of the muckraking movement. Before graduating from newspaper journalism to writing for the popular periodicals, Phillips was reared in a small city, raised in a Protestant, upper middle-class family, and college educated. When he entered journalism, he brought with him a small-town Midwestern vision of a simpler and cleaner America, an America that needed to be purged of its industrial ills and returned to its agrarian roots. Journalism, Phillips thought, was a profession where good things could be done. When it came to choosing a career, financial considerations were less important than idealism and ideology. As did so many other young men after the Civil War, Phillips viewed reporting as a noble profession but also, he felt, as the field that could prepare him for his long-range goal—the writing of fiction.[20]

Typical also about Phillips were his experiences as reporter and editor from 1890 to 1900. He could not help but become caught up in the intellectual currents and journalistic trends that affected all the thoughtful young writers of his generation: the Populist clamor for an assault on the trusts; the notion that a collectivist social approach could offset the atavistic Social Darwinists; and the rise of a naturalistic brand of American literature that depicted the real America. Add to this his professional experience which placed him in the middle of the sensationalism of yellow journalism, a scourge which plunged the press into a dark but exciting period and which helped shape the muckrakers' approach to their material. Finally, however, there is another important reason for focusing, at least initially, on Phillips' journalism: his work from 1901, when he left daily journalism, to 1906, when he wrote the attack on the Senate, epitomizes the contradictions that characterize the muckraking movement and typifies a confusion of purpose in journalism itself.

There would seem to be various ways to explain why confusion and contradiction dominated muckraking. But primarily the muckraking writers, who wrote nearly 2,000 articles over the Progressive Era years of 1900 to 1915, were tugged and pulled by the contrasting demands of a dichotomous American society.[21] The culture of commercialism begged from these journalists readable and safe imagery but, at the same time, their profession, modernizing along with the rest of society, demanded an emerging brand of responsibility in the form of objectivity. Among other things, this professionalism began to seek certain thresholds of proof and of facts over rhetoric. A journalist could no longer just say it was so, he had more and more to prove it. At the least, he had, more and more, to use consensually validated techniques or methods to write his stories. Unsure of what constraints their profession's emerging rules and rituals were imposing upon their ability to reach conclusions and to advocate, the muckrakers responded—quite naturally—with confused and varied approaches.

What becomes clear in looking at the work of Phillips and the other muckrakers is that they moved freely between conflicting journalistic ideals. On the one hand, their muckraking writing was dramatic, fiction-like and literary, with an emphasis on human interest. The "story ideal," as one author has called this trait, dominated much of their writing. The muckrakers embraced the theory of Will Irwin, who wrote that "[b]ehind every tragedy lies a whole novel, behind every movement for human good a poem."[22] On the other hand, the muckrakers were obsessed with dispassionate investigation, with the search for the facts that would inform public opinion. The larger truth that might come in the freedom of fiction was indeed an important thing to the muckrakers, but the actual truth brought by factuality was equally, if not more, important. And while this information ideal of muckraking certainly did not constitute the objectivity of today's journalism, it showed that many of objectivity's attributes were emerging. Thus, while the story ideal urged the muckrakers in one direction, fledgling objectivity, pushed the movement in another direction.

FIVE OTHER MUCKRAKERS

In this chapter, the confusion of function found in muckraking can be seen from a scrutiny of selected books and articles by Phillips and five other muckrakers. First, from the early period of muckraking, come Ida Tarbell and Samuel Hopkins Adams. Tarbell was one of the most famous women of the Progressive Era because of her articles in *McClure's* magazine on John D. Rockefeller. *The History of Standard Oil*, a chronicle of this quintessential American capitalist and his company, was serialized from 1902 to 1903 and brought out as a book a year later.[23] The exposé brought more infamy to Rockefeller than anything else ever had, and it brought fame to Tarbell. She spent the rest of her career alternately expanding on and discussing these articles.[24]

Samuel Hopkins Adams was a bold and crusading reporter, a champion on behalf of labeling and regulating America's drugs and medicines. Writing in *Collier's* between 1905 and 1906, he exposed the dangerous chemicals that existed in over-the-counter medicines. The American Medical Association reproduced thousands of copies of the articles, collectively entitled "The Great American Fraud." Adams was probably more responsible for the arrival of federal drug regulation than any other one person, and he spent parts of the next twenty years of his career fighting for reforms in medicine.[25]

Next, from the middle part of the muckraking era, came Phillips and Ray Stannard Baker. Phillips was the only muckraker of the Progressive Era whose work was appearing often in fiction and nonfiction. While one magazine was publishing an installment of his latest novel of finance and romance, another popular periodical was printing his journalism. His "Treason of the Senate" articles present a unique chance to compare the influence of the fictive imagination on the journalistic product. Phillips muckraked from 1902 to 1906, and then wrote only fiction until his death. The harsh "Treason of the Senate" was ignored for many years after its publication until it was reproduced as a book in 1954.[26]

Ray Stannard Baker, described as "one of the most resolutely objective observers of American life," earned fame in the early 1900s as a fastidious

researcher, good reporter, and clear thinker. His articles on labor relations and his muckraking of railroad corruption won praise even from
Roosevelt. In 1904, writing for *McClure's*, he tackled the controversial
subject of race relations with two articles about lynchings of black men
in the South.[27] With a moral fervor that resembled more a minister than
a journalist, Baker took up the subject again when he joined the *American*
magazine in 1906. *Following the Color Line*, which is analyzed in this
chapter, began publication in April 1907. Thanks to Baker's articles, the
February and March issues of the *American* sold out completely. In 1908,
this pioneer work in the study of race relations was published as a book.[28]

Finally, from the last stage of muckraking, came Will Irwin and Charles
Edward Russell. Throughout the century's first decade, the muckrakers
provided a fairly comprehensive critique and exposé of the ills of American society. No institution was sacred, as Irwin and Russell made clear.
Irwin, for example, muckraked the press itself in a prescient, tough, and
precedent-setting series of articles in *Collier's* on "The American Newspaper" (1911–1912). These articles, as much essay and analysis as exposé,
placed a check on the checkers, and foreshadowed numerous contemporary press issues. Although Irwin went on to write thirty four novels,
he is still best remembered for his history of the press.[29]

Perhaps the most prolific of the muckrakers was Russell who, in suc-
cession, was reporter, editor, publisher, muckraker, socialist, poet, and
Pulitzer Prize–winning biographer.[30] Much like Upton Sinclair, Russell
was driven by ideology. His conversion to socialism was much publi-
cized, and he brought home the need for change with his journalism.
Six of his magazine articles are analyzed in this chapter. His exposé of
prison conditions in Georgia and of tenement conditions in New York
(both printed in *Everybody's* in 1908) led, respectively, to an uproar in a
Southern legislature and to the acute embarrassment of Trinity Church
which owned some of New York's worst slums. Showing in his writing
a strong dose of economic determinism, Russell followed in Irwin's
footsteps in 1914 with four articles on the corruption of the press (published in *Pearson's*, 1914).[31]

THE APPROACH OF MUCKRAKING

Studying the work of the muckrakers is certainly nothing new. For
fifty years scholars have been trying to categorize and understand their
writings. "A near wilderness of facts, notions, surmises, unknowns and
generalizations" about muckraking has resulted, writes one researcher.
Some view the muckrakers as conservatives, others see them as liberals;
some call them anxious middle-Americans, others say they were shrewd
profiteers. Just as there is no consensus on how to understand the
Progressive Era in which they wrote, there is no agreement on how to

understand muckraking itself.[32] This chapter sheds light on the issue of who they were by looking at their work from journalistic, technical, and professional standpoints. Although what they wrote about is important, of course, the way in which the muckrakers approached their subject matter is more significant in this chapter. What journalistic norms did they apply in their writing? How did they work as journalists? How did they present their findings? Where did they put themselves in their stories? What was their point of view? Did the routines of journalism in Progressive Era America constrict their view of the issues and affect their ideology?

By analyzing their work and writing, it is clear that journalists in the Progressive Era were indeed confused about what role they should play. Hence, the muckrakers were different things at different times, even within the same article. At times, the muckrakers greatly resembled the contemporary reporter by wearing the hat of objectivity and by using aggressive, activist, enterprising research techniques. At other times, the muckrakers were at odds with the ideals of objectivity—I call this characteristic anti-objectivity—and more in tune with the harsh partisanship of the earlier days of journalism or with a literary form of journalism. To the thousands of readers of the popular magazines in the early twentieth century, whose views of where America should go in the twentieth century were being shaped by the press, journalism must have seemed confused. The muckrakers were offering a variety of points of view, and journalism was halfway between where it had been and where it was going.

That the muckrakers were confused should not be altogether surprising. The Progressive Era in which they were working was a dynamic, complex and confusing time. The central fact of American life was that the machine had entered the Garden of America. Ever since the Civil War, America had seen its industry grow, until by 1915, as historian Samuel P. Hays has written, "industrialism pervaded every segment and every activity of American life."[33] Rural America gave way to urban industrial America, and the pattern of life for everyone—from the threatened farmer to the factory worker to the "new woman"—was changing. New forces emerged everywhere, in labor, literature, politics, ideas, medicine, and journalism. In labor, for example, the unions were busy organizing and bitterly confronting capital. In politics, the spirit of reform was energizing both Democrats and Republicans, from state capitals to the White House, as politicians were forced to mobilize government efforts to regulate industry.[34]

Part of this stimulus for regulation was intellectual; there was a Progressive optimism about man's capability to alter the environment, to perfect social forms that would eliminate America's problems. This optimism brought great energy to reform, an energy that was only spurred by a new view of the world offered by a realistic brand of literature that had been brewing ever since William Dean Howells dethroned romanticism in the 1880s.[35] The dynamic of change in Progressive Era America was head spinning, and, depending on your perspective, America was either a nation on the move or in turmoil. The muckraking journalist, the most visible of Progressive Era professionals, was there both to capture the turmoil and speed the movement. But, like much of America, the muckrakers presented a blurred vision; they were unsure whether they wanted the garden back or wanted simply to keep the machine under control. Their journalism, at times, reverted to the days before the garden was despoiled; at other times, it looked ahead to a new age.

To show how journalism and journalists were confused during the Progressive Era, the various approaches the muckrakers took in their work are discussed. First, I will trace how the muckrakers were "objective"; that is, how they used many of the accepted characteristics of the modern objective journalist. Next I will contrast this fledgling objectivity with the ways in which, quite clearly, muckraking deviated from the norms of objectivity, ways that harken back to earlier times in American journalism. Then, to show still another, very different side of journalism, one which has a long history of its own, I will describe how muckraking was a literary phenomenon, how it borrowed techniques, and how it blurred the lines between fiction and nonfiction. Finally, coming almost full circle, I will discuss how the muckrakers were modern in another sense, in their enterprising and activist methods of gathering and presenting information.

FLEDGLING OBJECTIVITY

Michael Schudson, who traces the development of objectivity in his book, *Discovering the News*, asserts that not until after World War I "did the ideal of objectivity as consensually validated statements about the world, predicated on a radical separation of facts and values, arise."[36] Schudson cites two factors that led journalists to seek agreed-upon methods for writing news. The rise of the profession of public relations and the skepticism about facts brought on by wartime propaganda, he writes, made journalists wary of manipulated facts. Objectivity arose as a self-defense against those who would use the news pages for their own ends. This makes sense, but it does not explain why, in studying the muckrakers' work in the years before World War I, one can find numerous examples of how the rituals of objectivity had already begun to be practiced.

If, for example, one of the Ten Commandments of objectivity is the separation of "values" from "facts," then the turn-of-the-century muckrakers were, at the least, trying not to be sinners. Being thorough and establishing fact were fetishes with most of these journalists. "Look out for editorializing," Lincoln Steffens told his colleagues. "That's easy and it doesn't count for much without the facts." Ida Tarbell heeded the warning. She undertook research on John D. Rockefeller's Standard Oil Company in 1901. As she was pouring over various documents related to the company, word leaked about her investigation, and she was offered cooperation from some of the giant company's executives in New York. "I distinctly stated that I wanted facts," she told the company bosses.[37] Ray Stannard Baker, who recorded countless facts in tiny notepads kept stashed in his pocket, set a goal for himself when he decided to research the plight of blacks in America. "I want to set down every point of view," he declared. At the outset, he was determined that his opinions and conclusions would not influence his final product. Only "facts" would fill his articles, he declared.[38]

Charles Edward Russell went to the scene of a labor dispute in Northern Michigan in 1914 to ascertain whether the stories he was reading back East in the Associated Press were accurate. When he detailed his findings, he recounted the AP version and then compared it to what he called "the facts." Don't take my word, Russell said, listen to my facts. Not surprisingly, Russell's facts differed from AP's. Will Irwin perhaps spoke for many of the muckrakers when he wrote his 1911 articles on the press. Editorials, the opinion of the newspaper, mean nothing anymore, he wrote. People no longer discuss what Greeley or some editor says; they discuss only what facts from news stories tell them. Lincoln Steffens, considered the prototypical muckraking writer, said that the muckrakers learned their lessons on facts as newspaper reporters in the 1890s. "Reporters were to report the news as it happened, like machines, without prejudice, color, and without style; all alike." Facts are what count; not impressions, not opinion. Irwin, like Steffens, referred to the contemporary reporter as a "news machine"[39]—not only an apropos metaphor in the age of industrialism, but also a fitting term for the reporter who was emerging as a neutral technician who tinkered with the facts but tried increasingly to eliminate opinion.

Retrieving facts was the goal, but where did a reporter go to get those facts? The modern, objective journalist—muckraker or not—relies heavily on public documents, especially government documents. A fact is considered most reliable if it comes from an official source or record. The rely-on-government rule was less well established for the early muckrakers, in part because government was less pervasive. There were fewer federal and state agencies, fewer regulations, and fewer bureaucratic documents to consult. Nevertheless, when they could, the muckrakers relied on documents to make their cases. Perhaps the most reliant was Ida Tarbell, who viewed herself as a historian. "My first business," she said on beginning her research, will be "making sure of the documents in the case." When her articles appeared in book form, she included hundreds of pages of documents in an appendix. She often used an asterisk, much like a footnote, to let the reader know the source of her material. When Samuel McClure allowed her to hire an assistant to research Rockefeller's company, she told him to "draw almost entirely from original sources."[40] Dig into documents, she said, practicing what she preached by wading through thousands of pages of transcripts of court cases in which Standard had been a party.

Added to the court documents was testimony taken from legislative hearings which she meticulously studied. These two sources gave her the only on-the-record statements available from the reclusive Rockefeller. The search for documents drove Tarbell. From the outset of her research, she wanted to prove what everyone told her: that Rockefeller had sought and conspired to control the entire oil industry. Sources told her that at the beginning of his drive for power he had established a small company whose charter stated, in essence, that monopoly was the goal. Could she find the "smoking gun," the actual charter? Copies of it had been removed from every logical location until, of all places, she found it in an archive of the New York Public Library. The document that placed Rockefeller's hand right in the cookie jar had been found.[41] Tarbell did not charge illegal conspiracy; the record spoke for itself. It was not Tarbell's opinion that Rockefeller conspired to monopolize the industry; it was documented fact. Tarbell was neutral in the matter.

The investigative reporter's best friend is the government document, but what does a reporter do when the government has not yet acknowledged that a problem exists and there are no documents, no research, and virtually no interest in a public scandal? That was the problem faced in 1904 by Samuel Hopkins Adams who investigated America's $250-million patent medicine industry at a time when standards in American medicine were in transition. Medicines were virtually unregulated during the Progressive Era; there was no federal Food and Drug Administration.[42] There were only a bunch of quacks and get-rich schemers who were duping the public into buying various alleged medicines which, as Adams found, often contained addictive drugs or were placebos advertised as miracle cures. Included in the "conspicuous swindles," Adams said, were cures for heart disease, epilepsy, and cancer. "Relentless greed sets the trap and death is partner in the enterprise," Adams wrote.[43] Another partner "at the beck and call" of the quacks were the newspapers who were advertising the frauds and making a fortune in the process. Adams went to work to expose the patent medicine ingredients and the fraudulent advertising that hyped them. Documents played a key part in making his story believable.

In October 1904, Adams took on the makers of Peruna, a liquid nostrum that would cure, so said its advocates, bunions, heat rash, consumption, small pox, old age, sunstroke, and balding. Peruna's largest ingredient was alcohol. Even the government at times acknowledged this. At an obscure Indian reservation, Adams found a district attorney who had indicted Peruna's backers for illegally selling alcohol to Indians. Adams used the indictment to prove his case. In various state courts, Adams found documents which confirmed that judges had often agreed: alcohol constituted the bulk of Peruna and other dangerous patent medicines. When the government was no help, Adams let the nostrum owners reveal their own nefarious natures. He obtained letters they sent to consumers which showed that companies would pay substantial sums for testimonials about their products.[44] In response to his requests, physicians corresponded with Adams about the medicine company hucksters who went to hospitals seeking testimonials in return for free samples. When the American Medical Association documented a report of a young woman, in good health, who took Orangeine, a headache powder, and died, Adams used the coroner's report reprinted in the *Journal of the American Medical Association*. The official document, not Adams, made the case against this "subtle poison."[45]

Perhaps the most dramatic smoking-gun document that *Collier's* used came from a source in the newspaper advertising industry. Either Adams or his colleague Mark Sullivan was given a copy of the standard contract that the patent medicine sellers offered to newspapers—a "contract of silence," he called it. It stated that if any damaging or critical remarks appeared in any news pages about the patent medicines, all contracts, and thus considerable revenue, would be automatically ended. No wonder the newspapers were silent about the frauds and dangers of the industry; they had been bought off. *Collier's* then combined this with other damaging documents. From a New York criminal case, a doctor's seized records showed the extent to which the doctor relied on fraudulent advertising to earn his money. A bankruptcy case detailed the extent of a large patent medicine company's payments for newspaper advertising. Transcripts of private statements made by patent medicine industry lobbyists revealed their huge public relations budget. Copies of letters to newspapers from the nostrum makers showed that they warned newspaper owners how their revenue would suffer if pending regulatory legislation was approved.[46] Just as Tarbell did not have to accuse Rockefeller, Adams and *Collier's* did not have to say that the press had been bought off by advertisers. The documents made the case. The "strategic ritual" of objectivity was a key part of Adams' mode.

None of the other muckrakers studied here was as fastidious as were Tarbell and Adams in documenting their allegations, but all used documents to some degree. Will Irwin, for example, spent most of his time tracing the press' history by interviewing newspaper owners and reporters and by looking closely at the newspapers themselves. Once he made good use of a court case to prove that newspapers would omit unfavorable stories about their advertisers. When Minnie Akers, who was pregnant and shopping in a Manhattan department store in 1907, was falsely accused of shoplifting, she was so upset "she all but died," Irwin wrote. She sued the police, and when her lawsuit came to trial in 1910, it was the biggest news of the day. Irwin searched the news columns of some of the city's biggest newspapers, all of which carried considerable advertising from the sued department store. There were no stories about Minnie Akers' trial and her victory. "Had the defendant been a saloon-keeper," wrote Irwin, "it would have been good for an item anywhere."[47]

Russell, too, made occasional but effective use of documents. When he visited slum buildings on the Lower East Side of Manhattan in 1907, the tenants told him that Trinity Church, one of the city's oldest, wealthiest, and most prestigious religious institutions, owned the neighborhood. Off Russell went to view the property records kept by the city and to confirm the tenants' charges. His article began by sketching the tombs-like buildings, and then he asked: "Who owns these terrible places? Who draws the wretched profit of their existence?" Trinity Church was the answer. "This is the heart of her possessions," and the documents told the tale.[48]

Even though the muckrakers were clearly trying to name names and point blame, they often strove to be balanced, to give the benefit of doubt to those they were exposing. Ida Tarbell could balance points of view in a classic way. The oil producers "believed in independent effort and fair play for all. They wanted competition, loved open fight," she wrote. "Mr. Rockefeller's point of view was different. He believed that the good of all was in a combination. . . . Thus on the one hand there was an exaggerated sense of personal independence, on the other a firm belief in combination."[49] Will Irwin used a similar dual lens in his view of the press. "The condemners say" was balanced by "The defenders answer." He portrayed yellow journalism as, on the one hand, a scourge of the press, but also as a weapon against privileged autocracy.[50] Some of Irwin's best exposé material was about William Randolph Hearst, who was so worried when he heard about the articles that he threatened a large libel suit against *Collier's*. Irwin called Hearst a ruthless liar who often sold his news pages to the highest bidder. Still, he conceded, Hearst's brand of underdog journalism had to be admired. "The historian of the year 2000 cannot ignore" Hearst, he wrote.[51]

ANTI-OBJECTIVITY: THE FLIP SIDE

Ray Stannard Baker operated very much like Tarbell and Adams in his pursuit of facts, documents, and balance. "The people," he wrote, need "economic facts. . . . My job is illumination."[52] In *Following the Color Line*, Baker used police reports, court transcripts, census figures, and state and county records. Because commissions to monitor civil rights violations did not exist, Baker needed more than the documents, and he supplemented them with interviews and personal observations more extensively than the other muckrakers. Thus, one finds Baker often using the first person: "I saw . . . I was told . . . I heard." He also regularly balanced viewpoints. When blacks complained bitterly about paying first-class prices on trains but receiving second-class accommodations, Baker sought out railroad officials to get their side. "It is important to hear what they have to say," he wrote, and they explained that if there were enough black riders, the railroad would provide an entire car.[53]

When Baker began his research, he intended to report every point of view . . . to let the facts do the talking. When he was ready to write, however, he began to do an about-face. Perhaps what he had written three years earlier became clearer now in his mind: "After seeing men and things and thinking about them for some years, a writer develops a desire to put down some of his conclusions, something that will be more than a report on the facts."[54] And so, Baker added a final chapter to his work, a chapter of personal conclusions. Objectivity, then, is evident in various ways in the reporting of Baker, but so, too, is the antithetical desire to let the facts be submerged at times to logical conclusions and personal values. In this Baker was typical of the muckrakers, who were by no means stuck in the narrow trough of objectivity.

Steffens articulated what at least some of the muckrakers were thinking by 1908, midway through this era of reform. "We have the facts," Steffens insisted. "The time has come to discuss the cause of our American corruption—and cures."[55] Steffens wanted to advocate solutions, although some colleagues on the *American* magazine split with him on this issue. Being neutral, he felt, was not the antidote to what ailed America. How about a little dose of anti-objectivity? That, too, was in the muckrakers' writing. Strains of an ideological, almost dogmatic advocacy, intemperate rhetoric, partisanship, and personal involvement can be seen running through the muckrakers' work, before and after 1908.

David Graham Phillips and Charles Edward Russell provide the best examples of anti-objective stories. Phillips and Russell were two-of-a-kind reporters. Both were reared in the Midwest in professional families; both went to elite Eastern colleges. Phillips became a reporter in Cincinnati, Ohio; Russell went to Minneapolis, Minnesota. After coming to New York in the late 1880s, the two men became colleagues and confidantes at Pulitzer's *World*. Both had similar schizoid experiences in the newsroom: they began as reporters where facts were paramount, but then switched to writing editorials (Phillips for Pulitzer, Russell for

Hearst) where opinions about the facts were what counted. When they began to muckrake, the two traditions merged.

Russell was Hearst's first choice for the "Treason of the Senate" articles, but Russell declined, suggesting that Phillips be given the assignment. Russell might have written the articles in a similar fashion; both men saw a conspiracy against the people by an alliance of business and elected officials as the overriding issue in America. According to Phillips, the Senate was "the eager, resourceful, indefatigable agent of the interests, as hostile to the American public as any invading army." Senators "serve the master, the plutocracy." "The common enemy," he wrote, " 'the interests,' dominate the political as well as the industrial machinery of the nation."[56] To Russell, the "Controlling Interests" held the reins of power in America. Their invisible tentacles penetrated the Associated Press in Calumet, Michigan, the newspapers in Boston, and magazines all over the country. "The real editors are the advertisers," he wrote. "And back of them [are] the Central Financial Interests" who have the nation in a "stranglehold." "Nothing," Russell declared, "can escape it."[57] Russell's writing was smooth, colorful, and filled with anecdotes, but there was often little convincing reportage to buttress his case. The partisan editorialist spoke more than the objective reporter.

Phillips was given two researchers for the Senate articles and yet, when reading the "Treason," one has to search to find the facts. Rhetoric, intemperate language, and unsubstantiated allegations dominate, a far cry from the objective tone of Ida Tarbell, for example, who wrote about "Mr. Rockefeller." In his first article, Phillips called New York Senator Chauncey Depew a "traitor to the people . . . the sly courtier-agent, with the greasy tongue and greasy backbone." Like all lawyers, Phillips wrote, Depew is a mere "fetcher and courier for the plutocrats," a "buffoon" and "spineless sycophant," "the Vanderbilt's creature." As for Rhode Island's Nelson Aldrich, the next senator attacked, he was the organizer of the treason, a briber and swindler, "the chief exploiter of the American public." He was typical, Phillips wrote, "of the utter rottenness" of the leaders of Congress, one of the "thieves" whose "stupendous robbery" makes them a "scurvy lot."[58] Restrained this was not. In fact, two scholars assert, "rarely outside of campaigns had such blunt words been used about august public officials by a respected journalist." The harshness is akin to what can be found in the early nineteenth-century press, the "dark ages" of journalism.[59] One of the attacked senators was not far off the mark when he responded to Phillips' writing by saying that the articles were "manifestly designed to prejudice, rather than inform the public."[60]

Before the "Treason" was published, Hearst read galley proofs to see what his recently purchased magazine had gotten from Phillips. Hearst, never one to demand extreme factuality from his reporters, was upset.

"I had intended an exposé. We have merely an attack," he wrote in a telegram to Phillips. "Violence is not force. Windy vituperation is not convincing. . . . The facts, the proof, the documentary evidence are an important thing, and the article is deficient in them. We want more definite facts throughout."[61] What the reader got, however, was more rhetoric than substantiated fact. Henry Cabot Lodge of Massachusetts, who publicly supported civil service reform, had "tried to fill the Charleston navy yard with his heelers . . . [with]Lodge boys," Phillips declared.[62] How did he know this? What was his source? Not a hint of attribution. In this, Phillips differed from Tarbell and Adams, who made clear the source of much of their material. Baker, too, was likely to preface his findings with his attributions. But Phillips, Russell, and to some degree, Irwin, were more likely to assert and conclude than to document. Typical also of Phillips was to tell the reader about the "scores" of examples he could have given about a senator's wrongdoing, but, instead, he invariably said that "one most notable instance will suffice." Objective style would have called for less rhetoric, more examples.

Since a reporter is supposed to be a neutral observer, objectivity calls for a dispassionate approach. Reporters are not to be allied with parties on either side of a dispute, and they must avoid obvious involvement, in research and in the eventual writing. Others are players in the story, not the reporter. On this score, Phillips maintained the objective posture. On occasion he used a first-person plural approach, as in "We have now seen the Aldrich-Gorman merger of the two party machines."[63] However, he avoided using the first person singular throughout the "Treason" articles. This was typical also of Tarbell, who, if she had to refer to herself, wrote of "the reporter." In a similar fashion, Russell was often an invisible guide, smoothly bringing the reader into a tenement or a prison with no evidence that he was leading the tour. His focus was on the subject—the slum dwellers, the accused burglar—not on the reporter.

In contrast, Ray Stannard Baker was the most anti-objective of the muckrakers: he was boorishly evident. Baker told the reader not only what he believed and what he had concluded, but also where he went, with whom he spoke, and why he did what he did to piece a story together. Much of it, at least in hindsight, seems unnecessary. What follows is one segment from *Color Line*, the opening paragraphs from an article that readers of the *American* magazine read in June 1907 on the condition of the rural Southern black man. I have edited (in brackets) the article as a contemporary editor might.

After my arrival in Atlanta, and when I had begun to understand some of the more superficial ramifications of the colour line, I asked several Southern men whose acquaintance I had made where I could best see the poorer or criminal class of Negroes. So much has been said of the danger arising from this element of Southern population and it plays such a part in every discussion of the race question that I was anxious to learn all I could about it. [Delete this whole paragraph. Tell the reader what you have found, not what you have done to gather your material. Save your personal anxieties for your memoirs.]

"Go down any morning to Judge Broyles's court," they said to me, "and you'll see the lowest of the low." [Delete this quote. Show us the "low."]

So I went down—the first of many visits I made to police and justice courts. I chose a Monday morning that I might see to the best advantage the accumulation of the arrests of Saturday and Sunday. [Delete again. Let the research show how many visits you made. Get to the point: the black men on trial.]

The police station stands in [on Atlanta's] Decatur Street, in the midst of the very worst section of the city, surrounded by low saloons, dives, and pawn-shops. The court occupies a great room upstairs, and it was crowded that [this Monday] morning to its capacity. Besides the police, lawyers, court officers, and white witnesses, at least 150 spectators filled the seats behind the rail, nearly all of them Negroes. [This shows potential as your lead paragraph; it sets the scene and leads to the courtroom where your focus is to be.] The ordinary Negro loves nothing better than to sit and watch the proceedings of a court. [Delete this unless you have an eminent authority to this generalization. If not, avoid such personal conclusions.] Judge Broyles kindly invited me to a seat on the platform at his side where I could look into the faces of the prisoners and hear all that was said. [Delete this sentence also. Thank the judge with a note, not in your story. Tell the reader about the faces you saw, but not where you sat to see them. They, not you, are the story.][64]

Baker wrote another five paragraphs before he made it clear that this was "the story about the country Negro," whose travails were made evident in the courtroom. Baker was, obviously, very much a part of the narrative, unnecessarily so if one invoked objectivity's standards. The point, however, is that the confusion of journalism is especially evident in *Color Line*. Baker wanted to be all things at once: he wanted to deliver untarnished facts and he wanted to give everyone's opinion, but he also wanted to give his own opinions and draw his own conclusions. Samuel Hopkins Adams took a similar tack in his articles on patent medicines, but, in contrast, his involvement was more interesting and relevant. When he entered the narrative, it seemed as if he belonged. A doctor told Adams to mix vermouth, gin, and bitters and to advertise the mixture as a cure for bunions and baldness. "That sounds to me very much like a cocktail," Adams responded. "So it is," the doctor replied. "But it's just as much a medicine as Peruna and not as bad a drink."[65]

Even though all reporters play detective in chasing down information, objectivity usually forbids writing about the pursuit. Adams did so, however, and it was effective. Certain patent medicine representatives told Adams that not all medicines were evil; investigate the H. E. Bucklen Co. of Chicago, he was told, for they are "above criticism." Bucklen did not interest Adams as much as "Dr. King's New Discovery for Consumption," then being widely advertised in Midwestern newspapers. In pursuit of this cure, "I ran unexpectedly on an interesting trail," Adams wrote. He found that Dr. King's cure was a "pretty diabolical concoction," an opiate "designed to shorten the life of any consumptive who takes it steadily."[66] The trail of this cure unexpectedly led straight back to the supposedly reputable H. E. Bucklen; they made the poisonous cure. Adams' clever uses of himself as a character in his narrative was an exception. More often, the use was unnecessary and clumsy in the work of the muckrakers, who were more compelling when they wrote their articles from the outside, when they avoided the folksy first person, and, instead, recreated scenes in story-like and literary fashion. But the literary inclinations of the muckrakers also raised journalistic problems.

ARGUMENT AND LITERATURE AT ONCE

When Samuel McClure came upon the idea of examining the "trust" problem in America by probing one company, Ida Tarbell, who got the assignment, knew she faced a difficult task. Rockefeller was a slippery quarry, and McClure was a demanding taskmaster. McClure wanted stories that would hike circulation as well as expose. Tarbell recalled; "We were after, as McClure always insisted, interesting reading material and if it contributed to the general good, so much the better."[67] The reader first, then the facts. Writing for popular magazines like *McClure's* imposed a readability burden on the muckrakers that was sometimes at odds with factuality. Statistics, attributions, and laborious explanations of complex situations with their necessary qualifiers—these all hurt the flow of a news story. The challenge for the muckrakers was to stick to the facts and yet still keep their readers. They responded to the challenge with a journalism that had a decidedly literary inclination.

The impetus for dramatic story telling came not only from the editors and publishers, like McClure, who had a commercial desire to reach broad audiences and sell magazines, but also from the muckraking writers themselves, almost all of whom secretly harbored the desire to write the Great American Novel. The muckrakers figured they could learn about writing and life while working as reporters, and then they would translate this rich experience into fiction, albeit, as it turned out, second-rate fiction. Their dreams were further encouraged by concurrent movements in literature and journalism. In journalism, the feature or human interest story, where a reporter could write with flair and freedom, had been evolving since the New York *Sun* pioneered its use in the 1830s. It reached its peak at the *Sun* under Dana, who urged his reporters to be creative and literary. Take the facts and make them sing, Dana told his reporters. Future muckrakers Phillips, Irwin, and Adams all worked at one time or another, not coincidentally, for the *Sun*.[68]

Russell, Tarbell, and Baker never worked for Dana, but they, too, had similar secret longings for the creative life. Although a political ideologue and a tough, hard news reporter, Russell dabbled in the writing of poetry throughout his reporting years. Tarbell, at least once, tried her hand at writing a novel, but quit, saying her work was inferior. As for Baker, the writing of fiction was on his mind from the outset of his reporting career in Chicago. Sometime in the middle of the muckraking era, using the alter ego David Grayson, he began to switch gears. The result was eight novels, which were, the critics agreed, like most of the muckrakers' fiction, of poor quality.[69]

In literature, the novel of romance was being replaced by a naturalistic style of writing that often relied on a factuality, a realism, that the journalists could easily find in their storehouse of memories and anecdotes. Beginning in the 1880s, fiction writers began using precise details and facts to depict rapidly changing social relations in an attempt, largely successful, to show the true character of institutions. This literary realism often relied on real events and people. Writers like Stephen Crane, Frank Norris, and Theodore Dreiser crossed successfully between journalism and literature.[70] Others, like Tarbell and Lincoln Steffens, were unable to make the transition. Nonetheless, the desire was evident and it effected muckraking journalism. Steffens, complaining once about his editorial chores, said he wanted to do "real work," that is, to write fiction.[71] When he couldn't, he and the other muckrakers did the next best thing; they wrote fiction-like journalism.

Colorful descriptions, anecdotes, dialogue—these were the literary traits of the muckrakers. After working for years as reporters, it all came quite naturally for the muckrakers were adept at building drama and telling stories. Tarbell, for example, could have just mastered the voluminous statistics about Standard Oil, but she added human interest by offering snippets of personalities. Rockefeller, she wrote, was "brooding, cautious, secretive, seeing all the possible dangers as well as all the possible opportunities." Once, she described Rockefeller as having a "scaly face like a lizard." In the midst of a fight with the oil producers, Rockefeller attended a meeting, she wrote, sitting silently, listening. One producer told her, "He took me all in, saw just how much fight he could expect from me, and I knew it."[72] The reader could feel Rockefeller's cold, steely glance and sense his ruthlessness.

Adams wrote not only the facts about the poisonous nostrums but also about the people behind them, the "shameful quackery" of Frank

A. Richardson; the infamous Dr. Kilmer of Swamp Root fame; Mrs. J. A. Koop of York, Pennsylvania, who was "drugging helpless babies." He told stories about the poor victims, like the counter girls from a Chicago department store who kept returning to a pharmacy for a cocaine-based medicine, and how desperate they became when the pharmacy stopped its sales. He told about the man in a restaurant who encountered a prominent publisher who declared that his newspaper was free of fraudulent and offensive advertising. Oh, really, the man countered, as he picked up the newspaper and began to read aloud the graphic ad columns. First, the children were asked to leave the table, then the woman, until, finally, the publisher conceded: the advertisements were raw; he must clean up his ad pages.[73] The scene could have been taken from a William Dean Howells novel.

Perhaps the most effective muckraking segment of Baker's *Following the Color Line* came when he recreated in short-story fashion two Southern lynchings. Using court documents and interviews, he described the brutal killing of the Hodges family in a small Georgia town. Two black men first murdered Mrs. Hodges "with peculiar brutality." The husband came upon the scene, and he, too, was murdered. Their six-year-old daughter at first hid in the back of a buggy. When she came out, the murderers yelled at her, "Where's the money?" She gave them a nickel, and they beat her to death. The three bodies were dragged to a house and the house was burned. The men were arrested and convicted, but the townspeople feared they would be set free on appeal. "In the court room," Baker wrote, "sentence had been passed. . . . Then the mob broke in." A minister, "with tears streaming down his face . . . begged the mob to let the law take its course." A voice yelled, however, "We don't want religion, we want blood." The two black men were dragged out as the mob "gathered volume and excitement." "Burn them! Burn them!" The mob was in "a frenzy of ferocity." Someone yelled, "They burned the Hodges and gave them no choice; burn the niggers." "Please don't burn me," one assailant pleaded. "Hang me or shoot me; please don't burn me." The mob paid him no heed, Baker wrote, and a photographer took pictures of it all. The townspeople posed next to the charred bodies, took souvenirs, and threw sticks at the writhing creatures. "This is the law of the mob," Baker wrote. After an equally effective account of another lynching follows, the reader is drained.[74] This was good story telling.

Will Irwin used numerous anecdotes to spice his analysis of newspapers. To emphasize the growing control over the media by financial interests, Irwin told of a Pittsburgh newspaper owner who was called to a meeting by the city's bankers. They were angry that the newspaper was advocating various reforms that were inimical to their needs. Irwin re-created the meeting. "Stop it!" one banker yelled at the owner. If you don't, we will wreck your finances. The publisher stood up, and yelled back: "You may break me. It is in your power [but you] can't keep me from writing. Gentlemen, my signature to an article is worth some attention. And if you force me out, I shall have enough money left to print and distribute a handbill . . . and it will be the most interesting reading in Pittsburgh." With the threat of exposure, the bankers never bothered the publisher again, Irwin wrote.[75]

One story Irwin told about yellow journalism came from his days as a newspaper reporter in New York City. After a boat sank in New York harbor killing many passengers, Irwin was sent to the city morgue. Relatives, impatient at the delay in identifying next of kin, grew angry. For a minute they "pushed and jostled." One small German man "shook his fist at the police," but then the morgue doors opened and "they filed soberly in." When Irwin arrived back at the newsroom, an edition of Hearst's *Journal* was headlined in red letters three inches high: "Riot at Morgue—Frantic Mob Charges Police!" The story was "typical . . . in the height of the yellow insanity," Irwin wrote.[76] Typical also of the muckrakers' writing flair.

Mostly the muckrakers used such anecdotes as small parts of their overall package of material. Only Charles Edward Russell used a short-story approach for an entire article. In "A Burglar in the Making," Russell took an inmate at a Georgia prison and traced his steps through the criminal justice system. The young man was convicted of stealing a few hundred dollars from his employer's cash register; thrown into a prison with hard-core criminals; rented out to a private company for torturous labor; and finally released, embittered. He vowed to get even with a society that had made him into an outlaw. Russell's moral play included scenes of brutal whippings, worm-infested lunches, and chain-gang, sweatshop workdays. So effective was this article that, after its publication in *Everybody's*, the Georgia legislature moved to end peonage.[77]

This literary side of the muckrakers' work made them appealing to a middle-class audience, which clamored each month for more real-life drama, the soap operas of the Progressive Era. Such public attention and wide exposure also put pressure on government to respond to the exposés, to get a leash on the industrial beast that had been loosed. The drawback was that, in their attempt to be interesting, the muckrakers may have, at times, shown the larger truth at the expense of the factual truth. The seeds of doubt which they undoubtedly planted about their facts may have aided those who wished to derail their reform writing. When Phillips' "Treason" appeared, the attack began (beware, Roosevelt warned, of the "sensational, lurid, untruthful"), and if the facts were not to be believed, then the muckrakers' desire for governmental intervention might also be attacked. Could they be believed? Or were they novelist-journalists who were "piping" their stories?

Phillips, after all, had for years been writing fiction and nonfiction. What about his persistent technique of using imaginary characters, composites, and conversations which blurred the line between journalism and literature? Could the democracy choose reform based on Phillips' "Mr. and Mrs. Climber," or his "Lord and Lady Bountiful"? Even worse, was his attack on the august U.S. Senate inspired by his imagination or his facts? In his novel *The Plum Tree*, published the year before he had even done any research for the "Treason" articles, Phillips portrayed the U.S. Senate as a collection of fetching boys for the powerful industrialists. "Graft was the backbone of the whole skeleton of legislative business," he wrote. One senator, much like Nelson Aldrich, controlled all the legislation in league with a syndicate of wealthy businessmen. His fiction differed little from his journalism.[78]

Phillips was not the only one who used fiction in his journalism. Tarbell, Baker, Russell, Irwin, and Adams all embellished scenes and created dialogue. "This scheme," Tarbell quoted Rockefeller as saying, "is bound to work. It means absolute control by us of the oil business." The tight-lipped Rockefeller, who was such a careful witness at legislative hearings, would never admit such a plan, and he had never given Tarbell an interview. The statement was what Rockefeller must have been thinking, but this was not clear from Tarbell's use. In other instances, she was elaborate in her made-up dialogues.[79] Russell, who used a visit to a jail and interviews with a prisoner to re-create prison life, fictionalized extended conversations between inmates. He went so far as to imitate dialect. "Aw, go on, don't give me none of that. Think I ain't fly? I seen you pinched many's the time." The dialogue, conveniently, allowed Russell to make the article's major point. "You're a crook now, if you never were before, and a crook you'll stay till the end of your days," the prisoner tells the young burglar.[80] The dialogue made for pulp-type reading, but it strayed from what objectivity would demand. Will Irwin may have had the work of some muckrakers in mind when he pointed out that when the reporter "sits down to tell in his most interesting fashion the story which he has found," it is then that he meets "his greatest temptations to depart from the truth." "An imaginary detail here and there" might make for colorful reading, as Irwin knew, but it must have further confused the reader.[81] Perhaps Roosevelt was right. Could these "muck-rakers" be believed? Were conditions really as bad as they were depicting them to be? Or did their vision of America come from their imaginations, and not from the streets, not from the sweatshops, not from the smoky back rooms where the tycoons, so it was said, were plotting against the people? The confused techniques of the muckrakers, the blurring of the line between fiction and nonfiction, and the switching from objectivity to anti-objectivity made it difficult to answer those questions with a ringing affirmation of journalism's veracity.

ENTERPRISE AND OBJECTIVITY:
THE FUTURE BECKONS

Looking at the work of the muckrakers is much like watching a Darwinian species in the throes of evolution for the work of the muckrakers both looked back at journalism's past and foreshadowed its future. The artifacts from the past give glimpses, for example, of the harsh partisanship that was characteristic of the press in the early 1800s. More evident is the journalism of the post–Civil War years when independence from state power and business developed and when an alliance grew with the perceived interests of the people. Only a fiercely independent press, flexing its muscles as never before, could attack the plunder and corruption of the monopoly businesses as did the muckrakers; only an alliance with the masses could lead the muckrakers to deal as they did with social injustice in prisons and factories and race relations; and only a mixed-motive, populist-commercial editorial sense would make the muckrakers write in such a literary manner so as to seek more readers for their crusades. The press' penchant for seeking larger and larger audiences, however, also led straight to the scourge of sensationalism, and that, too, is a part of journalism history that is evident in muckraking. Add to this mixture one more ingredient: a literary and human interest flair, a readability spice, which had developed in the 1880s alongside sensationalism. In their effort to reach large audiences, the muckrakers practiced what many of their famous editors had preached for decades: they sought not only news but also human interest.

Partisanship, sensationalism, independence, and human interest—these were all developments that occurred before the turn of the century. What, if anything, then made these twentieth-century writers new, different, and vital? Was their journalism simply the continuation of old forms of journalism? One is tempted to say that there is little that is new in the work of the muckrakers. The subjects they chose—anti-trust and corruption in government, for example—were certainly not new ones but rather continuations of concerns from the years before the new century arrived. Many of their techniques and styles of writing were also the continuation of old forms. Where they differed from the past and distinguished themselves for the future was in their mixing of fledgling objectivity and literary exposé with enterprising techniques. As progressive, activist journalists, the muckrakers moved significantly out of the past—and into the journalistic future. With a typewriter and a swagger, the muckrakers blended their facts and images, telling fascinating insider's tales each month to the largest audience ever assembled. In doing so, they operated much like modern investigative reporters. Independent of government investigations, the muckrakers made their own forays into the behind-the-scenes world of politics and industry. They acted as detectives, social workers, preachers, and educators to reveal an underside of America, an "invisible government" that both entranced and alarmed their reading public.

The muckrakers were not satisfied with simply observing the social process. They felt the need, through their journalism, to become active participants. Later in their careers, some of the muckrakers would leave journalism and actually join political movements. For now, however, they were content to try to shape the world—in what directions at times they were not quite so sure—with their writing. Will Irwin made perceptive observations about the need for press activism in his 1911 essays on the press. In the 1890s, the *New York Times* had been pulled out of bankruptcy and restored to a place as one of the best journals in America. "It comes nearest of any newspaper in New York," Irwin wrote, "to presenting a truthful daily picture of life . . . in the world at large." The *Times* is not particularly clever nor especially illuminating, he said, but it is "straight, uncolored, essentially truthful." This, as Irwin reported, was to be praised at a time when many newspapers were rigged and corrupt. Nonetheless, the *Times* also presented a great journalistic dilemma. The *Times* was good at presenting what happened in the world, but it never made news on its own, it never took the initiative, and it showed little enterprise. If reformers got their case before a commission or court, the *Times* would report it fairly and fully. "But until the case becomes . . . news in the conventional sense, [Publisher Ochs] would consider that the matter was no business of the *Times*," Irwin wrote. With the *Times*' approach toward news coverage, Irwin reasoned, "the guerrillas of special privilege" will devour the public before the public is even made aware.[82] Irwin was criticizing the emerging objective approach to journalism and advocating an activism that, in part, was the unspoken but clear method of the muckrakers. Take these examples of activism.

Samuel Hopkins Adams was sure that certain prescription drugs were being made in 1904 with dangerous additives and chemicals. Because ingredients were not listed on the products, which was his goal, he needed a way to prove his suspicions. The government was a little help. Today, the Food and Drug Administration, which came about in 1906 partly as a result of Adams' work, would have on file extensive documentation on food and drug ingredients. Before then, the government's role was limited to the crusading of a lone chemist, Dr. Harvey Wiley, who, working in the Department of Agriculture, was championing the cause of pure food.[83] The drug matter was left to the muckrakers. *Collier's* editors stepped into the vacuum: they agreed to hire their own chemists and scientists to test the suspected products. Since the government was not working for the consumer, someone else had to. Adams and Co. became the *Consumer Reports* of the Progressive Era, practicing an activist brand of watchdog journalism.

Charles Edward Russell read dispatches in the Associated Press from the scene of a labor dispute in Calumet, Michigan, but he did not believe them. The AP was reporting that laborers, the working people, were using violence against police and property owners to protest their unhappiness with working conditions. Russell, recently converted to a benevolent socialism, did not believe that the workers would turn to violence. He made a trip to Michigan to investigate. Fueled by his belief that capital was attempting to whitewash the public's perception of unions, he checked the AP version against eyewitness accounts of various hostilities. His detective work paid off: he found AP's version to be misleading and at times downright false, and he documented the "truth," as he called it. According to the AP version; at a town hall where the union held meetings, an unhappy worker had gone beserk and to protest had wrecked furniture, broken glass, and fired shots at the police who tried to subdue him. Source? The police. Russell's version, based on accounts of numerous eyewitnesses, told a different story. The unhappy worker, a union organizer, lived in an apartment above the town hall. The police came to his front door, knocked it down, started a fight, and then fired shots at him. Subsequently, they wrecked the meeting place.[84] The people's man on the scene set the record straight.

When Ida Tarbell began her research in 1902, sources were, at first, reluctant to speak with her; some were afraid of Rockefeller and others had been bought off in return for their silence. Once, at a party, Tarbell received a veiled warning that her life might be in danger if she went after Rockefeller. Nevertheless, she persevered, relying on public documents at the outset, until her articles got into print and new sources came forward. One source, in particular, gave her perhaps her most damning evidence against Rockefeller. The backbone of Rockefeller's control over the oil industry was his system of rebates, or kickbacks, to the railroad. In return for the rebates, Rockefeller got special treatment for his oil cargo while his competitors got lost in the shuffle. Everyone knew that the rebates, which were illegal, were taking place, but how could Tarbell document them? A cleaning boy at a Standard Oil office read a Tarbell reference to the rebates. Perhaps, he thought, the rebates could be explained by the carefully documented lists of payments he had seen in the company's wastebaskets. The boy collected the lists and, through an intermediary, made connection with the jubilant Tarbell.[85] She had her proof; she also had the modern equivalent of Woodward and Bernstein's "Deep Throat," a secret source who brought her the inside dope. A more timid and less activist reporter would have shied away from secret sources that accused the world's most powerful company; Tarbell did not.

These are just a few examples of the times when the muckraking journalists took it upon themselves to get the facts; they went beyond observations, beyond interviews. They were activist—and free—in ways that journalists had not been before. In fact, the muckrakers had a freedom that was probably unprecedented in the history of journalism. Their publishers gave them tremendous amounts of time to do their research and more than ample space to display their findings. Their salaries were fat. Even Phillips was surprised how much Hearst was willing to pay for his "Treason" articles. They were allowed great creativity in their writing—they could be literary when they liked, or personal if they chose. There is no indication that anyone limited their choice of subject. If something smelled foul, and their muckraking noses twitched, off they went. This freedom also encouraged their creativity in another way: the muckrakers began to utilize enterprising techniques that are associated more with modern investigative reporting than with the trolley-car turn-of-the-century press.

As free as they were, the muckrakers were not quite sure what to do with all their freedom because they were not quite sure who they were, what their function was. Journalism had yet to define itself since professional norms were still emerging and not yet fixed. The result was that journalism produced a potpourri of techniques and approaches during the Progressive Era. The muckrakers were, at times, observers, who gave the facts and described conditions without inserting their values. At other times, they were creative artists, journalists with a literary bent, who painted a portrait of people and institutions, with a brush that mixed facts and fiction. When the facts the muckrakers collected angered them, they went beyond observation and description to advocacy for Progressive reform. Some, like Ida Tarbell, denied they had any social goals, but deny as they might, the muckrakers were reformers who sought to bring the government further into the lives of businessmen and the public.[86] In order to do this, they had to step past simple observation and adopt a new posture of activism and enterprise.

As the muckrakers experimented with these various guises and, in the process, aided the forces of reform, there were, unknowingly, forces gathering to slow the movement. Behind the scenes—secretly, quietly— those who had been attacked were beginning to fight back. Meanwhile, in the profession of journalism itself, there was a growing sense that press independence also meant press neutrality. The rituals of objectivity, only partially developed, needed to be refined more, and as these rituals came more and more into practice, they would limit the perogatives of journalists. The freedom of muckraking would turn out to be short lived. The combination of a new professional code for journalists and the opposition of society's institutions would soon lead to the installation of objectivity as the god of journalism and to the decline of muckraking.

NOTES

1. The legend of David Graham Phillips as journalist is related in Allen Churchill, *Park Row* (New York, 1958), 167–93; Daniel Victor, "The Muckrakers and the Dandy: The Conflicting Personae of David Graham Phillips" (Ph.D. diss. Claremont Graduate School, 1976); and Granville Hicks, "David Graham Phillips: Journalist," *Bookman* 73 (May 1931): 257–66.

2. On Charles A. Dana's grace as an editor and teacher, see Edward P. Mitchell, "Mr. Dana of the Sun," *McClure's* 3 (October 1894): 92–93 and "The Newspaperman's Newspaper," *Scribner's* 76 (August 1924): 149. The Dana-Pulitzer feud is traced in W. A. Swanberg, *Pulitzer* (New York, 1967), 136–52.

3. The articles appeared in the New York *World*, April 3–8, 10–15, 1893. Phillips' early newspaper muckraking is discussed in detail in Robert Miraldi, "The Journalism of David Graham Phillips" (Ph.D. Diss., New York University, 1985), 20–117. A summary of this work is included in an article with the same name in *Journalism Quarterly* 63 (Spring 1988): 83–88. Richard Olney, then the attorney general, was a former railroad corporation lawyer. See Gerald G. Eggert, *Richard Olney: Evolution of a Statesman* (University Park, Pa., 1974), 87–100.

4. Isaac Marcossen, Phillips' first biographer, said that by 1896 Phillips' feature stories "had begun to be widely copied throughout the American press," *David Graham Phillips and His Times* (New York, 1932), 184. Phillips' feature writing is discussed also by Helen MacGill Hughes, *News and the Human Interest Story* (New Brunswick, N.J., 1940), 202. Phillips did not receive a byline from Pulitzer until the late 1890s.

5. Such is the opinion of Churchill, *Park Row*, p. 171, and Marcossen. A bibliography of Phillips' early journalism can be found in Miraldi, "The Journalism of David Graham Phillips."

6. On the quality and content of Pulitzer's editorial page, see John L. Heaton, *The Story of a Page: Thirty Years of Public Service and Public Discussion in the Editorial Columns of the New York World* (New York, 1913) and George Juergens, *Joseph Pulitzer and the New York World* (Princeton, N.J., 1966).

7. Phillips' comment on reporting is found in Churchill, *Park Row*, p. 175. The only novel Phillips published under his pseudonym, John Graham, was *The Great God Success* (New York, 1901). He used a pseudonym because Pulitzer forbade his writers from signing books or articles outside the *World*.

8. Bibliographies of Phillips' work are given in Abraham Feldman, "David Graham Phillips: His Works and His Critics," *Bulletin of Bibliography*, 19 (May-August 1948): 144–46 and (September-December 1948): 177–79; Paul C. Rodgers, "David Graham Phillips: A Critical Study" (Ph.D. Diss., Columbia University, 1955); and Frank L. Stallings, "David Graham Phillips: A Critical Bibliography of Secondary Comment," *American Literary Realism* 6 (Winter 1970): 1–35.

9. David Graham Phillips, *The Master Rogue* (New York, 1903).

10. David Graham Phillips, *The Deluge* (New York, 1905). A similar novel that followed close on the heels of a major news event was *The Light-Fingered Gentry* (New York, 1907) which was about fraud in the insurance industry. David Graham Phillips, *The Plum Tree* (Indianapolis, 1905).

11. See Robert Miraldi, "Fictional Techniques in the Journalism of David Graham Phillips," *American Journalism* 4 (1987): 181–90.

12. Quoted from a letter from Phillips to Bailey Millard, in Louis Filler, *The Voice of Democracy: A Critical Biography of David Graham Phillips: Journalist, Novelist, Progressive* (University Park, Pa., 1978), 95–96.

13. David Graham Phillips, *The Treason of the Senate*, introduction by George E. Mowry and Judson A. Grenier (Chicago, 1964). The articles are discussed also in Louis Filler, *The Muckrakers* (University Park, Pa., 1976), 245–59.

14. Filler, *The Muckrakers*, provides a chronology of the muckraking movement (pp. 417–24). When muckraking began is much disputed. Researchers have found many examples of muckraking well before the turn of the century. See, for example, Warren T. Francke, "Investigative Exposure in the Nineteenth Century: The Journalistic Heritage of the Muckrakers" (Ph.D. diss., University of Minnesota, 1974).

15. Phillips, *Treason of the Senate*, 145.

16. The speech is reprinted in, among others, *The Muckrakers*, eds. Arthur Weinberg and Lila Weinberg (New York, 1961), 58–65, and is discussed further in Judson A. Grenier, "Muckrakers and Muckraking: An Historical Definition," *Journalism Quarterly* 37 (Autumn 1960): 552–58; and John Semonche, "Theodore Roosevelt's 'Muckrake Speech': A Reassessment," *Mid-America* 46 (April 1964): 114–25.

17. Roosevelt to George Horace Lorimer, May 23, 1906, in *Letters of Roosevelt*, vol. 5, ed. Elting S. Morrison (Cambridge, Mass., 1952), 268–69.

18. Charles Edward Russell, *Bare Hands and Stone Walls/Some Recollections of a Side-Line Reformer* (New York, 1933), 145.

19. Louis Filler, "Murder in Grammercy Park," *Antioch Review* 11 (December 1946): 495–508.

20. The "Progressive profile" is constructed by George Mowry, *The Era of Theodore Roosevelt and the Birth of Modern America, 1900–1912* (New York, 1958), 85–105.

21. Bibliographies of muckraking are found in C. C. Regier, *The Era of the Muckrakers* (Chapel Hill, N.C., 1932); and Arthur Weinberg and Lila Weinberg, eds. *The Muckrakers*. Bibliographical essays on muckraking are found in Louis Filler, "The Muckrakers in Flower and Failure," *Essays in American Historiography* (New York, 1960); and Harry H. Stein, "American Muckrakers and Muckraking: The 50-Year Scholarship," *Journalism Quarterly* 56 (Spring 1979): 9–17.

22. Michael Schudson contrasts the "story" and "information" ideals in *Discovering the News* (New York, 1978), 88–120. Will Irwin, "The Reporter and the News," in *The American Newspaper*, eds. Clifford F. Weigle and David G. Clark (Ames, Iowa, 1969), 22. This is a reprint of Irwin's 1911 articles for *Collier's*.

23. Ida Tarbell's articles appeared monthly in *McClure's* from November 1902 to July 1903. Ida Tarbell, *The History of Standard Oil* (New York, 1904). She also wrote character sketches of Rockefeller in 1905, "John D. Rockefeller: A Character Study," *McClure's* 25 (July 1905): 227–49, and (August 1905): 386–98.

24. Tarbell's fame and career have been described in various biographies, including Mary E. Tompkins, *Ida E. Tarbell* (Boston, 1974); and Kathleen Brady, *Ida Tarbell: Portrait of a Muckraker* (New York, 1984). Both authors point out that Tarbell had earned considerable fame with biographies of Abraham Lincoln and Napoléon Bonaparte before she began her work on Rockefeller.

25. Samuel Hopkins Adams' articles appeared in *Collier's* on October 7, October 28, November 18, and December 2, 1905; January 13 and February 17, 1906. Filler, *The Muckrakers*, discusses Adams' work, pp. 152–56, but a better account of the significance of the articles is found in James H. Cassedy, "Muckraking and Medicine: Samuel Hopkins Adams," *American Quarterly* 16 (Spring 1964): 85–99. Stewart Holbrook, *The Golden Age of Quackery* (New York, 1959), provides detailed summaries of Adams' articles and an account of their effect. A more recent assessment of Adams' place in Progressive Era America is found in John Crunden, *Ministers of Reform: The Progressives' Achievement in American Civilization, 1889–1920* (New York, 1982), 163–99.

26. The *Treason* was reproduced as a pamphlet (Stanford, Calif., 1954) and then as a book. See note 13.

27. Robert H. Bremer, *From the Depths: The Discovery of Poverty in the United States* (New York, 1956), 140. Ray Stannard Baker's early career in journalism and at *McClure's* is reviewed in two major biographies: Robert C. Bannister, Jr., *Ray Stannard Baker: The Mind and Thought of a Progressive* (New Haven, Conn., 1966) and John Semonche, *Ray Stannard Baker: A Quest for Democracy in Modern America, 1870–1918* (Chapel Hill, N.C., 1969).

28. Ray Stannard Baker, *Following the Color Line/American Negro Citizenship in the Progressive Era* (New York, 1964), introduction, Dewey Grantham, Jr. The book remained a classic for many years and was quoted often and approvingly in the scholarly study of Gunnar Myrdal, *An American Dilemma: The Negro Problem and American Democracy* (New York, 1944).

29. "The American Newspaper" series appeared originally in *Collier's* from January 21 to July 29, 1911. Will Irwin's career is recounted in Robert V. Hudson, *The Writing Game: A Biography of Will Irwin* (Ames, Iowa, 1982).

30. Despite the fact that Russell wrote dozens of articles and nearly two dozen books, there has been no biography of him. However, his work is discussed by Filler, *The Muckrakers, passim*; David Mark Chalmers, *The Social and Political Ideas of the Muckrakers* (New York, 1964), 95–103; and Donald H. Bragaw, "Soldier for the Common Good: The Life and Career of Charles Edward Russell" (Ph.D. Diss., Syracuse University, 1970). Russell wrote two autobiographical accounts, *These Shifting Scenes* (New York, 1914) and *Bare Hands and Stone Walls*.

31. Charles Edward Russell, "A Burglar in the Making," *Everybody's* (June 1908): 753–60, and "The Tenements of Trinity Church," *Everybody's* (July 1908): 47–57, both of which are reprinted in *The Muckrakers*, Arthur and Lila Weinberg, eds., 325–37 and 311–19. Russell, "The Associated Press and Calumet," *Pearson's* (January 1914): 437–47; "The Magazine Soft Pedal," *Pearson's* (February 1914): 179–89; "The Keeping of the Kept Press," *Pearson's* (May 1914): 34–43.

32. Stein, "American Muckrakers and Muckraking," 9.

33. Samuel P. Hays, *The Response to Industrialism, 1865–1914* (Chicago, 1957), 23.

34. As the historians Irwin Unger and Debi Unger point out, "The concept of Progressivism turns out to be curiously elusive." *The Vulnerable Years* (New

York, 1978), 97. The entire historiography of the Progressive Era is fraught with revisions and reversals. Once thought of as an era of liberalism and reform, "many historians now in the last twenty years have judged the movement as essentially conservative," write the editors of *Twentieth Century America*, Barton J. Bernstein and Allen J. Matusow (New York, 1969), 2. Viewing the era as one of liberal reform are Eric Goldman, *Rendezvous with Destiny* (New York, 1955); and John Chamberlain, *Farewell to Reform* (New York, 1932). Seeing it as conservative and reinforcing of the status quo are Gabriel Kolko, *The Triumph of Conservatism* (Glencoe, Ill., 1963); and James Weinstein, *The Corporate Ideal in the Liberal State 1900–1918* (Boston, 1968). On the confusion of Progressivism, see David Noble, *The Paradox of Progressive Thought* (Minneapolis, 1958); on intellectual currents, see Henry May, *The End of American Innocence* (New York, 1959); and Henry Steele Commager, *The American Mind* (New Haven, Conn., 1950).

35. Edwin Cady, *The Realist at War: The Mature Years of William Dean Howells, 1837–1885* (Syracuse, N.Y., 1958); Werner Berthoff, *The Ferment of Realism: American Literature, 1884–1919* (New York, 1965); Jay Martin, *Harvests of Change: American Literature, 1865–1914* (Englewood Cliffs, N.J., 1967).

36. Schudson, *Discovering the News*, 122.

37. Letter from Lincoln Steffens to Ray Stannard Baker, March 3, 1904, quoted in Bannister, *Ray Stannard Baker*, 106. Preface to Tarbell, *History of Standard Oil*, xii.

38. Herbert Shapiro, "The Muckrakers and Negroes," *Phylon* 31 (1970): 78. The muckrakers' need to focus on facts is emphasized also by Whitney Cross, "The Muckrakers Revisited: Purposeful Objectivity in Progressive Journalism," *Nieman Reports* 7 (July 1952): 10–15.

39. Russell, "The Associated Press and Calumet"; Irwin, "The Dim Beginnings," *The American Newspaper*, 16; Lincoln Steffens, *The Autobiography of Lincoln Steffens* (New York, 1931), 179.

40. Ida Tarbell, *All in a Day's Work* (New York, 1939), 207. Tarbell included 232 pages of documents in the appendix to *The History of Standard Oil* (subsequently called *History*). Tarbell to John Siddall, September 11, 1901, as noted in Brady, *Ida Tarbell*, 125.

41. The discussion of the charter is in Tarbell, *History*, 56–60. Brady discusses how Tarbell found the document, *Ida Tarbell*, 123–24, 136–38.

42. James H. Young, *The Toadstool Millionaires* (Princeton, N.J., 1961) discusses the patent medicine frauds, as does Holbrook, *The Golden Age of Quackery*.

43. In citing Adams' work, I will give the date of publication in *Collier's* but the page numbers will be from a reprinted collection of the articles in Adams, *The Great American Fraud* (New York, 1906). January 13, 1906, 58.

44. Adams, October 28, 1905, 17, 21; February 17, 1906, 68–69.

45. Adams, February 17, 1906, 69; December 2, 1905, 34–35. He used a coroner's report in one other instance, on October 28, 1905, 17.

46. Adams, "The Patent Medicine Conspiracy against Freedom of the Press," *Collier's* (November 4, 1905). The Weinbergs say that the article was written by Sullivan (*The Muckrakers*, 179), although it has been reprinted in editions with Adams' work.

47. Irwin, "All the News That's Fit to Print," in *The American Newspaper*, 24.

48. "The Tenements of Trinity Church," quoted in Weinberg and Weinberg,

The Muckrakers, 312. Russell wrote two other articles on Trinity: "Trinity: Church of Mystery," *The Broadway Magazine* (April 1908): 1–12; and "Trinity's Tenements—The Public's Business," *Everybody's* (February 1909): 278–79. Russell's fictionalized the tenement problem in a play: "The Writing on the Wall," in *The Best Plays of 1899–1909*, eds. Burns Mantle and Garrison P. Sherwood (New York, 1947).

49. Tarbell, *History*, 102. She used the same technique at other times (pp. 209, 274–75).

50. Irwin "The Power of the Press," in *The American Newspaper*, 15.

51. Ibid., "The Unhealthy Alliance," 18; "The Spread and Decline of Yellow Journalism," 21. Irwin gave an equally balanced assessment of Adolph Ochs and the *New York Times*, "The Editor and the News," 19.

52. Quoted from the notebooks of Baker. Chalmers, *Social and Political Ideas*, 122, note 5.

53. Baker, *Color Line*, 87.

54. Baker papers, November 24, 1901.

55. Lincoln Steffens, "What the Matter is in America and What to Do About It," *Everybody's* (June 1908), 723.

56. Phillips, *The Treason of the Senate* (subsequently called *Treason*), 48.

57. Russell, "The Associated Press and Calumet," 438; "The Keeping of the Kept Press," 36.

58. Phillips, *Treason*, 64, 67, 80, 91, 96.

59. Mowry and Grenier, introduction to Phillips, *Treason*, 30. See William David Sloan, "Scurrility and the Party Press, 1789–1816," *American Journalism* 5 (1988): 97–112, on the early partisan press.

60. Senator Joseph W. Bailey in a speech to the Senate, June 27, l906, printed in an appendix to Phillips, *Treason*, 228.

61. Quoted in John Tebbel, *The Life and Good Times of William Randolph Hearst* (New York, 1952), 150–51.

62. Phillips, *Treason*, 168.

63. Ibid., 114.

64. Baker, *Color Line*, 45–46.

65. Adams, October 28, 1905, 13.

66. *Ibid.*, January 13, 1906, 47.

67. Brady, *Ida Tarbell*, 139.

68. Phillips showed his literary orientation early in his career at the *Sun*, writing sixteen articles for *Harper's Weekly* in 1891–1892. The articles were mostly dramatic rewrites of stories Phillips had covered on assignment for the *Sun*. Irwin, too, made his name early in journalism with his stylistic recreations for the *Sun* of an earthquake that had struck San Francisco, Irwin's hometown. Irwin wrote the stories based on sketchy wire service accounts and his personal knowledge of how San Francisco looked before the quake. Adams, who wrote thirty-six novels, fictionalized the patent-medicine frauds in a novel, *The Clarion* (New York, 1914). Although he crusaded for drug regulations for many years, he spent most of his career writing fiction. On the *Sun* and the feature story, I recommend Howard Good, "The Literary Journalism of Dana's Sun," unpublished manuscript, 1988.

69. Baker's alter ego, David Grayson, is discussed by Semonche, *Ray Stannard*

Baker, 160–93; and Bannister, *Ray Stannard Baker*, 108–25, 148–87. Russell's reporting and writing skill culminated in 1928 when he won the Pulitzer Prize for his biography, *The American Orchestra and Theodore Thomas* (New York, 1927). Tarbell never completed a novel during this period of her career as she noted, sadly, in *All in a Day's Work*, 203.

70. On muckraking's connection to literature, see Jay Martin, "The Literature of Argument and the Arguments of Literature," in *Muckraking: Past, Present and Future*, eds. John M. Harrison and Harry H. Stein (University Park, Pa., 1973). See note 34 on literary realism. The nonfiction of Theodore Dreiser is discussed in Shelly Fisher Fishkin, *From Fact to Fiction* (New York, 1985), 85–134. The best account of Stephen Crane's journalism is in R. W. Stallman, *Stephen Crane: A Biography* (New York, 1968); and Joseph Kwiat, "Stephen Crane, Literary Reporter: Commonplace Experience and Artistic Transendence," *Journal of Modern Literature* 8 (1980): 129–38.

71. Lincoln Steffens, *The Letters of Lincoln Steffens*, eds. Ella Winter and Granville Hicks, vol. 1 (Westport, Conn., 1974), 267.

72. Tarbell, *History*, 71, 106. See also 127, 147. Her description of Rockefeller's looks came in her 1905 character sketches. See note 23.

73. Adams' article, "The Fundamental Fakes," February 17, 1906, is a good example of his use of feature-writing techniques. The restaurant scene is on p. 71.

74. Baker, *Color Line*, 179–92. Baker originally published parts of this chapter in two articles. See "What Is a Lynching?" *McClure's* 24 (January-February, 1905): 299–314, 422–30.

75. Irwin, "The Foe from Within," in *The American Newspaper*, 25.

76. Ibid., "The Fourth Current," 24.

77. Russell, *Everybody's* (June 1908). Russell wrote other articles on prison life. See "Beating Men to Make Them Good," about the Ohio prison system, *Hampton's* (September, October and November, 1909). Partially reprinted in Harvey Swados, ed., *Years of Conscience: The Muckrakers* (New York, 1962), 331–34.

78. Phillips wrote at least fourteen articles which used fictional techniques. See Miraldi, "Fictional Techniques." Phillips, *The Plum Tree*, 31.

79. Tarbell, *History*, 63. See also, 117.

80. Russell, "A Burglar in the Making," 321, 328.

81. Irwin, "The Reporter and the News," in *The American Newspaper*, 23.

82. Ibid., "The Editor and the News," 18.

83. On Dr. Harvey Wiley, see Filler, *The Muckrakers*, 144–48; and Oscar E. Anderson, *The Health of a Nation: Harvey W. Wiley and the Fight for Pure Food* (New York, 1958). The Food and Drug Administration was officially created in 1931. Its predecessor was created in 1906 as part of the United States Department of Agriculture's Bureau of Chemistry.

84. Russell, "The Associated Press and Calumet." A more favorable view of the Associated Press is found in Oliver Gramling, *AP: The Story of News* (Port Washington, N.Y., 1969).

85. Brady, *Ida Tarbell*, 144–45. Reporters have been using secret sources for many years, as noted by Charles W. Whalen, *Your Right to Know*, (New York, 1973), 17–72, but their use came to particular attention and became controversial especially in the late 1960s. Carl Bernstein and Bob Woodward focused attention

on their use with their "deep throat" secret source who provided much information in their Watergate reporting.

86. Tarbell denied she had any social or reform goals, in a letter to Alice Hegan Rice, January 21, 1933, quoted in Brady, *Ida Tarbell*, 263.

3

The Muckrakers Are Chased Away

For more than a decade, the literature of exposure had thrilled and depressed the American reading public. The writing of Josiah Flynt, the adventuresome rich kid they called "Cigarette," had brought people into the violent underworld of cops and criminals. The little man with the goatee, Lincoln Steffens, had ripped the lid off payoffs and bribes in cities from St. Louis to Minneapolis. Ida Tarbell, wearing her high-button collars and using a historian's diligence, transformed John D. Rockefeller's oil empire from American dream to American nightmare. Upton Sinclair, bent on bringing socialism, made a Lithuanian immigrant suffer so much in his fictional urban morass that the public agitated for a cleanup of American's meat products.

From Wall Street "bucket shops" to backroom political deals; from poisoned medicines to diseased animal carcasses; from illegal rail rebates to brutal lynchings of blacks in the South: for a decade, the muckraking writers and magazines had unraveled the invisible government that Progressive Era America knew had to be reshaped. With their faith in the ultimate good sense of an aroused public opinion, the muckrakers acted as journalistic professors, the magazine as their blackboard, the exposé as their textbook. "Educate, educate, educate," chanted Ray Stannard Baker about his work as a muckraker.[1]

For their part, the people had never known that the real story of the trusts could be so interesting. At first, of course, they responded to the stories told by this band of would-be novelists. This exposé stuff was much better than just plain old newspaper journalism; it was fun to read, as well as enlightening, and the serialized exposés helped lure thousands of readers to *McClure's*, *Everybody's*, and *Collier's*. The muckraking exposés appearing each month were the equivalent of today's television soap operas; the drama built, and the audience looked each month for the next installment. Muckraking became an integral, if not key, part in building and keeping huge audiences and in spurring legislators to act on the nation's problems.[2] Gradually, however, the response of the public to exposé began to wane, and the desires of magazine publishers, editors, and the muckraking writers themselves began to change along with public taste. Muckraking, whose life cycle closely parallels the Progressive Era in the century's first decade, reached a peak in the middle years of Theodore Roosevelt's first elected term, about 1906. In the last years of the Taft administration, muckraking flourished again but then faded once more as Woodrow Wilson and the nation debated entry into World War I. Before the onset of war, muckraking journalism had declined and virtually disappeared from the mass circulation periodicals. Whereas soon after the turn of the century there had been a dozen magazines that could be classified as muckraking, by the advent of World War I none remained. In the years between 1905 and 1911, *Era, Ridgway's*, and *Human Life* went out of business, and between 1911 and 1916, *Hampton's, Success, Twentieth Century*, and *Harper's Weekly* failed. By 1912 conservative business interests had taken control of *McClure's*, the *American*, and *Collier's Weekly*, and they, too, halted muckraking.

For those who wanted to continue attacking the political establishment, one word summed up what was stopping muckraking: conspiracy. A conspiracy by the "interests" that the muckrakers had exposed. To muckraking writer Charles Edward Russell, a reasonable man, a good journalist, and the most prolific of the muckraking writers, the conspiracy was simple to explain. "Several chuckling gentlemen" had met in New York City and decided to halt the exposing of the facts. "The Interests set out resolutely . . . to bring in the fiery untamed muckraking magazine and tether it in the corporation corral," he wrote in 1914.[3] Russell, who eventually became a leading American socialist, offered no documentation and did not name the "gentlemen," but his charge fit with what Progressives had been whispering for a decade. Walter Lippmann, who as a young man had been an aide to Steffens before beginning his own career as columnist and political philosopher, said he was told "not once but twenty times" about a "nation-wide scheme by financiers to suppress every radical and progressive periodical."[4]

The whispers of conspiracy began as early as 1905 when the staff of the most famous muckraking periodical in America, *McClure's*, broke up. Ever since Tarbell, Steffens, and Baker had led an assault on corruption and the trusts, *McClure's* had combined good writing, research, and editing to become a popular success. Muckraking was a key part of the success formula. But *McClure's* was not a happy ship. Publisher Samuel McClure was a brilliant editor and idea man, but he was also whimsical and erratic. Lincoln Steffens described McClure as the magazine's "wild editor," a man who was enthusiastic but unreliable. In about 1905, when McClure, who was always looking for new investment schemes, sought new investors for the magazine, he told his stockholders that he would temporarily halt muckraking. From outside the publication, it appeared that the interests had penetrated the once attacking *McClure's* magazine, that money had won out over muckraking. *McClure's* staff did not tolerate the boss' antics, and they quit en masse to start their own magazine, the *American*.[5] The *McClure's* breakup could have been cited as evidence that the interests were conspiring to stifle muckraking activity.

Samuel McClure's staff did not immediately go public with their suspicions about corporate meddling . . . but others did. At the height of its exposé of patent medicine frauds in 1905, *Collier's* magazine told its 500,000 readers how the businesses which bought advertisements for various medicines—fraudulent and otherwise—had engaged in a "conspiracy against the freedom of the press" by paying $1 million a year to the newspapers that promised not to print "any matter" critical of the industry. The payoff amounted to a "contract of silence," *Collier's* declared: a conspiracy to silence the Fourth Estate.[6] A similar claim came from the editor of a minor muckraking magazine, *Era*, who stated that the banker, J. P. Morgan, often identified as the leader of the "money trust," had set out to ruin his magazine after it exposed fraud in the insurance industry. After 1904, he wrote, his "news agents were threatened, printers were intimidated . . . customers were warned, advertisers . . . were menaced, our employees were watched, [and] bribes were boldly offered."[7] Typical of those who invoked conspiracy, however, the author offered little proof of his chargers.

In 1911, *Collier's* made it clear that the attack was genuine by publishing a threatening letter from a wool trust representative to its advertising manager. Do not print writer Mark Sullivan's muckraking material, the letter warned, because we "do not feel [we] should give this advertising . . . to publications who try to take . . . the bread and butter on which [we] must live." Here was the smoking gun, proof that, as one magazine declared, "the displeasure of the big interests" will eventually silence the muckrakers.[8] To the believers of conspiracy, the *Collier's* letter confirmed their suspicions. After all, didn't the interests force the *American* magazine only two years before to halt its exposé of the reactionary methods of suppression being used in Mexico? John Kenneth Turner's articles, which had been widely promoted before publication, were halted before the series was half over; tongues wagged that Rockefeller interests, fearing that the articles would hurt investments, had forced their termination. Hardly true, the *American's* editors countered. There was no pressure, no conspiracy; the articles were simply unreliable.[9]

When the muckraking magazines were at their height, charging politicians and corporations with despoiling the marketplace with corruption, it was logical to believe that the accused might strike back and call a halt to the exposés. That the political bosses might conspire with the corporate chiefs was a scenario that the public could believe. In 1906, David Graham Phillips wrote his popular novel, *The Plum Tree*, and in it he sketched out how the conspiracy worked. The businessman needs favors in Washington, D.C., so he spends his money to get the right senators elected. Then, with his butler in Congress, he orders him to deliver favorable legislation. If a legislator should balk, he would be recalled and another would be elected. All government business was controlled by "the machine," and the machine, in turn, "was a creature and servant of corporations." "Graft," Phillips wrote, "was the backbone of the whole skeleton of legislative business." It was that simple . . . if you believed Phillips' fiction, and if you wanted to believe that business chicanery operated so blatantly.

Conspiracy was—and is—a convenient and sensational way to explain the decline of muckraking, and it was a popular theory in the Progressive Era.[10] Pressure from business, however, provides only a partial explanation, and one must resist the temptation to look, as some have, for easy explanations. The factors that led to the demise of muckraking were complex and subtle; business pressure was only one of the elements that eclipsed the writers of exposé. Certainly, businesses and advertisers did apply pressure at times to the magazines, but muckraking's decline was brought on by a cumulative toll of institutional factors—from commerce to the courts—which combined, albeit with no central planning, against this harshly critical, adversary culture that had developed in the popular press. Society's elite did not knowingly work together, for John D. Rockefeller and J. P. Morgan did not sup with Teddy Roosevelt and conspire to call off the muckrakers. In their desire to maintain state-corporate hegemony, the capitalistic status quo, however, the effect was the same—they called off the attackers.

The triumph over muckraking was accomplished through organizations that were created to orchestrate opposition to reform and regulation; through a critical rhetoric—the Rooseveltian criticism that muckraking was a destructive force—that became common in popular culture; through the courts which toughened libel laws and scared off the investigative zealot; through isolated but persistent pressure from advertisers who were upset with critical articles; by a steady takeover of magazines by corporations which would not support continued exposés, especially in light of waning public interest; by the slow emergence of a new profession, public relations, staffed by refugees from journalism who knew the "enemy" and learned to take the bite out of the sharpest attacks; and by journalism itself which, by beginning to enshrine objectivity as a professional ideal, narrowed the range of journalists and put muckraking on the fringes of responsibility.

Pressures on the muckrakers were exacerbated by the natural evolution of muckraking writing which turned from Ida Tarbell's staid but fair prose to David Graham Phillips' accurate but sensational rhetoric. Muckraking writing often became shrill, preachy, and filled with advocacy; and this poor imitation of the earlier work brought much of muckraking into disrepute. Perhaps also after a decade of reading attacks on the interests and the system, after so many of the "shames" had been exposed, the hidden histories uncovered, and the political "plum trees" revealed, the public had just gasped one too many times. As early as 1908, Ray Stannard Baker sensed that muckraking was in disfavor. "The public had begun to be satiated," he wrote.[11]

The muckraking writers, too, had tired of exposé well before 1915. Many went from being newspaper reporters to well-known magazine writers and then to public figures who could command handsome fees for articles and books, who lectured in public, who became confidantes of prominent elected officials, and who often wrote novels, usually of a second-class nature. Had there been great demand, of course, other muckraking writers would have moved into their place, but the magazines whose audience and approach made them most likely to muckrake—*New Broadway* (later named *Hampton's*) magazine is the best example—were beset by management and financial problems, and they failed before they could undertake new investigative ventures.[12]

By the end of World War I, exposure was little to be seen in mass periodicals; it has been supplanted by "happy talk." Orison Swett Marden, whose *Success* magazine had muckraked just a few years before, declared in 1918 about a new magazine he was starting: "It will be filled from cover to cover with sunshine, encouragement and gladness. It will give its readers only that which will help and inspire. . . . It will engage in no pessimism, no muckraking."[13] It had come to this: after more than a decade of criticizing, exposing, and accusing, the press was ready to go back to being safe. Happy talk. Sunshine. Avoid the bad news; don't tear down the system, build it up. The combination of factors working against investigative exposure had become too much in the years before World War I. If you want to stay out of court, be careful about what you write. If you don't want to lose advertisers, be cheerful, not gloomy. If you want to keep old audiences and develop new ones, follow the lead of George Horace Lorimer's *Saturday Evening Post*: a little romance, some genteel fiction, a mix of news and interpretation. Then, watch your circulation soar. Muckraking did not fit into the new formula. The publishers and the audience were ready for a new direction; and the interests which had been under attack could rest easy for a while.

ADVERTISING: PAYING THE PIPER, CALLING THE TUNES

When Ralph Ingersoll began to publish *PM*, his famous newspaper experiment of the 1940s, he wrote a prospectus that explained why his new newspaper would not take advertising. "The pressure exerted by . . . advertising," Ingersoll wrote, "works consistently and without interruption against the interest of the reader. It works so efficiently . . . that publishers and editors and writers censor themselves 100 times for every once their advertisers censor them." Management, Ingersoll concluded, cannot forget "on which side their bread is buttered."[14] Ingersoll, a veteran editor with the *New Yorker*, *Time*, and *Fortune* magazines, knew that it was an uneasy coexistence, to be at once a business enterprise and a critic of business methods and policies. Although Ingersoll was writing some twenty-five years after the muckraking movement had declined, his words are especially applicable to the journalism of the Progressive Era.

The Progressive Era was a pivotal time for journalism. The press had established its independence from political parties, professionalism was emerging among reporters, and the ideal of objectivity was beginning to take hold. The press was just coming out of its yellow journalism phase, the sensationalism borne of commercialism that dominated the 1890s, and it was entering a dangerous period when advertising was bringing great revenues along with the threat of business dominance. Although they contained exemplary journalism and were often principled critics of business and political corruption, certainly the muckraking magazines were also businesses. Muckraking editor Edward Bok declared quite candidly in 1902 that "a magazine is purely a business proposition . . . published to earn money for its owners."[15] Would the muckrakers turn away from exposing tyranny if their profit was threatened by principle? Could an advertiser's pressure, the threat of canceled advertising space, make the muckrakers go easy on certain offenders? Even more pertinent, if the corporations attempted to silence the muckraking magazines with buyouts, would the principled publishers, like McClure, nod yes, take the money, and allow their exposés to be silenced?

Pressure from business on the muckrakers came in direct and indirect ways, usually behind the scenes. The obvious way that business could attempt to alter editorial content was through cancelling advertising. Joseph Pulitzer, whose New York *World* was America's dominant newspaper in the 1890s, once told an employee that if an advertiser ever requested changes in a news story the advertiser should be thrown out of the newspaper's building.[16] With his prosperous New York *World*, Pulitzer could afford to be tough on advertisers, but the muckraking magazines were particularly vulnerable to advertiser pressure. By the turn of the century, advertising affected virtually all aspects of the magazine industry. From 1890 to 1904, advertising revenue in magazines had doubled, from $360 million to $821 million a year. By 1908, the average magazine was more than half filled with advertisements. "It was not an overnight transition," wrote one chronicler of the magazines in America, but generally speaking it was advertising that had come "to dominate the media."[17] If they wanted to survive, magazines had good reason not to offend advertisers. Nonetheless, muckraking attacks on business in general and on certain businesses in particular were offensive, and advertisers did respond on occasion.

In April 1906, for example, at the time when President Roosevelt was making his celebrated public criticism of the muckrakers, F. J. Armour, the powerful meat-packing industrialist, canceled advertising in *McClure's*. Piqued by Ray Stannard Baker's history of the rail industry's illegal rebates to, among others, the meat packers, Armour killed his ad in *McClure's* for six months. Burton J. Hendrick's articles on life insurance company rip-offs of consumers prompted the Life Assurance Company and Mutual Life also to cancel their advertising in *McClure's*, at a time when the magazine was already rife with dissension.[18] Usually, the advertiser resumed his advertising, but his message had probably gotten through by then. If a reporter's story caused an advertiser to cancel, he or she might see this as a badge of honor—at least at first. Knowing, however, that the publisher is a businessman first and a newshound second, if at all, might make the reporter wary in the future. At the least, it might take the bite out of any future attacks. Self-censorship was the likely alternative course.

Canceling advertising was the negative way to influence editorial content; buying more ads—a payoff in essence—was the flip side. And that happened, too. U.S. Senator John F. Dryden was running for reelection in 1906 when he learned that David Graham Phillips' attack on the Senate, soon to appear in William Randolph Hearst's *Cosmopolitan*, would include damaging information against him. Dryden was a wealthy member of Congress, the president of the Prudential Life Insurance Company, and an owner of the Public Service Corporation in New Jersey which operated public utilities in the state. Prudential revenues had helped finance the utilities, and Phillips—at the urging of his researcher Gustavus Myers—wanted to call for a legislative investigation of the Dryden connections. Since bruising hearings into insurance industry practices had been held the previous year by a Senate committee, Dryden wanted no more revelations. Phillips' article, which profiled six senators

and which included some of the most intemperate language of the muckraking era, was set to appear in October; in fact, it had already been set
in type. A few weeks before publication, however, *Cosmopolitan* business
manager George Van Utassy told Myers that the material on Dryden
would be suppressed. Prudential Insurance had just bought an addi-
tional $5,000 worth of advertising space. Even worse than that the bribe
had suppressed the facts about Dryden was that the ad Prudential purchased, typeset to appear as if it were a staff-written nonfiction article,
spoke in glowing terms about Dryden. Only the fine print revealed that
it was an advertisement.[19] Advertisements that resembled news stories
were not uncommon during this period in journalism history. What was
unusual in this case was that the purchase of the advertising space also
meant the killing of a critical news story.

C. W. Post perhaps spoke for many businessmen when he urged in
an article he wrote for *Leslie's Weekly* in 1913 that advertisers boycott
antibusiness, un-American muckraking magazines.[20] How many did is
impossible to say, but certainly at the very least the pressure from potential and real advertisers, as Ingersoll suggested, planted the seeds of
hesitation in writers and editors. Some, like Post, were making their
threats in public; behind the scenes, unknown to the muckrakers, businessmen were urging each other to monitor the magazines and, as Post
suggested, avoid the most offensive and critical periodicals.

The leader in this business counteroffensive was the National Civic
Federation (NCF), an organization begun after the turn of the century,
which turned into a powerful lobbyist for business and a dogged op-
ponent of radicalism. Made up of representatives of business and labor,
the NCF wanted, initially at least, to improve relations between capital
and labor and subsequently to spur reform that would make the marketplace more profitable and safe for business. To bring this about, public
opinion against the trusts, whose success epitomized to many the ruthlessness of business, would have to be assuaged. That could not happen,
one businessman commented, with "continued agitation of yellow journals, professional muckrakers, and demagogues."[21] The NCF was particularly concerned that, if the attacks on business continued and labor
relations worsened, workers might embrace a radicalism that would
overthrow capitalism. President Roosevelt, of course, shared this fear
and, in part, shot his arrow at the muckrakers in 1906 to slow their
criticism. The "lurid sensationalists," he wrote to William Howard Taft,
the next president, are building up a revolutionary fervor in the nation.
By all means, let out the "sewer gas," Roosevelt said, but let in light
and air also.[22]

Beginning in 1905, the NCF was active in counterattacking the critics
of business; in 1912, the NCF allotted $50,000 for a propaganda campaign
against what it considered socialism. To the NCF conservatives, almost

anyone who criticized business methods was a socialist. The NCF, which prided itself on behind-the-scenes manipulations, had begun in 1909 to plan committees to combat socialism, including one on the press to be composed of editors of various publications. Soon letters complaining about stories began to go out. "If I were an advertiser myself, I would see that none of my money went to papers and magazines that were promoting anarchy in this country," stated one letter sent to a newspaper in 1912.[23] In 1915, NCF member F. G. R. Gordon, a self-styled industrial expert and ex-socialist, attempted to convince a number of large companies not to advertise in *Metropolitan*, a magazine which in 1911 had adopted a moderate socialist editorial policy and published some muckraking articles. The success of the *Metropolitan* policies "would mean the confiscation of all your property," he told such companies as Beech-Nut, Campbell Soup, and Hudson Motor. The president of Beech-Nut promised to "study more carefully" the magazine's editorial policy; an executive of the Chalmers Motor Company responded: "We think they have a right to run their magazines in their own way."[24] There is no way to judge the success of the NCF campaign, but if it merely made writers and editors more careful and less adversarial—and it probably did this—then the businessmen had succeeded.

THE ULTIMATE CENSOR: BUSINESS BUYOUTS

Editor and Publisher (E&P), a trade publication, summed up a fear that had long been discussed in the publishing industry when it asked in 1911, "Shall the Bogey Man Get the Magazine Publisher?" *E&P*, along with other observers of journalism, was wondering aloud about the existence of a "magazine trust," a combine which, much like a modern newspaper chain, could buy up magazines and thus dictate editorial content. The question was raised when Crowell Publishing Company announced its purchase of the *American* magazine which had been owned and operated by the most famous of the muckrakers—Steffens, Tarbell, and Baker—until financial woes forced its sale. A top official of Crowell, Thomas Lamont, was also an executive with the banking interests of J. P. Morgan, the financier whose name was always linked to covert industry takeovers. Would the bank trust "put a stop to what the Morgan element calls muckraking"? *Editor and Publisher* asked.[25] This was not the first time that the fear of corporate money's interfering with the muckrakers' editorial perogatives had daunted Steffens and Company. The breakup of the original McClure staff came, in part, because in 1906 McClure began, as already noted, to seek outside capital. The muckrakers felt that the new business interests would be hostile to their reporting. The internal dissension at *McClure's* led U.S. Senator Dryden, who was looking for an outlet for favorable publications, to attempt to buy stock in the magazine. Using as his intermediary J. Walter Thompson, head of the advertising company which represented Prudential, Dryden offered a McClure associate $125,000 and then increased the offer to $200,000. McClure refused the Dryden offer, however.[26] In the meantime, gossip made its way to Baker that the new financial backers that McClure had lured to the magazine were rich businessmen, some with railroad interests. Baker knew the railroad crowd from his muckraking exposés of rail industry practices, practices that had included regularly bribing editors and paying for news space.[27] The new association for McClure, whether it was true or not, rankled the muckrakers and they exited *McClure's* for the *American*. Financial woes continued to plague McClure, and in 1907, with advertising revenue decreasing, he listened to but declined offers from the American Tobacco Company. In 1908, Crowell Publishing tried to purchase the magazine; McClure refused that offer also.[28] After a series of bad investments weakened McClure's hold on the magazine, the inevitable occurred in 1911: the magazine was reorganized and taken over by American Tobacco Company money. The "bogey man" had gotten *McClure's* magazine.

With Crowell in control of the *American* and American Tobacco in control at *McClure's*, journalists feared the worst. "We cannot be blamed for viewing with apprehension the acquisition of independent magazines by interests in any way allied with financial factors of Wall Street," wrote crusading editor E. A. Van Valkenburg.[29] The fears seemed to become reality in 1912 when an article by Baker on a textile workers' strike in Lawrence, Massachusetts, was harshly edited. "Some of the cuts were only the normal editorial deletions, others most decidedly were not," concluded Baker's biographer. Sarcastic references to Boston philanthropists were changed to praise for their activities; statements questioning capitalism were deleted as were various critical facts about the mill owner's treatment of workers. When the article appeared in May 1912, Baker saw that many of the changes he had rejected had been made nevertheless. "Does not this raise the question as to who is really editor of the *American* magazine?," Baker asked in a letter to Ida Tarbell. Baker said that once Crowell's "business men taste blood, they'll pare us down to utter colorness, utter mushiness. Everything must be smooth, sugary, inoffensive."[30] Baker was, of course, correct in his assessment: muckraking was on its way out in the pages of the *American* and in most of the nation's other magazines. The final blow for Baker and his muckraking colleagues came in 1915 when his attempt to write critically about Henry Ford and the auto industry was completely censored. Baker quit; his muckraking career was essentially over.

A similar fate befell *Collier's*, one of the classiest and most respected of the magazines. For a decade, *Collier's* had been an independent voice of journalistic integrity, attacking yet constructive. Samuel Hopkins Adams' exposé of the patent medicine frauds, for example, had coupled sensational and interesting exposure with an almost scholarly examination of sensible legislative alternatives to the problems he had revealed. Nonetheless, when financial woes struck *Collier's*, the bankers who stepped in to bail out the periodical sought an end to muckraking—constructive or not. To keep the magazine afloat, *Collier's* owners had borrowed money from Harry Payne Whitney, a family friend who was an industrialist. The banking house which managed Whitney's money had complete authority over his loans. One day, recalled muckraking writer Mark Sullivan, "strange auditors appeared in *Collier's* offices," attempting to guard Whitney's interests by altering editorial content. "There must be less muckraking, greater amiability toward business," the bankers declared.[31] If ever there was a smoking gun, this was it. The bankers couldn't care less about journalistic principle or independence; they cared about their client—and he was a businessman. A businessman could do without criticism, especially if he is paying the bills of the critic.

Norman Hapgood, *Collier's* editor, resisted, but only for a while. He quit in 1913 to edit *Harper's Weekly* and later, despite this experience, he said he doubted any conspiracy lurked to halt muckraking. If *Harper's* fails, he wrote in 1914, "it will be because the present management lacks sufficient brains." Others too doubted the business conspiracy. "Mr. Morgan's partner," wrote one magazine editor, "has not yet been to see me with a proposition for the purchase of *Pearson's*, and I am not expecting him."[32] Subtly, however, business had already had its effect. As Ray Stannard Baker put it after his experience with the corporate-inspired cuts in his stories, when he sat down to write he felt as if businessmen were watching his every word. Not only were businessmen keeping a watchful eye, however, so too were some judges. Baker and the muckrakers learned—sometimes the hard way—that the law of defamation was another weapon being used against the muckrakers.

LIBEL: A BRUISING LEGAL CLUB

From the turn of the century until World War I, the muckraking journalists "shrank from libel suits," wrote Will Irwin in his 1942 autobiography. No wonder since, as Charles Edward Russell said of one muckraking exposé, "[e]very paragraph contained material for a libel suit."[33] The recollection of Irwin, who in 1911 had written a precedent-setting series of muckraking articles about the American press, sums up the muckrakers' fear that they would end up in court because of their tough prose. "We dealt with libelous material all the time," said John S. Phillips, *McClure's* top editor, to explain why the magazine spent so much time confirming its allegations.[34]

As early as 1901, when muckraking was just beginning, fear was evident. William Allen White, a young journalist who had made his name in the Midwest, wrote an article for *McClure's* on an aging senator from New York, Thomas Platt. The article alleged that Platt controlled the New York State legislature by soliciting campaign contributions from businesses and then paying them off with favorable legislation. White also made a personal attack on Platt as "narrow, both morally and intellectually."[35] The unusually intemperate language enraged Platt who threatened a six-figure defamation lawsuit against McClure and White. The threat alone proves how forceful a tool a lawsuit can be. The threat, White wrote, "scared me to death." A month after the article's publication, White recalled, "I was going into nervous exhaustion." For the next four months, White could not work; he left Kansas and slipped away to California to recuperate. McClure hired a prominent Republican, Thomas B. Reed, to defend the magazine, but Platt backed off and never filed his lawsuit.[36] The die had been cast; libel was one way for the attacked to strike back.

Lincoln Steffens' October 1902 article, "The Shame of Minneapolis," drew the ire of a former county prosecutor who objected to being called a "politician" and threatened to sue. McClure, the publisher in whose magazine the articles were appearing, worried that the politician "will stick us for $2,000 before we are through with him."[37] Steffens, for his part, used defensive tactics. "Don't shoot all your ammunition at the first attack," he told one journalist. "Hold back a few of the most damning facts." This way, he explained, whomever you have attacked will feel "relieved to find you haven't told the worst." In his autobiography, Steffens wrote: "My readers thought that I had been hard on Cox, [Boss' Cox of Cincinnati] but Cox thought I had gone easy to spare him. He may have feared that in a libel suit I would bring out the rest of my evidence."[38] Although it is only one example, Steffens' cautious approach shows that the whole truth could suffer under threat of a libel lawsuit, a real fear of the muckrakers.

Steffens' biographer concludes that McClure and the muckrakers "lived with the constant threat of lawsuits." The threat became reality apparently only once for McClure when, in 1906, he and Ray Stannard Baker were sued. Baker had written "The Railroads on Trial," one of the most quoted exposés of the entire movement. He charged that a Milwaukee industrialist was involved in receiving illegal rebates. His source had been Wisconsin Governor Robert LaFollette, for whom Baker would later work when LaFollette ran for the presidency. LaFollette said he had been told about the industrialist in a report prepared by his railroad commissioner. Baker did no further checking before he included the information in his article. The industrialist, who denied the charges and produced considerable contrary evidence to Baker, asked for a retraction. Baker listened, but in a subsequent article reiterated his original charge. Baker felt that although his facts might have been in error, the essence of his charge was correct. Furthermore, he felt that the industrialist would not dare sue. He did sue, however, and hauled both Baker and McClure before a federal court in New York in 1908. A jury heard both sides and found against McClure who had to pay $15,000 in damages and $40,000 in court costs. McClure, already reeling from the loss of many of his reporters to the *American* magazine, cut back on muckraking. After the trial, one attorney reported, McClure told him that "muckraking was ended as far as he was concerned."[39]

Other editors had similar experiences with libel. Edward Bok's *Ladies Home Journal* was sued because of his crusading against bogus medicines. In 1903 the *Journal* published an article attacking one Dr. Pierce's Favorite Prescription which, the *Journal* alleged, contained 61 percent morphine. Bok, who had already refused to carry any patent medicine advertising, had taken on a powerful industry which retaliated in court. The named company claimed it was not using any morphine and sued Bok for $200,000. Bok believed that the company had used morphine but had subsequently removed the drug from the prescription. That did not help Bok in the courtroom: he was forced to pay $16,000 in damages.[40]

The year 1906 was a tumultuous one for the muckraking movement: Sinclair's *The Jungle* appeared, Phillips wrote an attack on the U.S. Senate, and Roosevelt criticized the muckrakers for being too harsh on capitalism. Libel came close to touching both Sinclair and Phillips. Sinclair, an avowed socialist, chose fiction for his brand of exposé, even though the story he told was correct in virtually all its particulars. Follow-up researchers said they were able to confirm all but one of his startling exposures.[41] Nevertheless, when he sought a publisher, he encountered problems. Norman Hapgood of *Collier's* turned down Sinclair for fear of libel lawsuits. "We had been winning our libel suits in spectacular fashion," he wrote in his memoirs, but *The Jungle* "would obscure what we are doing . . . telling the exact truth about important things."[42] The fiction, he felt, might be dangerous and invite attack, both legal and other kinds.

When it was published, *The Jungle* did cause an uproar and drew the ire of Armour, who challenged Sinclair's account of conditions. In a letter to the New York *Times*, Sinclair invited Armour to sue him for libel, saying the issues would be settled in open court. Armour did not sue, although he did temporarily cancel advertising. He continued to bluster about lawsuits and threatened McClure after he published Baker's articles which linked the rails and the meat packers in a corrupt alliance.[43] A libel threat confronted Hapgood five years after he rejected Sinclair's book. *Collier's* was leading the fight against an attempt to sell public land in Alaska. Hapgood learned that the Republican leaders of a congressional committee had secretly decided to investigate *Collier's* charges, find them to be false, and thus clear the way for the named public officials to sue the magazine for a million dollars. The goal was to put *Collier's* out of business. Only the dogged research and defense of attorney Louis Brandeis foiled the committee and saved *Collier's* from the courts and potential financial disaster.[44]

Although Hapgood feared that fiction about real events and people might bring a libel lawsuit, others felt that turning news events into fiction would be a safer way to write. Phillips, the most prolific of the muckrakers to use fiction, often wrote about real events and people in his novels between 1901 and 1907. *The Plum Tree* (1905), in particular, used a series of corrupt characters who closely resembled elected officials.[45] In his magazine writing during the early muckraking period, Phillips made caustic attacks on the social establishment, but he used imaginary types and composites instead of real people. Certainly Phillips was aware of the risks of libel lawsuits. For nine years he had been a reporter and editorial writer for Pulitzer's *World* which was sued dozens of times for libel. In one year alone, 1894, Pulitzer was sued twenty-one times.[46] This was typical of what was happening to many newspapers and magazines in the 1890s. After several decades of decline, criminal indictments for private and political libels had begun to rise, and state courts were hearing a greater number of all types of libel cases. The number of criminal libel cases reached an all-time high between 1896 and 1905.[47] Thomas Lawson's 1905 muckraking of Wall Street and insurance companies, for example, prompted a threat of a criminal libel lawsuit in New York and an attempt to bring one in Boston. The top executive from Standard Oil, who threatened Lawson, never followed through, and a Boston grand jury refused to indict Lawson, which caused him to brag; "At last the issue is clinched and the American people will know the truth."[48] Lawson, a wealthy man, was probably not deterred by the lawsuits. The same cannot be said for publishers who were worried over profit margins and revenues.

Phillips avoided libel suits, but his 1906 "Treason of the Senate" articles worried his editors. After the articles had been type set and were awaiting publication, *Cosmopolitan* publisher Hearst read them. He was angry: the articles needed more facts and less rhetoric, he told his editors, and he feared libel lawsuits because of Phillips' angry but unsubstantiated allegations. When the articles appeared, after Phillips had added more substantiation, there were many angry responses, but no lawsuits were filed.[49]

Hearst was not above using libel laws in an attempt to intimidate muckraker Will Irwin who had undertaken a project on the press for *Collier's* in 1910. His history and analysis included exposés of how Hearst's newspapers had cozy relationships with advertisers and how, at times, they buried or refused to publish articles unfavorable to certain advertisers and even potential advertisers. Hearst learned of the investigation, and his attorney wrote to Irwin threatening civil and criminal libel suits.[50] Irwin was not slowed by Hearst's threat, but, his biographer wrote, he "braced for Hearst's reaction." The reaction was a $500,000 civil libel lawsuit. The outcome of that lawsuit is unclear. Irwin's biographer states that "the preponderance of evidence is that it was never brought to trial," but, he added, it might have been settled.[51] One way or the other, at a time when muckraking was clearly waning, it might have been a death blow to editors who were contemplating more detailed investigations. Prominent First Amendment lawyer Floyd Abrams has made it clear how the press is likely to deal with the threat of libel. "The ultimate way to avoid the risk is not to write the story," Abrams said.[52] Undoubtedly, that is what some of the muckrakers did.

Just as what happens in journalism is inseparable from what happens in society, what happens in the nation's judicial system is also tied to external events. The nation's legal policies and doctrines are shaped in response to political and social occurrences. The political events of the late nineteenth and early twentieth centuries—a time of economic unrest, political turmoil, and the emergence of the modern regulatory state—inevitably affected emerging legal doctrines. Journalism's crusades and yellow phase in the 1890s and its bold muckraking after 1900 undoubtedly alarmed many, particularly those who felt that the "best men" would avoid public life.

The courts worked during this period to restrain rather than encourage political discussion. In the area of libel law the courts revived tight controls over the press. One prominent libel case that came before the U.S. Supreme Court in 1907 was probably not lost on the muckraking writers and their editors. The court upheld a contempt citation against a newspaper for printing cartoons and articles which were critical of the Colorado Supreme Court. The federal court said that the First Amendment did not limit a state's power to punish people who published statements which "may be deemed contrary" to the general welfare.[53] Coming in the same year as the Phillips and Sinclair exposés and coupled with the Roosevelt attack, the court decision can only be viewed as a further warning to the press to pull back on its criticism of the establishment. Americans in the Progressive Era still exalted the value of free expression, but social and political tensions had forced influential citizens to expect the law to provide reasonable restraints against dangerous expression. The judiciary, for the most part, responded by allowing libel lawsuits to flourish.

A RESTRAINT FROM WITHIN: PROFESSIONALISM

By the middle of the muckraking period, the public had a fixed and dual view of journalism. Journalists were, on the one hand, stereotyped as crude inquisitors and callous purveyors of sensationalism. On the other hand, they were also champions of the underdog and the dynamos of the democracy. The muckrakers, who can be seen as fitting either sterotype, considered themselves serious professionals. Journalism, to them, was a noble and important practice; it deserved recognition as such, and it needed to be further refined and defined in order to earn the public's admiration. One way to gain public respect was to be associated with science and to use scientific methods and techniques. The science of journalism, as it began to develop, was objectivity. The true professional did not simply shoot from the hip; he or she used consensually validated methods of presenting evidence. In other words, journalists prove their professionalism by being objective.[54] When they were not objective, reporters left themselves open to criticism. While this emerging ethic of professionalism is not explicitly stated by any of the muckrakers, it can be seen implicitly in the reaction to David Graham Phillips' "Treason of the Senate" articles.

Roosevelt's criticism of the muckrakers received the lion's share of publicity, but Roosevelt was aiming less at journalism and journalists than he was attempting to further his own goals. He concluded his speech by calling for reforms in inheritance laws, and more than one author has speculated that TR probably wanted to press his own legislative agenda by defending the Senate in public and then privately goading the legislators to implement his policies. The more telling criticism was that which came from Phillips' muckraking colleagues.[55] *Collier's* editor Norman Hapgood was especially harsh in his view of Phillips' articles. *Collier's*, a respected journal, had already published Adams' patent medicine fraud series, and it would go on to expose the Taft administration's land grab cover-up. Thus, when Hapgood spoke, journalists listened. This was a voice of, if not reason, certainly credibility.

"The Treason of the Senate" has come to a close. These articles made reform odious. They represented sensational and money-making preying on the vogue of the literature of exposure which had been built up by truthful and conscientious work. . . . Mr. Phillips's articles were one shriek of accusation based on the distortion of such facts as were printed, and on the suppression of facts which were essential.[56]

This was the voice of fledgling objectivity, arguing on behalf of a new and narrow professional ethic. David Graham Phillips' attack on the Senate had gone too far, beyond neutrality, beyond what he could document, and beyond professional responsibility. No matter that, by most accounts, he was on target in his criticisms, and no matter that his overall goal, direct election of Senators, was embraced by most progressives.[57] Objective journalistic method would not allow such a partisan attack; the facts must speak for themselves.

Eventually, even Phillips' muckraking colleagues joined the chorus of criticism. Will Irwin said that the muckrakers, in general, "guarded carefully against letting artistic imagination run away with judgment," but Phillips, "good reporter though he was . . . [was] given to see life in terms of the picturesque. If the fact was striking, then it must be true." Ida Tarbell said that Phillips "always put into his discussions an emotion and an imagination we did not indulge ourselves much on *McClure's*." Because the muckrakers stuck "to the facts . . . as nearly as we could establish them by research, the public gave us confidence and respect," she said.[58] Despite Phillips' claim to the contrary, his rhetoric and partisan attack strayed not only from the almighty documented fact, but also from the muckrakers' apparent self-definition. There were too many undocumented allegations, and there was too much angry rhetoric to suit the emerging journalistic ideal of neutrality. Phillips simply did not follow the "strategic ritual" of objectivity that his fellow professionals seemed to be demanding. If in 1906 one was a hopeful muckraking journalist, ready to expose the misdeeds of the powerful, one might have to reexamine one's goals in light of the response to the "Treason" series, which was a defining moment for journalism. The reaction to the "Treason" articles encouraged neutral reportage and discouraged muckraking activism.

THE PUBLIC TIRES AND WAR INTERVENES

As the nation debated whether to enter World War I, and if so, on what side, America's magazines began to change direction. For nearly fifteen years many of the periodicals had been, in various ways, raking muck. At the same time, of course, publications like the *Saturday Evening Post* were combining slick features and upbeat portraits of self-made businessmen to produce huge circulation gains and healthy revenue. The *Post* ran occasional pieces of journalism that bordered on exposé, but genteel fiction was its bread and butter. The *Post* set the trend for national magazines. Sensing a changing public opinion, the *Ladies Home Journal* shifted its content to war preparedness, becoming at times almost a mouthpiece for government propaganda.[59] Some magazines tried in vain to continue hard-nosed journalism; *Pearson's* and *Hampton's* were perhaps the most notable examples. Like the spirit of Progressivism, however, muckraking journalism was wearing thin with the public as the war drew near.

Charles Edward Russell, committed to revamping society, saw the change in public attitude. People concluded that "the whole thing was part of the helter-skelter insanity of modern life," he wrote, and "they turned to something else." As early as 1906, Lincoln Steffens predicted, "I expect to see the people get tired of 'exposure' and seek a more 'optimistic' prospect." Ermin J. Ridgway, editor of *Everybody's*, wrote in an editorial that "when a man has read about the same crimes for years, he begins to tire reading about them. . . . They are not so interesting." Benjamin Hampton, launching the magazine *New Broadway* in 1908, said, "The country likely has had its fill of 'muckraking.' " Even America's socialists, who had used the muckrakers' facts to press their argument that capitalism was fatally flawed, felt that the muckrakers' attacks on business had served their purpose. "Muckraking has largely spent its force," *Wilshire's*, a socialist magazine, concluded in 1911.[60]

If the public was tired of and perhaps a bit disgusted with muckraking, it would not be surprising. Why should journalists keep muckraking commerce when, as Hearst editor Arthur Brisbane said, "it has been done by Upton Sinclair in shrill spiritual falsetto; by Lincoln Steffens in grumbling bass; by Alfred Henry Lewis with Texas foam and fury; by Ray Stannard Baker in lawyer-like reportorial coolness; (and) by Ida Tarbell with Lady MacBeth fury."[61] The repetitive attacks probably had the public believing that many of the issues with which the muckrakers had been dealing had been solved. The appearance of vigorous government investigations—in 1912 alone eleven congressional committees were holding what some have called muckraking hearings—added to the public perception that the problems were on their way to resolution. After all, federal and state governments had dramatically enlarged their functions and their control over business, and recalls and direct elections gave the impression that things were cleaner in government. Simply the appearance in print, over a period of years, of news about scandal provided a catharsis for the public, and it created an impression that things had improved.[62] In reality, the system that had produced the problems to start with had changed very little; many of the same problems would appear again in the years to come.

By 1910, the public reasoning was simple: the problems had been exposed and solutions were being implemented, so why not halt the attack on capitalism. Stop beating a dead horse, unless, of course, as some feared, the press was only interested in sensationalism and profiteering; unless "buckraking" was now more important than "muckraking." Alfred Henry Lewis, who edited *Human Life* in its muckraking phase, contended that some of the magazines had "turned to muckrakes . . . wholly for the sake of private gain,"[63] exposing a sensationalist and profiteering streak that has always been a part of journalism. Could the public have missed this streak? What were people to think when they saw sensational publicity campaigns surround upcoming muckraking stories? In 1904, for example, *Era* proclaimed that its articles on life insurance frauds would "be the most profoundly interesting, important and vital ever printed in a monthly periodical . . . an epoch in magazine making." After William Randolph Hearst lured David Graham Phillips in 1905 to muckrake the Senate, his *Cosmopolitan* magazine ran bombastic advertisements, saying it would soon produce the revelations of the century.[64] Other magazines used similar circulation-building techniques revolving around their muckraking exposés. "[W]hen exposure became a prescription for manufacturing magazine circulation," declared *Everybody's* editor John O'Hara Cosgrove many years later, "muckraking was ended." Muckraking became its own worst enemy. The fact-based tone of the early days was taken over by something different. The *Nation* magazine charged that certain magazines had created "a vast appetite for horrors ... and to satisfy that appetite editors grew reckless; then they grew desperate; then they grew ridiculous."[65] Ida Tarbell noted the difference between the work of some, like Phillips, and the work of *McClure's* writers. Baker agreed, saying the public needed to distinguish between honest and sensational exposés.[66] Even the muckrakers were confused about the direction of their work as the movement unfolded. At first, Steffens wanted to stick to the facts. He told Baker: "Look out for editorializing. That's easy and it doesn't count for much without the facts." But when Steffens joined the staff of the *American* in 1906, he began to sing a different tune. In 1908 he left the magazine because he wanted conclusions and the others still wanted facts.[67] As World War I approached, the confusion was evident, and the public was caught in the middle.

If the combined effect of business pressure, libel lawsuits, and a tired public was not enough to put muckraking out of business, then the cataclysmic war in Europe applied the final blow. As the march toward a Progressive society was halted by the mounting death count, so too was muckraking journalism. "The war in Europe swallowed Progressivism," sighed William Allen White.[68] All eyes turned away from the flaws of business to the business of winning the war. Peter Finley Dunne, known to millions of Americans for his "Mr. Dooley," the Chicago bartender whose wit, irony, and irreverance poked fun at America's flaws and foibles, found the war so depressing that he found he could not make fun of it in his satiric essays.[69] The muckrakers followed suit; America needed boosting, not attacking, as the war unfolded. Perhaps the muckrakers would simply take a break during the war, and then they could return to Progressive reforms when the boys returned home. But it did not work out that way. Muckraking disappeared and, except for isolated muckraking episodes over the next forty years, it did not reappear as a movement until the world had gone through a period of business idolatry, through a stock market crash and a depression, and through another world war.

NOTES

1. Quoted in David Mark Chalmers, *The Social and Political Ideas of the Muckrakers* (New York, 1964), 67. The statement comes from the unpublished notebooks of Ray Stannard Baker.

2. Although many magazines adopted muckraking to boost circulation, it did not necessarily mean success. *McClure's* was more profitable before it began muckraking. See Peter Lyon, *Success Story: The Life and Times of S. S. McClure* (New York, 1963), 251–252. *Everybody's* circulation soared from 150,000 to 700,000 when it published Thomas Lawson's "Frenzied Finance," and it dropped by 200,000 after the series ended. The *American's* circulation stayed at 300,000 until after 1914 when it stopped muckraking, and then the circulation rose to 1,500,000. See Peter Barry, "The Decline of Muckraking: A View from the Magazines" (Ph.D. Diss., Wayne State University, 1971), 23–24, 26–27.

3. Charles Edward Russell, "The Magazine Soft Pedal," *Pearson's* (February 1914): 182. Others invoked a theory of a conspiracy against the muckrakers. See Upton Sinclair, *The Brass Check* (Pasadena, Calif., 1919), passim. A contemporary critique of the book's view of journalism is found in Judson A. Grenier, "Upton Sinclair and the Press: The Brass Check Reconsidered," *Journalism Quarterly* 49 (Autumn 1972): 427–36. Louis Filler writes in a matter-of-fact fashion about conspiracy, but he provides little documentation. See *The Muckrakers* (University Park, Pa., 1976), 359–78.

4. Walter Lippmann, *Drift and Mastery* (New York, 1914), 3.

5. There are various accounts of the breakup of *McClure's*. See Ida Tarbell, *All in a Day's Work* (New York, 1939), 254–59; and John E. Semonche, *Ray Stannard Baker: A Quest for Democracy in Modern America, 1870–1918* (Chapel Hill, N.C., 1969), 154–58. The description of McClure is found in Lincoln Steffens, *The Autobiography of Lincoln Steffens* (New York, 1931), 361.

6. See "The Patent Medicine Conspiracy against the Freedom of the Press," *Collier's* (November 4, 1905): 13–16, 25; and "What Is Yellow?" *Collier's* (March 31, 1906): 20.

7. John W. Ryckman, "Despotism of Combined Millions," *New England Magazine* (July 1908): 547–48. Muckraker Charles E. Russell said that he was shadowed by detectives when he researched his articles; see his *Bare Hands and Stone Walls/Some Recollections of a Side-Line Reformer* (New York, 1933), 183–87. Mark Sullivan said, too, that detectives from the patent medicine industry trailed him when he probed bogus medicines. See his autobiography, *The Education of an American* (New York, 1938), 186–87.

8. "Can the Wool Trust Gag the Press?" *Collier's* (March 18, 1911): 12; "The Wool Trust and Collier's," *Collier's* (March 18, 1911): 9. The statement about the "big interests" is quoted in Sheila Reaves, "How Radical Were the Muckrakers? Socialist Press Views, 1902–1906," *Journalism Quarterly* 61 (Winter 1984): 763–70.

9. John Kibbee Turner, *Barbarous Mexico* (Chicago, 1910). John Semonche, "The American Magazine of 1906–15: Principle vs. Profit," *Journalism Quarterly* 40 (Winter 1963): 39–40; and Filler, *The Muckrakers*, 364, discuss the incident.

10. David Graham Phillips, *The Plum Tree* (Indianapolis, 1905), 31. Phillips offers a similar view in *The Master Rogue* (New York, 1903). The best analysis of a conspiracy against the muckrakers is found in Michael D. Marcaccio, "Did a Business Conspiracy End Muckraking? A Reexamination," *Historian* 47 (November 1984), 58–71. Despite business pressure, he concluded there was no conspiracy. Historian Richard Hofstadter first suggested the need for a full-length study of the decline of muckraking in *The Age of Reform* (New York, 1955), 196, note 5. Studies of muckraking's decline include Edwin H. Lundberg, "The De-

cline of the American Muckrakers: A New Interpretation" (Master's thesis, University of Vermont, 1966), and Barry, "The Decline of Muckraking." Barry and Lundberg both reject the notion of the existence of a conspiracy to end muckraking.

11. Ray Stannard Baker, *American Chronicle: The Autobiography of Ray Stannard Baker* (New York, 1945), 206.

12. Scholars Marcaccio and Barry conclude that it was possible but implausible that a conspiracy existed to destroy *Hampton's*. See Marcaccio, "Did a Business Conspiracy," 62–64; and Barry, "The Decline of Muckraking," 320–31.

13. Orison Swett Marden, "A Foreward," *New Success* (January 1918): 13. Marden had previously edited *Success* magazine which, according to his biographer, was put out of business by the financial community. See Margaret Connolly, *The Life Story of Orison Swett Marden: A Man Who Benefited Men* (New York, 1925), 226–29. A conspiracy against the magazine was ruled out by Frank Luther Mott, "The Magazine Called 'Success,' " *Journalism Quarterly* 34 (Winter 1957): 49.

14. Roy Hoopes, *Ralph Ingersoll: A Biography* (New York, 1985), 398.

15. Salme H. Steinberg, *Reformer in the Marketplace: Edward W. Bok and the Ladies Home Journal* (Baton Rouge, La., 1979), 65.

16. W. A. Swanberg, *Pulitzer* (New York, 1967), 336–37.

17. Theodore Peterson, *Magazines in the Twentieth Century* (Urbana, Ill., 1964), 18; John Tebbel, *The American Magazine: A Compact History* (New York, 1969), 195. Tebbel says that when advertisers became the main source for magazine revenue "editorial independence" was "virtually ended," (p. 196). Richard Hofstadter agrees with Tebbel on press vulnerability to advertiser pressure; see *The Age of Reform*, 195.

18. Lyon, *Success Story*, 300–301.

19. Prudential and Dryden used this ad in many other publications. See Robert D. Reynolds, Jr., "The 1906 Campaign to Sway Muckraking Periodicals," *Journalism Quarterly* 56 (Autumn 1979): 513–20, 589. A fuller discussion of advertising news is found in Linda Lawson, "Advertisements Masquerading as News in Turn-of-the-Century American Periodicals," *American Journalism* 52, (1988): 81–96.

20. C. W. Post, "A Great Power If Patriotically Used," *Leslie's Weekly* (January 23, 1913): 94.

21. Gordon M. Jensen, "The National Civic Federation: American Business in an Age of Social Change and Social Reform, 1900–1910" (Ph.D. Diss., Princeton University, 1956), 119. Jensen argues that the NCF was a progressive force, spurring business to help in the reform effort. A different view of the NCF is contained in James Weinstein, *The Corporate Ideal in the Liberal State, 1900–1918* (Boston, 1968), 3–39. Weinstein saw the NCF as a conservative group that sought a more efficient, i.e., less regulated, marketplace for businessmen. The NCF was composed of labor leaders, as well as businessmen.

22. Theodore Roosevelt to William Howard Taft, March 13, 1906, Elting S. Morrison, ed., *Letters of Roosevelt*, vol. 5 (Cambridge, Mass., 1952), 183–84.

23. Unsigned letter, September 4, 1912, Box 51, National Civic Federation papers, New York Public Library.

24. Box 82, NCF Papers, March, April, 1915.

25. "Shall the Bogeyman Get the Magazine Publishers?" *Editor and Publisher* (February 11, 1911): 8. A similar question was raised in "A Word to the Muck-rakers," *Independent* (February 6, 1911): 319; "The Rumored 'Magazine Trust' " *Literary Digest* (February 25, 1911): 344; "Magazine Facts and Rumors," *Fourth Estate* (February 11, 1911): 2, 16. The same view was expressed in "Do 'The Big Interests' Control Our Magazines?" *Current Literature* (July 1912): 103–5. Those who championed the conspiracy theory naturally assumed that Thomas Lamont was an agent of J. P. Morgan. Lamont became a partner in J. P. Morgan and Company in 1911 and he did own substantial stock in Crowell Publications; however, Marcaccio concludes that his interest in magazines was not to thwart muckraking but to make money.

26. Reynolds, "The 1906 Campaign," 520.

27. Robert C. Bannister, Jr., *Ray Stannard Baker: The Mind and Thought of a Progressive* (New Haven, Conn., 1966), 210.

28. Lyon, *Success Story*, 321.

29. E. A. Van Valkenburg to Ray Stannard Baker, February 13, 1911, Baker Papers, Library of Congress, quoted in John Semonche, "The American Magazine," 41. Subtle business pressure on editorial content was explored in a series of articles in 1912 in the militant *Twentieth Century* magazine. See George French, "Masters of the Magazine" (April 1912): 501–8; "Shall the Tail Wag the Dog?" (May 1912): 19–26; "The Damnation of the Magazines" (June 1912): 99–111; "Everybody's Business" (July 1912): 241–49.

30. Semonche, *Ray Stannard Baker*, 42. Baker's comments are found on p. 279.

31. Sullivan, *Education of an American*, 286–87.

32. Quoted in Barry, "The Decline of Muckraking," 339; "Reflections of the Editors," *Pearson's* (April 1911): 549–80.

33. Will Irwin, *The Making of a Reporter* (New York, 1942), 155. Russell, *Bare Hands and Stone Walls* (New York, 1933), 132.

34. Quoted in Robert S. Maxwell, "A Note on the Muckrakers," *Mid-America* 43 (January 1961): 56, note 2.

35. White, "Platt," *McClure's*, December 1901, p. 152. This article is in marked contrast to two earlier flattering profiles of "Hanna," Marcus Hanna, powerful Republican senator from Ohio, *McClure's*, November, 1900, pp. 56–64, and "Croker," about New York City's political "boss," Richard Croker, *McClure's*, February 1901, pp. 317–326.

36. William Allen White, *Autobiography* (New York, 1946), 346–49. Thomas Reed, a Republican congressman from Maine, was a prominent candidate for the presidency in 1896 and speaker of the House from 1899 to 1901.

37. Lincoln Steffens' article appeared originally in *McClure's*, in January 1903, and was reprinted in *The Shame of the Cities* (New York, 1957). Justin Kaplan, *Lincoln Steffens: A Biography* (New York, 1974), 123, discussed the threat. Mc-Clure's response and Steffens' strategy are included in Kaplan, 124.

38. Steffens, *The Autobiography of Lincoln Steffens*, 486.

39. Maxwell, "A Note on the Muckrakers," 59, note 8. Baker's version of the lawsuit is found in Baker, *American Chronicle*, 206–12.

40. Steinberg, *Reformer in the Marketplace*, 102–3.

41. Jon A. Yoder, *Upton Sinclair* (New York, 1975), 11; Filler, *The Muckrakers*, 167.

42. Norman Hapgood, *The Changing Years: Reminiscences of Norman Hapgood* (New York, 1930), 171, 183.

43. "Mr. Sinclair Would Be Sued," *New York Times*, 4 May 1906, p. 8. The threat to McClure is recounted by Baker, *American Chronicle*, 207.

44. Filler, *The Muckrakers*, 334. Hapgood, *Reminiscences*, 183. Hapgood was sued again in 1915 and again in 1916. Barry, "Decline of Muckraking," felt that the lawsuits may have deterred *Harper's* from muckraking, 338.

45. The best account of Phillips' life and work is found in Louis Filler, *The Voice of Democracy: A Critical Biography of David Graham Phillips: Journalist, Novelist, Progressive* (University Park, Pa., 1978). Phillips' journalism is discussed in Robert Miraldi, "The Journalism of David Graham Phillips," *Journalism Quarterly* 63 (Spring 1988), 83–88.

46. George Juergens, *Joseph Pulitzer and the New York World* (Princeton, N.J., 1966), 82, note 89.

47. Norman L. Rosenberg, "The New Law of Political Libel: A Historical Perspective," *Rutgers Law Review* 28 (1982), 1157, 1182. Rosenberg's expanded account of the evolution of libel law is found in *Protecting the Best Men: An Interpretive History of the Law of Libel* (Chapel Hill, 1986). See especially "Legal Science and Hamiltonian Principles: Libel Law, 1818–1920," 178–206.

48. "News Company Warned against Lawson Story," *New York Times*, 20 December 1904, p. 1; "Fails to Indict Lawson," *New York Times*, 10 December 1905, p. 2.

49. John Tebbel, *The Life and Good Times of William Randolph Hearst* (New York, 1952), 150–151; Filler, *Voice of Democracy*, 99. The Phillips articles are collected in *The Treason of the Senate*, introduction, George E. Mowry and Judson A. Grenier (Chicago, 1964).

50. Criminal libel was a tactic that Hearst's nemesis, Roosevelt, had tried to silence Pulitzer's *World* in 1908 after the newspaper criticized Roosevelt's handling of the Panama Canal. See George Juergens, *News from the White House: The Presidential Press Relationship in the Progressive Era* (Chicago, 1981), 79–90. That lawsuit failed.

51. Robert V. Hudson, *The Writing Game: A Biography of Will Irwin* (Ames, Iowa, 1982), 70–71. Hudson speculated on the lawsuit's outcome in a personal communication, February 23, 1986.

52. Floyd Abrams is quoted in the *New York Times*, 17 February 1985, p. 72.

53. *Patterson v. Colorado*, 205 U.S. 454 (1907). Rosenberg discusses the relationship between the courts and society in "The New Law of Political Libel," 1141.

54. Robert Wiebe points out that professionalization of both the legal and medical professions took place during the Progressive Era and that a similar occurrence was evident in journalism also. See *The Search for Order, 1877–1920* (New York, 1960), 116–17, 113–15, 120. Opinion surveys of how the public felt about journalists were not available during this time, but a clue to public sentiment about how journalists were viewed can be seen in literature, as detailed by Howard Good, *Acquainted with the Night: The Image of Journalists in American Fiction, 1890–1930* (Metuchen, N.J., 1986).

55. Phillips, *Treason*, 44.

56. *Collier's* (November 17, 1906): 9. Even Phillips' friend, George Horace Lorimer, criticized him in the *Saturday Evening Post* (April 17, 1907): 17.

57. Richard Hofstadter asserts that Phillips' assessment of the Senate was essentially correct; see *The Progressive Movement, 1900–1917* (Englewood Cliffs, N.J., 1963), 108. An amendment to the Constitution that provided for direct election of the U.S. Senate was approved in 1913.

58. Irwin, *The Making of a Reporter*, 170–71; letter by Ida Tarbell to Louis Filler, *Voice of Democracy*, 77. Ray Stannard Baker also criticized Phillips' articles, *American Chronicle*, 245.

59. John Tebbel, *George Horace Lorimer and the Saturday Evening Post* (Garden City, N.Y., 1948). A typical shift in approach toward war preparedness, for example, can be seen in magazines such as the *Ladies Home Journal*. Edward Bok's memoirs, *The Americanization of Edwin Bok* (New York, 1930), 394.

60. Russell, *Bare Hands and Stone Walls*, 132; Lincoln Steffens, *The Struggle for Self Government* (New York, 1906), xxii; Ermin J. Ridgway, "What Do You Know About Rum?" *Everybody's* (October 1907), 506–8; "Four Hundred Stockholders and What It Means," *New Broadway* (September 1908), 399–400; Unsigned, *Wilshire's* (February 1911): 2–3.

61. Quoted in Oliver Carlson, *Brisbane: A Candid Biography* (New York, 1937), 188–89.

62. See "The Craze for Commissions," *Saturday Evening Post* (March 2, 1912): 3; and "Congressional Muckraking," *Saturday Evening Post* (November 30, 1912): 24.

63. Alfred Henry Lewis, "Mr. Lewis' Editorial on the 'Muck-Rakers,' " *Human Life* (June 1906): 20.

64. *Era*, (October 1904), i; the *Cosmopolitan* ad is reprinted in Phillips, *Treason*, 56.

65. "The Popular Magazine," *Nation* (February 23, 1911): 187.

66. Baker, *American Chronicle*, 204.

67. Letter from Steffens to Baker, March 3, 1904, quoted in Bannister, *Ray Stannard Baker*, 106; Steffens' reasons for leaving the *American* are discussed in Kathleen Brady, *Ida Tarbell: Portrait of a Muckraker* (New York, 1984), 183; and Steffens, *Autobiography*, 575–76.

68. Walter Johnson, ed., *Selected Letters of William Allen White, 1899–1943* (New York, 1947), 185. On the effect of the war on Progressivism, see Arthur S. Link, "What Happened to the Progressive Movement in the 1920s?" *American Historical Review* 64 (July 1959): 833–51.

69. Although Dunne wrote nearly fifty essays on war, he "generally refused to write about" World War I, says his biographer, Grace Eckley, *Finley Peter Dunne* (Boston, 1967), 100.

4

An Awakening: Murrow and the Migrants

The eyes of the nine-year-old boy are large, saucer-like, innocent, and empty. There is no smile on his black face as he gazes around the ramshackle room that is his home for the harvest. Cinder-block walls, an open window, a few mattresses. Jerome King sits on a bed, his three sisters, Beulah, Katherine, and Lois, nearby; they appear to be from three to six years old. The boy is babysitting while his mother, Ailean, works in the fields where she picks beans from 6 in the morning until 4 in the afternoon. Jerome points to his sister, looks at the television camera, and tells the interviewer that the hole in the bed where she is sitting was made by a rat. Jerome is protecting her now. What about food, asks the interviewer, David Lowe, in a gentle voice. What are you going to feed your sisters? "I don't know, sir," the boy answers, and then he shrugs.

Lowe, a producer who works for CBS News, eventually finds the mother kneeling in a furrow, picking crops; a bandana is wrapped around her head to catch perspiration. She confirms that yes, indeed, her son is the babysitter while she goes out and earns the $1 a day that isn't even enough to pay for their food which costs $2 a day. A nursery school would cost 85 cents, so that is out of the question. Besides, Ailean King, who is twenty-nine, has seven children to feed.[1]

The year is 1960, and the King family is the poorest of the poor, part of the perennial underclass of two million farm laborers who are known as migrant workers, nomads who travel up and down America in what the sociologists call "streams"—the East Coast, Midwest, and West Coast streams. As the cliche goes, they follow the sun and the ripening crops.[2] The U.S. Secretary of Labor calls them "excluded Americans"; a senator from New Jersey labels the migrant workers "a voiceless and voteless minority of poverty"; a presidential committee calls them "children of misfortune"; and the New York *Times* in an uncharacteristic break with objectivity pleads in a pictorial essay for help for the "landless, luckless army."[3] David Lowe, on his first assignment for CBS, had followed the migrant workers for nine months, along the Atlantic seaboard and then to farms and camps in California. When he was done, he turned over his findings to Edward R. Murrow, the newsman, who stood before a camera and told a shocked audience, in that resonant voice America knew so well, about these lowest paid laborers who pick fruit and vegetables for the "best fed nation on earth." She worked as hard as she could all day long and Ailean King, migrant worker, still could not feed her children—a claim hotly disputed by farmers after the November 25, 1960, showing of one of the most controversial and heralded muckraking documentaries in television history: "Harvest of Shame."

Blink the camera, and skip ten years. Add color to the picture, change the name of the interviewer from David Lowe to Martin Carr, and switch the network from CBS to NBC. Focus the camera this time on Ernest Jarvis, a brown-skinned man with a graying stubble of beard. Creases run down his cheeks, his eyes are bloodshot, his voice is hoarse, and he coughs, a hacking, unhealthy cough, as he sits on the edge of a cot in a cell-like room. Ernest Jarvis is a migrant worker. He looks old, although he is only thirty-nine. Been pickin' and stoopin' in the fields my whole life, he tells Carr, but times are rough. "I owe my landlady money and I owe my bossman money," he says. Never do catch up, he adds, seeming more tired than embarrassed.

And the future, the questioner asks. Do you worry about the future? "All the time," Jarvis says, and then he mumbles something about Social Security money that someone told him he should get in his old age. There is silence as the camera focuses on Jarvis' weathered face. He coughs again. The distinctive voice of broadcaster Chet Huntley, the narrator, intones that for many workers like Jarvis, the time to collect will never come. Migrant workers die, on the average, at the age of forty nine.[4]

In the nationally televised 1970 documentary, called "Migrant," Huntley replaced Murrow, but the story was virtually the same—poverty, wretched housing, low wages, disease, early death. Huntley ended the broadcast by saying, "We hope that no one will need to make a film about migrants ten years from now." He did not get his wish. Ten years later, there stands black-haired Chris Wallace, the son of the well-known CBS broadcaster, with a camera crew in tow, pacing in front of a row of migrant houses owned by a local farmer. A representative of the owner tells Wallace to leave. There will be no filming. "You gonna have to go to the office," the man says. "What office?" Wallace asks, baiting the man to say more for the camera. The man responds, "Elberry's office. This Elberry's Camp. This is private property. Y'all go down there and talk with them. We're working for Elberry." "He owns this camp?" Wallace asks, innocently, as the camera films, and then the man waves angrily at the camera. "I told you, man, don't be filmin' me."

In this 1980 documentary, the migrants seem less important than the constant confrontations that occur between Wallace's NBC camera crew and those who employ the migrants. The show's producer, Morton Silverstein, takes a crew to a grove where a job action is taking place. The migrants, protesting low wages, are replaced by children, a violation of Florida labor law. A sheriff and the owner's foreman tell Silverstein to leave. "The bossman said run 'em off, run 'em out. They don't have no business in here," the foreman says. Subsequently, Wallace interviews a judge who handles worker-landlord disputes, and he confronts the judge with information that the judge owns some of the worst migrant housing in the area. The judge stands up, takes off his robe, and asks Wallace to leave. Wallace goes next to a sheriff who is allegedly hiring illegal aliens. The sheriff denies the charge, but Wallace confronts the sheriff with documents that make his denial look foolish. "The Migrants" 1980-style is done in prosecutorial fashion, with Wallace, who chased the bad guys, acting as judge and jury. Nonetheless, the point is clear: migrant workers were as badly off in 1980 as they were in 1960. Wallace concludes with moral indignation, "How many more harvests will it take before we understand that the migrants' shame is our own?"[5]

A better question might have been, how many more muckraking exposés will it take before the unmitigated misery of the migrant worker in America is ended? Why haven't hundreds of newspaper stories and four major televised documentary exposés revolutionized the lives of the thousands of migrant workers in America? Why is the average age of migrant death still forty-nine? Why are they America's lowest paid workers? Why are malnutrition and disease still rampant? Why do they still live in shacks that reporters for forty years have been describing as "hovels"? The answer may be that the press can muckrake and expose forever on certain questions, but that try as it might, it cannot solve a complex problem which has roots in the nature of American capitalism, one where solutions do not come in small legislative steps. Ever since 1947, when the Taft-Hartley Act excluded farm workers from the protections of labor legislation, migrant farm workers have been trying to eke out a living. The average worker worked 136 days a year and earned $900, Murrow reported in 1960. Certainly, no one could argue that the migrants' plight has not gotten attention. "We have been well, and often, informed," one social worker wrote. "The many words that have been written about migrant workers add up to a mountain of paper," another added.

The fictional portrayal of a migrant family by John Steinbeck in *The Grapes of Wrath* first brought the migrant family into the American consciousness in 1939. Congressional inquiries and a scandal over the use of Mexican aliens followed in the 1940s. Two reports by presidential commissions and ballyhooed hearings by social workers brought more attention in the 1950s.[6] Then, in 1959, Howard Van Smith, a reporter for the *Miami News*, began an onslaught of news coverage when he championed the cause of migrant farm laborers in Florida. He won a Pulitzer Prize and stirred media interest, highlighted by "Harvest of Shame." More exposé followed, reaching regional and national audiences but, despite thirty years of muckraking and the resulting public indignation, real change still has not arrived. The migrant worker today, probably either black or Hispanic, is poor, powerless, and, some contend, worse off.[7]

The story of muckraking journalism and migrant workers is one of heroic effort and empathy, of activism, and of an effective press. It is, nonetheless, a story of failure. This chapter tells that story—of the crusaders for change, of the journalistic techniques used to expose conditions, of the powerful impact of the exposés, and of the angry counterreactions. Why has it failed? Three episodes of news coverage between 1959 and 1961 may help to answer the question. Two are regional—the reporting of Howard Van Smith in the *Miami News* and Dale Wright in the New York *World Telegram and Sun*—and one is national—the Edward R. Murrow–Fred Friendly documentary "Harvest of Shame." All three garnered national attention and awards, and all three were closely connected with the flurry of legislative activity and reform that resulted in the mid–1960s. A separate study, beyond the scope of this work, is needed to understand why the plight of migrant workers has defied significant change. This chapter, instead, explores how journalists revealed and combated a social injustice, continuing in the tradition of the Progressive Era muckrakers. Moreover, it explores how journalism's unwritten code, its strategic ritual of objectivity, shapes and limits what the audience eventually sees and reads, and how the conventions of objectivity constrain and narrow press coverage, keeping the focus on exposé and not on insight, analysis, and solution.

"SHACKTOWN"—WORSE THAN THE DEPRESSION

Much of America's vision of migrant workers was shaped by Steinbeck's fictional Joad family, a decent lot of Okies who traveled to California in search of work. All they found, however, was poverty and trouble. Howard Van Smith, a small, dark-haired man and a diligent reporter, stumbled on a 1957 version of migrant poverty and trouble when he discovered hundreds of hungry farm families in a small Florida farming town near Miami. Van Smith, then forty-eight, had been a reporter and editor for twelve years with the *Miami News*, the little kid on the block (circulation 122,691) compared to the *Miami Herald* (275,067). Van Smith worked in a bureau south of Miami, an agricultural area where he first encountered migrant workers. Always on the lookout for stories, Van Smith regularly drove around the Miami area in his tiny black Volkswagen while his large collie sat panting in the backseat. As a result of his surveillance, he knew the area "like the back of his hand," recalled a photographer who worked with Van Smith. "If he was looking for some fruit grower who was dumping rotten tomatoes, he knew where they were dumped."[8]

Van Smith received a tip one day that a freeze in the farming town of Immokalee, 125 miles northwest of Miami, had wiped out the tomato crop and, in the process, had put thousands of migrant workers out of work. As many as 4,000 laborers, mostly American blacks in town for the harvest, were stranded in what was called "Shacktown," described by Van Smith as "a nondescript group of miserable hovels where . . . whole families, without furniture, sleep on the floor." Even when there was work, the living conditions of the migrants were pitiful; "human beings living like pigs," wrote Van Smith. The shacks the workers lived in were made of cardboard, rags, old linoleum, rotting lumber—"tiny, flimsy hovels thrown together with as little care and expense as possible. Most farmers," Van Smith said, "wouldn't keep a goat in one of them." Disease was common because, he wrote, "[g]arbage and refuse lie on the ground, feeding the flies, and amid this filth, children play." Raw sewage and drinking water sat side by side in the sun. Shacktown, a public health nurse told Van Smith, "is something just beyond belief."[9]

Before he could begin a crusade, Van Smith had to overcome the reluctance of his own editors. Immokalee was not his "beat"; in fact, it was out of the *News*' circulation area. The city desk wanted Van Smith to stick to South Dade County. This he did, but then, for weeks, after his workday was completed, Van Smith made the forty-five-minute drive over to Immokalee to document conditions there. "It was pretty shocking," recalled Van Smith's son, William, who was twelve at the time. "There were babies running around in only diapers, and the temperature was 25 degrees."[10] Van Smith finally convinced the *News*' city desk that he had a story, even if it was out of the newspaper's normal area of coverage. One editor explained that the city desk wanted Van Smith to have much of his research completed before the paper began to publish any of the stories. A reporter who worked with Van Smith at the time said that the story was held so long because the editors did not think it would help circulation very much.[11]

On January 12, Van Smith's weeks of leg work began to pay dividends. He wrote a page-one story for the *News* that described "the tragedy of Immokalee" as "something even the bottom days of the Depression couldn't equal."[12] Using the words of public health officials to warn about disease and starvation, Van Smith began an eight-month, thirty-five story crusade. His immediate goal had become clear by the second day when he wrote three stories. He described the conditions to a doctor, who was the chairman of world health of the American Academy of General Practice, and the physician demanded of the federal government: "Send doctors, send nurses, send food."[13] In the following days, Van Smith, playing social worker as well as reporter, called, among others, the president's commissioner on migratory labor to describe the conditions. The response was immediate; the federal government said it would send surplus food that should last for two weeks. Van Smith noted, however, that the migrants would not have a work opportunity for at least six weeks. More aid—and more stories—would be needed.[14]

Over the next two months, while Van Smith kept a barrage of stories before the public, more than $100,000 in donations were received. The U.S. Public Health Service responded with medical care; Miami fuel dealers delivered free kerosene; a baby-food company donated 10 tons of infant supplies; and a Miami radio station made round-the-clock appeals for donations. "It's a near miracle," a minister told Van Smith, "to think all this could happen to save these poor people in so short a time."[15] Despite its initial reluctance to run the stories, the *Miami News* wasn't bashful about taking much of the credit, but Van Smith's work was not over. His second goal was to place blame. "Many people here . . . are asking why government agencies failed when asked for help before the Miami *News* brought attention to the town's wants, suffering and disease," Van Smith wrote. He pursued the answer and found that "someone reported to the governor that conditions were all right in Immokalee." Embarrassed by the state's foul-up, Florida's Governor Leroy Collins secretly visited Shacktown and ordered aid to begin immediately. As soon as word came that Collins would visit, a source tipped off Van Smith. He arrived at the scene twenty minutes too late; the governor had already left. Van Smith sped off in pursuit, driving at high speeds up the Tamiami Trail. Van Smith caught the governor's car, pulled him over to the side of the road, and conducted an interview which appeared in the next day's edition. Two of Collins' aides, as Van Smith wrote, had failed to report the dangers at Shacktown.[16]

With the pressure on the governor and with the migrants' health and medical needs taken care of, Van Smith sought his third goal: the construction of decent housing. After the state promised funds for housing, Van Smith wrote, "Some people are already asking if this is just another brushoff made to look more important by the release of some state funds—and if next year the filthy little shacks won't be there as much as ever before." The chairman of the Immokalee chamber of commerce told Van Smith that the reporter was the migrants' only hope: "[K]eep a fire under them. Keep it burning. Don't let them forget this time." Van Smith started by reminding state officials of a report filed five years earlier by the county health department. He quoted it at length, showing that the presence of disease, filth, rodents, and building code violations had been well known for years. Van Smith wrote that he feared that after the exposés were over, a few drainage ditches would be dug, but Shacktown would remain, "growing more rotten, dirtier and crowded than before."[17] Less than a month later, however, Van Smith's reporting paid dividends.

On Monday, March 24, the *Miami News* published a photograph of Van Smith, with a hammer in his hand, tacking a condemnation notice to the wall of a Shacktown hut. County officials declared 597 houses unfit; 151 were ordered torn down, and the rest were to be closed unless they underwent major repairs. It was an empty victory at first, because it simply meant that hundreds of migrant families would have no place to live. The growers balked at the county order, and asked the governor to intervene, but he would not. Finally, faced with a shortage of workers to pick their ripening crops in the winter of 1960, the growers began to make repairs. The biggest health threat was tackled first by plumbing crews which installed flush toilets. With federal, state, and private money, construction began on dozens of new units for the workers. "It's a modern miracle—the kind that comes when good finally triumphs over bad," declared an Immokalee minister.[18] The "miracle" did not go unnoticed; Van Smith received the Pulitzer Prize for national reporting in 1959 for cleaning up what the Pulitzer committee called this "cesspool of America." "[I]f so much could be done in Immokalee," declared the committee, "the final phase in helping these migrants might begin"[19]

DAVID LOWE FINDS MISERY

It was springtime in Florida, 1960, just months after Van Smith's crusade; David Lowe was on his first assignment as a producer for "CBS Reports," the documentary arm of the television network's news division. As the new decade began, CBS News was closely identified with one person: Edward R. Murrow, a tall, dark-haired man who constantly had a cigarette dangling from his fingers and who had a *Casablanca*-like mysteriousness about him. His wartime broadcasts from besieged England, his tough "See It Now" television news show throughout the 1950s, his popular "Person to Person" celebrity interview show, and his integrity had made him into a legend, a mass cult hero. He was the biggest star in news broadcasting.[20] Along with Fred W. Friendly, who was the producer, organizer, and catalyst behind so much of Murrow's television work, Murrow had tackled a slew of difficult and controversial social issues. Murrow and Friendly were perhaps best known for their 1954 attack on the witch-hunting politics of Joseph McCarthy, the Republican senator from Wisconsin. Their weekly news broadcast had given way to hour-long documentaries, known as "CBS Reports," which since October 1959 had been appearing every few weeks in prime time.[21]

Lowe, who was thirty-seven years old, had approached Friendly seeking a job. Friendly was not sure he had a position for Lowe; after all, he already had four producers. "But David was very persuasive," Friendly recalled. So Friendly made a proposal. The previous evening, while driving home from Manhattan, Friendly had heard a radio broadcast from Washington, D.C. by Edward P. Morgan who was bemoaning the condition of American's migrant farm workers. "We should do something about that," Friendly told himself. The next day, appeared the eager Lowe. Friendly, unconvinced that either the farmers or the workers would cooperate, told Lowe to go to Florida for a month and see if he could make some inroads. "If we couldn't film, we couldn't do a program," Friendly said.[22] He promised Lowe $1,000—$250 a week for four weeks. If Lowe could get cooperation, he would then travel with and chronicle the life of the "stoop workers," the laborers who pick tomatoes in Florida, beans in the Carolinas, corn in New Jersey, and apples in New York. Lowe headed for Florida where he found that many of the migrant farm workers would not talk. Reporters, most of whom are white, often learn that farm laborers, most of whom are black and Hispanic, will not talk openly, if at all, with strangers. The Harvard-educated Lowe, who dressed in tailor-made clothes, was a world removed from the migrant experience. Despite his appearance, Lowe knew about poverty; he was reared a poor boy in Brooklyn, the son of immigrant parents. He had worked his way through college, pumping gas and then, after graduation, when he was only weeks away from a law degree, he walked out of Harvard, decrying the practice of law as something that rich people used to protect their money.[23]

Lowe had to show the farm workers where his heart was. "At first the workers were embarrassed," Lowe recalled. "Then one man spoke up. 'Are you with us or against us?' [a farm worker asked Lowe]. I said, 'I'm with you,' and they let us take their pictures."[24] For Lowe, this was a pivotal point: it allowed him to start filming the migrant workers and winning their trust, and it was an affirmation that this was to be a sympathetic portrait of the laborers. The documentary that in nine months would, as Lowe put it, "shock the consciousness of the nation" was not to be strictly objective journalism, a balanced account that showed how farm ownership could be as rough as farm labor. Lowe was setting out to expose a lifestyle that made him angry.

"David's politics were always left-liberal," said Harriet Van Horne, Lowe's widow, a prominent television critic at the New York *World Telegram and Sun.* "David really cared about social issues," added his second wife, Sue Davidson Lowe, an author with whom Lowe produced Broadway plays.[25] Sue Davidson met Lowe (who had changed his name from Lowenthal in 1944) when they produced shows together beginning in 1948. Lowe's first Broadway play, before World War II, depicted the life of a black Army man who lived in a society without prejudice. Between 1948 and 1950, Lowe and Davidson produced a half-dozen plays, all critically acclaimed social statements; all commercial failures. In the spring of 1950 Lowe went to work at the Dumont Studios, a television station in Manhattan sometimes called the "fourth network." Television was in its infancy and Lowe was in on the ground floor as a producer. Before long he was producing and directing "Captain Video," one of America's first popular children's shows. "Captain Video," about the adventures of a high-technology space ranger, appeared live six nights a week, from 1950 to 1954.[26] David Lowe Jr., who was eight years old at the time, recalls being a hero in school because his father was associated with Captain Video.[27] Lowe produced and directed other shows, including a quiz show for ABC, "Who Do You Trust?," which starred Johnny Carson.

Lowe had little experience with documentaries before he went to CBS. After World War II, during which he coordinated troop entertainment for the U.S. Air Force, Lowe filmed the testing of the atomic bomb at Bikini Island in the Pacific. For The Dumont Co. he assembled material for a program about victims of the holocaust and for one on diversity in America; and he worked for six months as a consultant to Granada Television, Britain's first commercial station. In 1958 he produced a documentary for NBC called "MD International." The show, which was about world medical care, won a Peabody Award. With those somewhat slim news credentials, Lowe approached Friendly. By 1959, the desperate state of life for migrant workers was coming into public focus. A comprehensive report on migratory labor was issued by a presidential commission in 1951; in 1954, President Eisenhower used a Cabinet committee to coordinate migrant relief; and in the late 1950s some New York City newspapers published exposés. The biggest awakening for the nation's opinion leaders came in 1958 when the nonprofit National Advisory Committee on Farm Labor held hearings in Washington, D.C. The time was ripe for the marriage of media, migrants, and reform. "This was Murrow's kind of story," Friendly said, a "story about the little people, about the oppressed. This story was what journalism is all about."[28]

Wearing a cashmere-colored jacket that was his constant companion for nearly eight months on the road, Lowe started in Belle Glade, Florida, to watch the migrant life unfold. First came the shape-up, a daily occurrence whereby the workers—mostly black—would line up in front of hawkers who would yell out the going wage rate. These crew leaders would hustle workers for the farmers, often with false promises of high salaries and good housing. This was the beginning of the journey to the fields for many of the migrants. One farmer told Lowe, "We used to own our slaves. Now we just rent them." When "Harvest of Shame" appeared, the shape-up was the opening scene of the documentary. Murrow, off camera, said, "This scene is not taking place in the Congo. It had nothing to do with Johannesburg or Capetown. It is not Nyasaland or Nigeria. This is Florida. These are citizens of the United States, 1960. This is shape-up for the migrant workers."[29]

Florida's conditions were worse than Friendly had imagined, and the migrant workers both fascinated and depressed Lowe. In a Florida migrant camp Lowe met Jerome King and his sisters, a visit that stuck with him for the rest of his life. "When he returned from Florida," recalled Lowe's daughter, Ellen, "he told me about that boy and that interview."[30] The interview with Jerome King, one of the most poignant in the broadcast, showed off Lowe's sensitive and graceful interviewing techniques.

"What happened to your foot, Jerome?" Lowe asked.

"I drove a nail in out there by the wash house," Jerome replied.

"So, you drove a nail in out by the wash house? What did your mother do for that?"

"Put some alcohol on it."

The exchanges were not profound, but it was clear to the viewer that Jerome was growing up alone, and he was bound to get in trouble, or worse, while his mother picked beans. Jerome's chances of going to school were slim. The report of a presidential commission revealed to Lowe that only one of every five hundred migrant children ever finished grammar school. "Beans are in competition with school in this country, and beans are winning out," one Florida educator said.[31] Other interviews were more dramatic. A Mrs. Doby stood in the sunshine at the Okechobee, Florida, labor camp while Lowe questioned her. She was thirty-four, the mother of nine children; her face was lined, her teeth prominent, her hair pulled back tightly.

"What is an average dinner for your family?" Lowe asked.

Mrs. Doby replied, "Well, we just—you mean what do we have in . . . "

"Yes," Lowe said.

"We—well, I cook a pot of beans and fry some potatoes," answered Mrs. Doby.

"Yes," Lowe said, urging her to talk.

"Some corn or something like that," Mrs. Doby responded.

Lowe elicited from Mrs. Doby that even her smallest children had to make do with a quart of milk a week ... maybe. The camera slowly panned the faces of her children—no one smiled—and Mrs. Doby bit her lip as she talked.

Lowe's persistent but dignified questioning of the Roaches, a white family, which had traveled 1,600 miles to find work in Florida, brought this exchange.

"Mr. Roach, where did you spend the night last night with your family?"

"Over in the woods. Pulled off on the side of the road—on a little dirt road—and slept in the woods outside the car."

"May I ask you, sir, what did you have for dinner and your family last night?"

"Well, we had bologna sausage and a loaf of bread."

"That isn't very good for a growing family, is it?"

"Well, we made on it."

"How much money do you have in the world right at this moment?"

"Oh, I have about a dollar and forty-five cents."

"Well, what do you intend to do about food for your family today?"

"Well, I've always worked and I always figured I could get work. I have never been where I couldn't get a little something to do."

The Roach family stood next to the father, a man who appeared to be about fifty years old, throughout the interview. They were quiet, polite; not embarrassed, but not happy.

"Lowe had a way of interviewing, a way of asking very difficult questions, and yet he would allow people to keep their dignity," said John Schultz, who was the film editor for "Harvest of Shame." "He was sensitive," explained Palmer Williams, Friendly's right-hand man, the director of operations, "but he also had a con man's ability to cuddle up to people." David Lowe Jr., who followed in his father's footsteps and became a producer for CBS' "60 Minutes" where he won two Emmy awards, said the key to his father's interviewing ability lay in the fact that he liked the migrant workers: "He was comfortable with them."[32]

When the crops were all picked in Florida, Lowe boarded the broken-down buses with the migrant workers, and headed north, his back stiffening from the terrible seats. "We didn't hear much from David in Florida," said Palmer Williams. "The pace picked up as he approached New York." It was Williams' job to keep track of producers and supply equipment to the staff in the field; he was the unsung hero on the

Murrow-Friendly team. "In those days," he recalled, "once you committed to a project, that was it. There was no doubt that it was going forward for an air date."[33]

GETTING READY FOR SHOWTIME

Had there been any doubt, it ended when the dailies—the footage that had been shot mostly by cameraman Marty Barnett—were viewed in one of CBS' two screening rooms on Ninth Avenue in Manhattan. Here, "everyone gathered, exchanged gossip, and watched incoming rushes while the producers sweated as the rough copy flashed across the screen," wrote a Murrow biographer. Schultz recalled the "Harvest" footage: "This was powerful stuff; everyone was quite impressed."[34] In some of the footage, Lowe seemed shocked and embarrassed by what he found. At a migrant camp in Elizabeth City, North Carolina, Lowe interviewed a Mrs. Blakely who showed him the straw on which they slept and the one faucet which supplied water for the large group. How many bathrooms are there, Lowe asked. None. "Where do you . . . where do you use the bathroom? Where is . . . where are the facilities?" "We haven't one. We use our tin tubes," Mrs. Blakely said. She laughed.

Finally, Lowe made his way through the fields of New Jersey and Long Island, and, after nine months, the filming and the interviewing were done. Murrow, Friendly, Lowe, and Williams gathered in New York—at the screening room. Every editor wanted to work on this documentary. "What do you think?" Friendly asked thirty-one-year-old John Schultz for his opinion about the rough copy. "I like it. I did migrant work in Washington State."[35] That settled it. Schultz, who had picked potatoes as a child in Washington, got the editing job. The close collaboration between editor Schultz and producer Lowe began with Murrow and Friendly offering ideas and suggestions for changes. By this point, Lowe was an expert on the migrants, and he had accumulated nearly 300,000 feet of film, of which about 5,000 feet, an hour's worth, would be used.[36] There was a finishing touch to be applied: Lowe and Murrow had to go to Florida to film Murrow in the fields. This film would then be used for the introduction and ending.[37] Murrow, increasingly estranged from CBS' management, had just returned from a leave of absence, during which he had traveled in Europe. Once back at the screening room, he was excited by what Lowe had produced. Schultz, who was editing the film, recalls seeing Murrow, day after day, "looking just rapt at the footage," this procession of American faces with their Depression-era looks. Friendly was not happy that Murrow would have to travel to Florida . . . the dust and heat would be bad in the late summer. Murrow's cough and his health were worsening; Friendly was not sure Murrow was up to the task, but Murrow insisted. "The subject was exceedingly close to him. [These were] people who worked with their hands; he identified with them. Don't forget, Ed had been poorer than anyone who worked on that program," Friendly said.[38]

Lowe took Murrow to some of the migrant camps and he spent some time in the fields talking to workers. Although it was their first project together, Murrow and Lowe got along well, playing cards at night, visiting the camps during the day. Both men, reared in poverty, could understand the plight of these workers; both wanted to tell this story to America. Moreover, Murrow was known for bending over backward to please producers who knew the material and the issues better than he. Murrow asked only two things in return for his cooperation. First, producer Jeff Beck said, "Better not give him a false direction, and don't push it too far. Do it right, do it professionally, and you had his respect. Get slipshod, goof off, and you wouldn't be giving him instructions much longer."[39] Finally, they filmed. Murrow stood in a dirt field, a small microphone hung around his neck; he looked like a combination of Henry Fonda and Woody Guthrie. He wore a light black shirt, and his dark hair was slicked back off his forehead. Deadly serious, his voice and face anguished, he recited the introduction and closing, most of which he had written himself, and asked a pointed question: "Must the two to three million migrants who help feed their fellow Americans work, travel and live under conditions that wrong the dignity of man?" Murrow's voice was especially raspy; the congestion in his lungs came right through on the sound track. Murrow finished filming, but when he returned to New York, he had pneumonia. No one knew at the time that Murrow had filmed his last documentary for CBS . . . or for anyone.

With Murrow now on film, the pace of the final cutting quickened under Friendly's loud urging. Lowe joined the others in the screening room. Schultz, the key man now, thought he had the perfect ending for the documentary: a migrant girl singing while the camera panned despairing faces. Those watching in the screening room cried. Murrow told Schultz to cut the ending and said to Friendly, who was seated to his left on a couch, "The migrant story has no ending." "You mean, the migrant story is endless?" asked Friendly, confused. "No, Fritzel [Murrow's nickname for Friendly], I mean that is not the right ending." Murrow was right, Schultz said. "He wanted anger, indignation, not the sort of 'tsk, tsk, those poor people.' "[40] They came up with a new ending, written mostly by Friendly. With the final product ready, Friendly, Murrow, and Lowe chose an air date of November 25. "We felt that by scheduling the program the day after Thanksgiving," explained Lowe, "we could stress the fact that much of the food cooked for Thanksgiving throughout the country was picked by migratory workers. We hoped the pictures of how these people live and work would shock the consciousness of the nation."[41]

ON THE AIR; OFF THE FENCE

David Lowe Jr., now forty-six, remembers the night, when he was eighteen years old, when "Harvest" aired. "I was in an apartment in Manhattan with my girlfriend," he said. "I wanted to watch the show and she wasn't the least bit interested. My eyes were glued to the television. I saw that opening segment and I said, 'I hope this isn't too dramatic.' "[42] "Harvest of Shame" was dramatic stuff . . . with a title that harkened back to Lincoln Steffens' "Shame of the Cities," with a narrator who had a national reputation, with its comparisons to the despised slavery and to the Depression Era Okies of Steinbeck's novel. The drama aside, however, the more important issue was, would it make a difference?

The documentary opened with the shape-up and Murrow's comparison to apartheid. A cut was made to Eisenhower's Secretary of Labor James Mitchell who said the migrants "cry out for some assistance and whose plight is the shame—the shame of America." Murrow had conducted this interview; the camera captured the smoke swirling up from his and Mitchell's cigarettes. Then the other side, the president of the American Farm Bureau, responded: "We take the position that it's far better to have thousands of these folks who are practically unemployable, earning some money, doing some productive work." Murrow made no rejoinder; he called the story of the migrants "an American story . . . a 1960 Grapes of Wrath." Lowe interviews followed: Mrs. Doby said, pitifully, "It don't look like we'll ever get ahead"; and an unnamed minister told Lowe, "They are just as bad off as the slaves . . . but in the way they are treated, they are worse than the slaves." Twice in the opening moments, the migrant workers were called slaves. Murrow's voice again: "They are the migrants, workers in the sweat shops of the soil, the Harvest of Shame." Bring in music, and cut to a commercial . . . from Marlboro cigarettes.

Throughout the eight years of the Eisenhower administration, the issue of migratory farm workers had concerned official Washington; little had happened, however. Now, their plight was on display for the nation, an opening salvo for a new decade. This documentary was a departure for the documentary and for the journalism of the time. The 1950s were prosperous but uncertain years for Americans, a conservative time when dissent—and an adversary culture in journalism—was hazardous. Murrow and Friendly had learned this after their 1954 attack on McCarthy; they were all accused of being too sympathetic with the Communist side. "The American documentary of the fifties clearly reflected these conditions," said Lewis Jacobs, a film historian. "Its outlook on life revealed itself in a neutralism that offered no challenge to the national temper."[43] That is one reason why "Harvest of Shame" was such a startling departure. The other reason lies in the state of journalism in the 1950s.

Muckraking, as the previous chapter indicated, disappeared as a movement in the years before World War I. After the war, no longer did a group of writers and mass circulation magazines attempt to expose the nation's problems. Even though the movement was gone, the muckraking tradition did not die. Exposé journalism continued to appear—at times in fiction, in some crusading newspapers, and in some of the small, left-liberal magazines, like the *Nation* and the *New Republic*. "The small-media magazines," wrote Carey McWilliams, who was for many years the editor of the *Nation*, "kept the muckraking tradition alive." McWilliams was one of those who saw journalism as a continuing way to alter social conditions. His 1944 book, *Ill Fares the Land*, in the muckraking tradition, described how the migrant workers were "visible evidence of breakdown" in a society.[44]

For the majority of the press, however, muckraking journalism was simply that thing that Steffens did many years ago. Crusading and investigation had taken a backseat to a new fetish—objectivity. This set of unwritten rules guided reporters and led them to rely on official, i.e., usually government, sources. Stories needed to be balanced and reporters needed to be essentially neutral fence sitters who simply moderated debates between feuding factions. For his part, Murrow had always relied on the unofficial sources and the little people more than on government sources. The press' easy acceptance of McCarthy's branding of people reminded him of how demagogues he had covered in Europe in the 1930s had used the press as a partisan tool. Yet, subjectivity and advocacy equally troubled Murrow. For many years he struggled over the question of point of view, that is, how involved a reporter—and, in his case, broadcasting—should be in putting a mirror up to the world, drawing conclusions, taking a stance, and urging the audience to action.

In 1937, as European director for CBS Radio, Murrow's thoughts on the role of broadcasting were forming. He told a group at the Royal Institute of International Affairs to be wary of the journalist who plays the role of propagandist or who is guilty of "under-emphasis or the complete elimination of unfavorable material." Rely less on the official voices, he said, more on the cabbies and the fisherman. Murrow backed off from saying that the journalist must advocate solutions and attack authority, warning of the potential power of the press, broadcasting in particular, and alluding to the manipulation of the media being made by Adolf Hitler and Joseph Goebbels. Radio, he said, had "enormous power . . . but it has no character, no conscience of its own."[45] Murrow wanted to provide its conscience, but could he do that without stepping over the fence that separated neutral reportage from muckraking exposé?

In 1954 Murrow had stood on the fence as he struggled with the form of his exposé of Senator Joseph McCarthy. McCarthy was a demagogue, Murrow felt, who reminded him of those who took power in Europe before World War II. He feared the beginning of a Nazi-like mass movement. Murrow's thirty-minute broadcast on McCarthy was "a virtual half-hour editorial ending in a call to action, the final step from TV news purveyor to TV activist, with all that implied," wrote a Murrow biographer. This activism worried him greatly. "The McCarthy program bothered the hell out of him," said a friend from CBS. Did he or anyone else have the right to use this tremendous power to attack one man?[46] Right or wrong, Murrow hopped off the fence in this documentary, on the other side from objectivity. The McCarthy documentary was a departure, however. Murrow was more bent on objectivity than activism. In fact, he had an objectivity clause written into his contract. "News . . . should be devoted to giving the facts," it said. The journalist should analyze only "in the light of known facts . . . without intruding the views of the analyst." Allow, it read, "the listener to draw his own conclusions."[47]

Despite the clause, Murrow felt that attacks and exposés were not being done enough on television, in part at least, because "the present system . . . the money-making machine" will not allow them. In his controversial criticism of broadcasting made in 1958 before the Radio-Television News Directors Association, Murrow complained that television "is being used to distract, delude, amuse and insulate" the American public. "I do not advocate that we turn television into a twenty-seven-inch wailing wall. . . . But I would like to see it reflect occasionally the hard, unyielding realities of the world in which we live."[48] "Harvest of Shame" was, in many ways, a culmination of Murrow's thinking since 1937.

"Harvest of Shame" was both a muckraking and an objective document. The broadcast was arranged chronologically, with the beginning and end taking place in Florida. In between, CBS' cameras followed the migrants up the East Coast, using various work stops along the way to focus on four major issues—wages, travel, housing, and education. Each section used Lowe's interviews and Barnett's carefully filmed migrant faces to expose conditions. The way the migrants looked and what they said, after Lowe's careful prodding, told their part of the story. Lowe's opinion did not enter the narrative as the story unfolded. The camera close-ups of desperate faces and the migrants' words revealed a hard-working people and a resigned futility. The migrant statements were then juxtaposed with interviews with policymakers and industry representatives. For the most part, those elements fit the formula for objectivity. The reporter was not talking; the subject told the story. Official sources in government and industry, combined with statistics drawn from government documents, fleshed out the rest. Although the emphasis was on the migrants' plight, there was also balance, the other side, another attribute of objectivity. Lowe and Murrow allowed the president of the American Farm Bureau to give the farmers' side moments after the documentary began (even though his comments about these "folks" were condescending and less than sympathetic). Later, Charles Schuman defended the farmer-provided housing, saying that no other employer was expected to provide housing for workers. A farmer in Florida echoed Schuman, offering the economic rationale for not building better housing; they simply did not make enough money to do so. The "other side" was offered other chances to explain its view, but the response of one farmer, an employer of hundreds of migrant workers, was damning. Asked if his workers seemed happy, a farmer said: "Well, I guess they got a little gypsy in their blood. They just like it. . . . They love it. They love to go from place to place. They don't have a worry in the world. . . . They're the happiest race of people on earth." Naiveté, and worse, racism, dripped from the statement, but it was the other side—or at least the other side that Lowe chose to use.[49] Murrow did not have to say that racism was a foe of the migrants; the farmers said it for him. A final balance was offered by Murrow who said he agreed that it did not seem to make any financial sense for the farmer to build good housing when workers would live there only six weeks a year. "The farmer claims he is trapped between what society expects and his market demands," Murrow stated. Murrow was defending the farmer, but his use of the loaded word "claims" was somewhat of a deviation from the norms of objectivity.

There were other deviations from objectivity. Especially effective—but out of bounds for objective journalism—were the analogies made by Murrow that none of the on-screen participants had seen fit to make. His analogies crossed the line between conventional, objective journalism and what amounted to a stronger muckraking-like attack. Normally, reporters are limited to describing things they have seen, parroting statements made by government or authoritative sources, and using with attribution material taken from official documents. Murrow did and did not keep within these limits. For example, when the camera showed migrant workers being transported north for ten-hour drives without stopping, Murrow said, "Government regulations say that cattle must be rested every six hours. There are no such regulations for migrant workers." This was a fact, but it was the joining of two, to some, unrelated facts that broke the objectivity barrier. Murrow deviated with another incisive but subjective analogy: "The Federal Government spends six and a half million dollars annually protecting migratory wildlife. This year Congress failed to appropriate three and a half million dollars to educate migratory children." Are birds relevant to farm labor?

In discussing housing, the cameras showed a labor camp in Princeton, New Jersey, where six people lived in one room. "Nearby," Murrow said, "a trotting raceway has new stables for horses." He added, "They cost $500,000."[50] Are these related facts? Moments later in the broadcast, an unidentified minister from Riverhead, Long Island, seemed to summarize the Lowe-Murrow view of migrant housing when he said, "This is as primitive as man can live." Other people's opinions are acceptable under the rules of objectivity, but when ones like the minister's are coupled with strong film footage and Murrow's analogies, the result is that the view could reach only one conclusion: the farmer was exploiting his workers.

The final and perhaps most obvious deviation from objectivity came in the documentary's conclusion. Secretary of Labor Mitchell, a champion of the migrant cause, identified the reason why it was so difficult to change the migrants' conditions. "They have no voice in the legislative halls," he pointed out. Meanwhile, "their employers are highly organized and make their wants and terms and conditions known to our legislators. I know of no greater pressure lobbies so-called than the farm group." A Cabinet member certainly was a legitimate person to interview—an official, objective source, even if he did pin the rap on the farm lobby. Objectivity here would have called for a farmers' response; there was none. Instead, the camera went back to the migrants who had returned now to Belle Glade, Florida, where it all began. One migrant told Lowe, "We broke even; we were broke when we left, broke when we got back." Murrow then listed all the recommendations a presidential commission had made to improve the lot of farm workers, pointing out that 150 attempts had been made in Congress to help the migrants. "All except one has failed," Murrow said. In terms of objectivity's dictum, the statement about being broke from a migrant worker, assuming it was representative, was acceptable as was the citation from a government report. Murrow's final words, which came next and which were probably written by Friendly, went beyond objectivity, past muckraking, and into advocacy.

Murrow stood in a field, the sun beating down on his head, and uttered in his raspy voice his final words in a documentary. "The migrants have no lobby," Murrow declared. "Only enlightened, aroused and perhaps angered public opinion can do anything about the migrants. The people you have seen have the strength to harvest your fruit and vegetables. They do not have the strength to influence legislation. Maybe we do. . . . Good night and good luck." Murrow's voice seemed choked with emotion; he blamed his oncoming pneumonia. As the credits rolled across the screen, Harriet Van Horne said she thought, "We've just seen an important television event."[51] A television broadcaster had rolled up his sleeves and had said: let's have a fight, let's get involved. If the 1960s produced the birth of guerilla documentaries, this may have been its beginning. "We" have to do something about this problem, Murrow said, a far cry from the detached tone that objectivity normally demanded. Even for Murrow this was a departure. He generally believed that the broadcaster's role was to "illuminate rather than to agitate," to cast light into dark places and let the public see the facts.[52] The public would decide what to do once it had the facts in hand. In "Harvest of Shame," Murrow and Friendly implored the public to take up the cudgels; it was clear whose side they were on and whose side the public should get on. The growers, the farmers, were the enemy. The enemy would soon counterattack.

"THE RESPONSE . . . WAS OVERWHELMING"

Murrow and Friendly were unprepared for the response to "Harvest of Shame." The big, gruff executive producer had done dozens of documentaries with Murrow, and many had been controversial, but "Harvest" was a blockbuster. Friendly wrote, "Not since McCarthy had we done a broadcast that created such impact, and never again would any of our programs create such clamor for change."[53] The overnight reviews in New York were good. Jack Gould in the New York *Times* called it "uncompromising in its exposure of the filth, despair and grinding poverty." *Time* magazine labeled the work "a moving muckraking masterpiece."[54] The night of the broadcast, CBS' New York switchboard lit up with calls, and letters poured in—2,700 in total, of which only 160 criticized the broadcast.[55] People in the heartlands were stirred. "[R]arely have I received such an outpouring of mail expressing concern about a social issue with which the correspondents had no direct connection," said Senator William Proxmire of Wisconsin. Edward R. Murrow's secretary, apologizing to a letter writer for Murrow's tardy response after the broadcast, explained that work in the office had backed up. "The response of the press and public to 'Harvest of Shame' was overwhelming," she said.[56]

David Lowe, too, was taken aback. "He knew he had something extraordinary," David Lowe Jr. said. "The basic reaction right off the bat—the next morning—people knew they had seen a classic. My father said, 'This is too good to be true.' " Today, Palmer Williams offered, with all the competition from cable and pay television stations, "there never could be such a response. The show would get lost in the shuffle."[57] But it didn't get lost in 1960. Perhaps the election of John Kennedy had unleashed a new energy for change in America; perhaps the show culminated years of consciousness-raising by social workers; or perhaps it was what one reviewer called the program's "action-arousal" technique. Whatever the reason, the public was stirred, but so were those who had been attacked. Months of controversy lay ahead.

CBS had gotten an inkling that its words and pictures would be watched closely when, on October 20, it received a letter from the American Farm Bureau Federation, a powerful farm lobby. The group complained about an October 19 press release in which CBS announced the documentary, citing a figure of three million migrant workers. The numbers were far less, the growers contended, and they told Lowe where to find accurate figures. Lowe checked, and lowered the numbers. His final figures, however, were still "grossly inaccurate," the growers later charged, adding, this is "not honest reporting."[58]

Lowe's position at "CBS Reports" was, of course, greatly strengthened after "Harvest." Friendly assigned him to another documentary with Murrow; he wanted them to document racial violence in Birmingham, Alabama.[59] In Alabama, however, Lowe got official word that his brief association with Murrow was over. Murrow took a call from an aide to President Kennedy. Would Murrow serve as director of the United States Information Agency (USIA)? Disgruntled by his steadily eroding relationship with CBS' management, especially President Frank Stanton, the whittling away of air time for documentaries, and his concern over CBS' commitment to news and public affairs, Murrow assented . . . reluctantly.[60] "Clearly," Friendly later wrote, "CBS wanted the competence of the Murrow unit but not his prestige and outspokenness." Some believed Murrow was pressured to quit.[61] The announcement came in Washington, D.C. on January 27: Murrow would go over to the government side, an odd choice for one so committed as an independent voice.

Three days later, in Washington's New Senate Building, the AFL-CIO sponsored a special showing of "Harvest of Shame" for legislators. On February 2, as Murrow's confirmation at the USIA loomed in Congress, the growers complained. Representative Robert H. Michel, a Republican from Peoria, Illinois, questioned from the floor of Congress this "strange type of reporting—the cub type—especially in a show that purports to be a documentary presentation."[62] Mouthing almost word for word criticism made by farmers in a just-completed report on the broadcast, Michel said "Harvest" was filled with "endless misstatements," was "wildly improbable," and was a "highly colored propaganda job." What the public needs, he said in a theme echoed by other critics, is a "more objective presentation." On February 6, the Democratic senator from Florida, Spessard L. Holland, who had close ties with the citrus growers, continued the attack. On February 26, Holland and Senator Harrison Williams, a Democrat from New Jersey, got into a testy debate before their colleagues. Williams, who chaired a subcommittee on migrant issues, was the sponsor of much of the legislation then before Congress.

Williams conceded only one point in his debate with Holland—"the film lacked objectivity in certain respects"—but on most particulars, and certainly on the overall plight of the workers, it was indeed an accurate picture. Holland demurred, calling the film "extravagant propaganda . . . extravagant overstatement." Holland and the farmers criticized each section of the film. The shape-up sequence was not the only way in which workers were recruited, and how else, after all, could workers be hired? The use of an unnamed source to call the migrant life akin to slavery, well, this was an old "propaganda trick." Lowe's numbers, they contended, were "grossly inaccurate." He should have known better; we gave him the correct figures. As for wages, CBS had wrenched its figures out of context—"not honest reporting" again. If Aileen King earned only $1 a day, then she must have been a lousy worker. If she couldn't afford to feed her family, what could she expect when she had so many children, and whose fault was that? Moreover, her husband, the farmers said, had a job also, and he earned $83 a week. Transportation? There were federal regulations, despite what Lowe implied. The accident that the film had shown? It was three years old, and accidents happen to everyone. As for housing, CBS' "producers must have sought far and wide to discover the most dilapidated housing they could find," the farmers charged. There had been progress. Echoing a criticism that would be made a decade later by Vice President Spiro Agnew, the farmers wanted to know why the "television program fails to give credit for the progress that has been made in recent years." Why only the bad news?[63]

The farmers' most serious charge against CBS revolved around a scene, near the end of the documentary, that showed migrant workers standing in a bread line after a freeze had wiped out crops in Florida. The farmers said this scene was filmed several years ago, but it had been made by CBS to appear as if it were a recent occurrence. "Rigged documentaries are a much more serious abuse of responsibility than rigged quiz programs," the board of directors of the Farm Federation declared.[64] At a time when broadcasting was still recovering from the falsifications that had taken place on quiz shows, charges of news fakery were not taken lightly. The nation, the sponsors, and the Federal Communications Commission, which regulated broadcasting, watched closely for a response.

Harriet Van Horne recalls that Lowe "was quite cut up by all these charges. They were calling him communist and such. He felt quite badly."[65] CBS replied quickly and quite effectively to the charges. The farmers' "so-called analysis," wrote Thomas K. Fisher, a vice president and attorney for CBS, does not change the basic issue: " 'Harvest of Shame' addressed itself to a bona fide problem, national in scope."[66] One by one, CBS dismissed the farmers' charges. The "breadline incident" was filmed on January 29, 30 and 31 and February 1, 1960; Lowe was present. Your charge "is without any foundation and is contrary to fact," Fisher wrote. Quoting extensively from a 1960 presidential report, Fisher backed up Lowe's statistics on wages, transportation, and illiteracy. Without comment, Fisher repeated the farmers' racist remarks about large families and contented workers. CBS was aware that, as Friendly said, "most of [the farmers] were their own worst witnesses." Contrary to the farmers' charges, Fisher said, the documentary "used considerable restraint." Fisher concluded by rejecting the growers' request for response time, saying that the program was, in the end, "fair and balanced."[67] CBS eventually found only one "fact" that needed to be corrected: Murrow had said that "there is no case upon the record of the child of a migrant laborer ever receiving a college diploma." The farm lobby provided evidence of twelve college graduates.

While CBS easily handled the complaints of the farmers, it could not have been happy that their outrage landed on the floor of Congress, and that copies of the farmers' complaints went to the Federal Communications Commission. Friendly said that "management was disturbed by complaints about such programs." Two years earlier, William S. Paley, the founder and chairman of the board of CBS, had told Friendly, "I don't want this constant stomach ache every time you do a controversial subject."[68] Making the brass equally unhappy was the reaction of the program's sponsor, Phillip Morris, the makers of Marlboro and a big advertiser. For years, the networks had routinely allowed sponsors to preview a documentary, allowing them to withdraw if they found it objectionable—or perhaps subtly to make suggestions for changes. "CBS Reports" had rejected that policy—no previewing—and Phillip Morris paid the price. After the show aired, and the sponsor incurred the wrath of the farmers, the sponsor investigated the farmers' allegations. "[T]hey buckled and sent representatives through the agricultural community apologizing for the program," Friendly said. Ironically, Friendly had given Phillip Morris a chance to back out ten days before the broadcast when he warned the company that the show would irk the farmers and draw the sponsor into a controversy.[69]

As if a company boss with gut ache, angry farmers, and an unhappy sponsor were not enough, Murrow added fuel to CBS' fire just when the blaze seemed extinguished. Murrow's confirmation was stalled while the Federal Bureau of Investigation (FBI) completed a background check, digging into the old charges that followed in the wake of the McCarthy broadcast. Meanwhile, Florida's Senator Holland, remembering his pledge that the "Harvest" broadcast "was an affront which our people will long recall," threatened to vote against Murrow's appointment and embarrass Kennedy.[70] Holland was joined by other conservatives who were still upset about the liberal Murrow's McCarthy attack. Despite the holdup in confirmation, Murrow went to work in Washington. He was now the man in charge of projecting a favorable image of America to the world, a move from objectivity to partisanship. One of his first orders of business was to see whether the television networks and the government—the mythological adversaries—could help each other. In a confidential March 2 letter to David Sarnoff, the chairman of the board of NBC's parent, RCA, Murrow wondered whether the network would be interested in producing documentaries and allowing the USIA to show them abroad. "I need not tell you," Murrow wrote, "that I have no desire to influence or control this export."[71] Murrow just wanted to use the networks' expertise in filmmaking—and presumably the credibility that would come along with their news products—to further America's goals abroad. Murrow, wearing his new hat as a government employee, apparently had forgotten his own words of years before, that "a reporter has to be against everybody, some." Maybe the government and the press could cooperate a bit. Sarnoff sent the proposal along to NBC President Robert Kintner who told Sarnoff that such a relationship was not desirable.[72]

As the FBI report in mid-February cleared Murrow of any Communist ties and as he prepared to testify before the Senate, a bombshell secretly brewed. Word came to Murrow that the Soviet Union had broadcast "Harvest of Shame" as anti-American propaganda. With his confirmation pending, this was publicity that Murrow did not need. He quietly asked his friend at CBS, Palmer Williams, to do some checking. Williams confirmed for Murrow that, yes, indeed, Moscow Home Service had shown eighteen minutes of the broadcast to a Soviet audience.[73] It was unclear how the film was obtained, but Murrow's news report, called propaganda by the farmers, had been used as propaganda by the Communists. Fortunately for Murrow, the Moscow broadcast was never revealed to the American public. Murrow was easily confirmed by the Senate, but the "Harvest" saga was not over yet. Murrow learned that the British Broadcasting Company (BBC) was planning a rebroadcast in late March, an embarrassment for the administration and its new image maker.

Perhaps because of the pressure from Congress about his confirmation or perhaps because he understood that his new role called for protecting America's image, Murrow decided that he needed at least to attempt to halt the showing. He placed a telephone call to his old friend, Hugh Carleton Greene, head of the BBC, asking for a cancellation.[74] "I can remember him sounding rather embarrassed over the telephone," Greene recalled. "I remember thinking to myself . . . that Ed had been caught in an intentional trap." If Greene refused the request, the critics would say Murrow was powerless, unable to convince even his friends. If Greene acceded, Murrow would be accused of censorship. Greene explained to Murrow that the program was already on the schedule . . . it could not be deleted. Murrow said he understood; there was no yelling or undue pressure.[75] Predictably, a furor erupted when Senator Holland leaked the story about the program and Murrow's request for cancellation to the press. The newspapers turned on Murrow as did the American Civil Liberties Union (ACLU). This was "attempted official censorship," said ACLU director Patrick Malin. "A dismaying start" for Murrow, opined the New York *Times*, a refrain joined by other editorialists who implied that he had bowed to pressure from either the White House or the Senate.[76]

Privately, Murrow offered his resignation, but Kennedy refused to accept it, saying it would all blow over. Murrow then faced the press. "Harvest of Shame," be began, was an "accurate . . . muckraking . . . exposé." Murrow added: "I have defended it and will continue to do so. . . . Had I been still employed by CBS, [however] I would have recommended that it not be shown abroad." Foreign audiences could not be expected to understand that the migrant plight represents only a part of America's agricultural activity, he explained. With his rationale expounded, Murrow then shot back at those who said he had caved in to pressure. "There is not enough pressure . . . in Washington to have caused me to do it," he said.[77]

When the BBC showed the film on March 30, Friendly said that the British were "impressed by the freedom which allowed American television to expose such a national scandal." They also were aghast at the condition of migrant workers. "Like finding a beautiful apple with a worm inside," one Britisher said. It's not clear that CBS—its famed eye a bit bloodshot after the broadcast—was so impressed. Paley, the man who called the shots at the network, met Friendly on an elevator two weeks after the broadcast, and Friendly asked how the boss liked it. The elevator reached the seventeenth floor, Friendly stepped out, and Paley replied; "Excellent. I thought I told you I liked everything but the ending."[78] The doors closed. The ending was Murrow's exhortation, his stepping over the line between objectivity and activism. Exposé was fine, but to go beyond the facts was not permissible. Paley did not want activist journalism. He wrote in his memoirs that "CBS has strictly forbidden editorializing by our regular newscasters. And this has caused persistent problems over the years about interpreting what is editorializing, commentary or analysis, even though it is clearly separated from hard news." Paley's insistence on objectivity led him to "heated arguments" with Murrow and other CBS broadcasters. In the end, however, Paley said, "I always insisted that when it came to straight reporting, it had to be as objective as possible."[79] "Harvest of Shame" didn't meet the credo, and the brass was not happy.

TO FOLLOW OR NOT TO FOLLOW

The New York *World-Telegram and Sun*'s concern for the problems of migrant workers predated "Harvest of Shame." Reporter Allan Keller had written of their plight in 1953, and the newspaper took credit for forcing the creation of a New York State legislative committee on migrants. After "Harvest," the paper's editors, spurred by conscience and circulation (then at 453,331), thought another probe was needed. How about an undercover investigation, a favorite trick of the *Telegram*'s, into migrant worker conditions? "I said sure, I'll do it," recalled Dale Wright who in 1960 was the first black reporter ever to be hired by the *Telegram*. "I was eager to get my hands on a big story." Wright wrote a memo to his editors, explaining how he would pose as a farm laborer and live and work with the migrants. "We had no idea how long it would take. They gave me carte blanche."[80]

The New York *World-Telegram and Sun* was a hybrid newspaper. Some of the most creative writers in journalism lurked in its past. The New York *World* was the first muckraking newspaper, the creation of Joseph Pulitzer whose turn-of-the-century crusades created the first one-million circulation newspaper. The New York *Telegram* was the afternoon companion of the innovative *Herald*, brainchild of James Gordon Bennett, the man who created sensationalism. The New York *Sun* was the first "penny" paper in America, where the human interest story was virtually invented. In 1927, the Scripps-Howard chain purchased the *Telegram* and, four years later, merged it with the *World*. The *Sun*, which had hovered for years far to the political right, never with enough audience to make money, was added to the fold in 1950.

By 1961, this newspaper with so many disparate traditions had an identity crisis. These were difficult times for newspapers in New York; there were simply too many of them to find enough readers and advertisers to go around. The *Telegram*, as it was known, was competing in the afternoon with the New York *Post*, the liberal, Manhattan-oriented tabloid, and the *Journal-American*, the Hearst-owned conservative broad sheet. The *Telegram*, positioned politically in the middle, liked to muckrake and was especially fond of guarding taxpayer money, making sure that every dime was being spent right, especially on those receiving welfare. The newspaper muckraked the issues that concerned the middle class. The newspaper knew also that its audience, although mostly in New York City, was increasingly moving to suburban Long Island, catching the train east and grabbing the afternoon paper on the way out of the city. Long Island, famous for its beaches, also had potato farms— farms that were populated every fall with migrant labor.

Wright was thirty-six years old in 1961, married, the father of an infant son. The five-foot, ten-inch 160-pounder had wanted to be a newspaperman since junior high school. "There was never any doubt," he said. "I enjoyed digging up information." After receiving a journalism degree from Ohio State University, Wright worked with the *Amsterdam News*, a weekly that covered the black community in New York, and then with *Jet* and *Ebony*, both black-oriented magazines.[81] After seven years of magazine feature writing, he went to the *Telegram*, not as their "black" reporter, but as a reporter who knew the back streets of New York City. Ironically, his first big assignment sent him from the streets to the farms.

Wright did three things before he went to Florida in April: he obtained a phony identification card from a Social Security office—his new name was Dave Wright; he purchased work clothes; and he read all he could on migrant conditions. "I was a little nervous," Wright admitted. "I didn't know very much about the South. I knew very little about farming."[82] He didn't even know where the streams of migrant workers began. That was his first chore after he flew to Miami. With a small amount of money hidden in his belt and a tiny notepad tucked in a pocket, Wright trekked through Dade County. After a few days he found the shape-up and took a job picking tomatoes. Shape-up began at five in the morning and the real work started at around seven; for the next ten hours, Wright kneeled in the dirt. Wright was in peak physical condition at the time; nevertheless, he wrote:

The muscles along the backs of my legs, across the small of my back and up into my shoulders and upper arms ached murderously. I hurt everywhere. My pant legs were ragged and stained with insect spray from crawling along on my hands and knees through the rows. Blood had scabbed over the many abrasions I'd acquired on my legs and hands in encounter with rocks. I limped slowly, wearingly, haltingly to the end of the row to make a final count of the stack . . . It was the end of a punishing day, perhaps the most strength-sapping labor I had ever done. It took all the reserve I could muster just to wait in the line, then shuffle up to the bossman for my pay.[83]

This was the beginning of six months on and off the road for Dale Wright. He spent, in total, six weeks actually working as a farm laborer. Where David Lowe saw misery, Dale Wright actually lived under the conditions that the laborers had talked about in "Harvest." "I was one of them," he wrote. "I saw it with my eyes, I felt it in my blistered hands, I smelled it with my nose and I rebelled at it in my conscience."[84] The hours were tortuously long, the pay ridiculously low; the housing consisted of "shabby, unkempt hovels and shacks"; children, starting at age six, worked in the fields for less pay than the adults; and the transportation, "under conditions inferior to those afforded cattle," came in "dilapidated, hazardous vehicles."[85] All of that was to be expected— "Harvest" had sketched it out and no one really denied the conditions—

but Wright's first-hand experience showed a human condition that out-side observation could not bring. "The working and living conditions were bad enough," Wright wrote on the day his articles began, "but it was the way he's cheated that outraged me. . . . He's overcharged for his squalid shack, his food, his clothing, his bottle of wine at the end of a hard week of work. And he's gouged on just about every other item he purchases."[86] Lowe's microphone and camera missed the inside view; Wright filled out the picture.

In a book on journalism ethics, a former newsman argued that un-dercover research is usually a waste of a reporter's time; the same in-formation can be gotten from interviewing and research.[87] On the contrary, some of Wright's encounters with workers could have hap-pened only in his undercover mode. In the fields, Wright met Red Fisher, a migrant worker who had tuberculosis and five small children at home to feed. Fisher took Wright to his house. "I had so much wanted to see and talk to them," Wright said, a feeling he had until he saw the family home.

The three youngest children lay sleeping crosswise on one bed. It was a sagging, mesh-spring piece of antiquity and the small forms were spreadeagled wherever they could find space. The stale odor of damp, moldy cotton was mixed with the moist tang of human perspiration in the tiny space. . . . A feeling of nausea crept up from my stomach into my throat. . . . I saw and smelled the hopeless-ness, the futility that lived in one man's chest, the same agony that—along with inadequate and improper food—had already sent two of his little ones to the grave.[88]

Some weeks later, Wright and a group of migrants were promised work at a picking site, but when they arrived there was no work. He described the mother of a family:

She pondered her plight: a long trip to nowhere, to poverty and hunger amid plenty. It was the way it had been before . . . it was the way it would be tomorrow. That was the way of a migrant farm family. At last the woman wept silently. Great tears welled up in her eyes, rolled heavily down both dark cheeks, and collected in pools in the wrinkles at the sides of her mouth.[88]

Just as in "Harvest," the migrants' sense of futility ran through Wright's reporting. At one migrant camp, Wright was sleeping when he heard cries from an infant in an adjacent room. He investigated and found "a column of large, beetlelike insects was marching . . . across his night clothes and over his brown face. One of the insects had crawled into the child's nostril and the little fellow was flailing aimlessly . . . to fight off the invaders." It was pay day. The mother was at a local tavern, the only diversion for the workers after ten-hour workdays. She had wrapped the child in a laundered burlap sack and left him sleeping. When she returned, her shoulders sank in exasperation. "Ain't no place you can get away from them," she said of the bugs. "What can you do? We got to live someplace. Jus' ain't no place else for us folks comes here on the season." On her face was the look of utter defeat, Wright wrote.[89]

Unlike the migrant worker, Wright could exit. Once or twice he went to a nearby hotel; three or four times he returned home. Sometimes, flight from work brought danger. "Harvest" showed the despair, but there was no indication that violence threatened the workers. "Walk away from this camp, boy," one of Wright's field bosses told him, "and the cops in town will beat you half to death! If they don't catch you, me or Rudy will come after you ourselves. . . . You got to work 'til you pays off everything you owes." Nonetheless, on that occasion, Wright left camp. "I was always fearful," Wright told me when I interviewed his twenty-seven years after the articles appeared. "A black reporter from a white paper in the Deep South . . . you know . . . confrontation. I was fearful."[90] Wright spoke with workers who had been beaten. No one ever suspected he was a reporter even though, at times, his inquisitiveness brought attention. "You must be from the gov'ment. Askin' all them questions. You an inspector or something. . . . You one of them people from the State that wants to know how my half is gittin' along?" a crew leader from New Jersey asked him. Another crew leader was not so gentle when he saw Wright talking with other workers. "Don't bother them people. You're keeping them from making their money and they don't appreciate it. Neither do I. Next time I ketch you with your nose in their business, I'm gonna knock some of them teeth out of your mouth."[91] For Wright, the threats brought home how "economic slavery" controlled every aspect of a migrant's life.

At CBS, there was an internal policy against editorializing. There was also the government-imposed fairness doctrine which mandated reasonable balance in a broadcast. The print media have no such edicts— the rules of objectivity are unwritten. They stem from common understandings about how the press is supposed to function. At times some of the rules can be suspended. Dale Wright said that there was never any thought that his ten articles, which appeared between October 4 and October 21, would be balanced. Wright, for example, never quoted a farmer or any farm industry spokesman. "I made no effort to get two points of view, to provide a balanced overview. I had read about the government regulations and rules. My job," Wright said, "was to find out if the rules were being enforced. They were not." Thus, the balance rule of objectivity was suspended for Wright, but in other senses, neutrality was not: Wright was simply a first-person observer.[92] As if he was a man from Mars, Wright went to view the migrant plight with little prior knowledge and with few preconceptions. The reporter simply recorded and retold.

When typewriter time came in October, the anonymous "Dave Wright" was replaced by an angry Dale Wright, the professional observer turned participant. He used a first-person point of view throughout his stories. Sometimes he was the main character; more often, other migrants took center stage. "It was an advocacy piece on my part," Wright said. That was only partially true. Nine articles present Wright's objective observations; only his final article offers his solutions. On October 21, Wright proposed some new laws and vigorous enforcement of old ones, but this was by far the weakest story of the series.[93] Perhaps this is understandable since the migrant situation is complex, but Wright's chance at analysis was greatly limited by the deadline that his editors foolishly imposed. After six months on the road, he returned and was beginning to write, mostly in a back office of a Baptist church in Harlem. Then, on Sunday, October 2, a fire in a migrant camp in Cutchogue, Long Island, killed four migrant workers. The *Telegram*, seeing a newspeg for its series, told Wright he would have to go to print the next day. The series began before Wright had finished writing—and certainly before he had had a chance to digest all that he had seen and learned. What resulted was another searing exposé, but no solutions came with it.

TODAY: STILL AT THE BOTTOM

"One of the hardest tasks facing those who have wanted to do something about the shocking living and working conditions of the migrant farm worker has been to make the public aware that the migrant worker and his problems even exist in prosperous twentieth century America," wrote New Jersey's Senator Harrison Williams in 1965.[94] That task has been made much easier by the press, which for two decades has been the biggest ally of those seeking to heighten awareness. With anger and eloquence, journalists have muckraked and exposed and put the plight of migrant workers on the public agenda. For a while, there was promise of significant change. State legislatures and the U.S. Congress responded—funding became available for rural health programs; education centers for migrant children were established; crew leaders were required to register; and sanitary facilities in the fields improved. On so many other fronts, however, legislation and enforcement were thwarted. By 1988, when I called the U.S. Congress to see what new laws were pending, no one even knew what legislative committee would handle such legislation. "That tells you something, right there," a lawyer with the Senate Judiciary Committee said. "Some issues fade."[95] Yet the needs of the nearly one million migrant farm workers have not faded . . . and conditions have not improved.

"Farm workers are the most neglected and disempowered work force in America," wrote four Cornell University researchers in 1988, adding, "[T]he conditions in which they live are as shocking as those of the refugees" of Africa. The average American lives to the age of seventy-three; the average migrant, forty-nine. They remain American's lowest paid workers. Average annual income, $3,025. Child malnutrition is ten times the national rate. By the age of four, most migrant children have already begun work. Pesticides in the field pose the greatest health hazard, perhaps explaining why the infant mortality rate is double the national average. "Very little has changed for the farmworkers in all these years," concluded the Cornell researchers.[96] The director of a farm worker advocacy organization in Washington, D.C., said, in fact, that, for a variety of reasons, migrant workers may even be worse off today than they were in the past.[97]

Should the press seek to improve the condition of America's migrant workers? Can it expect to bring about change? Professor Clifford G. Christians answers those questions convincingly when he writes that "the litmus test of whether or not the news profession fulfills its mission over the long term is its advocacy for those outside the socioeconomic establishment." Christian adds that "justice for the powerless stands at the centerpiece of a socially responsible press."[98] The only question then concerns how to achieve that goal, which may come in part by under-standing where the press has failed in its past coverage and what factors get in the way of improving future coverage.

The press, of course, can never expect to achieve social change if it acts alone; it needs to be supported by and to complement reformers from the government and private sectors. The press, acting in concert with other agents for change, is nevertheless a key part of the social process, and it can act as an inspirational force and catalyst, stirring both the public and the bureaucracy to action. For a serious reform effort to begin, proceed, and succeed in improving migrant conditions, the press would need to undertake a four-step campaign. First, with muck-raking exposé, the press would enlighten and outrage the public; facts and figures—documentation—would combine with the faces of migrant life. Next, with persistent and dramatic follow-ups—more facts, more faces—the press would introduce new and troubling aspects of the mi-grant lifestyle, thus keeping the problem on the public agenda. Third, as the issue unfolded via follow-up stories or broadcasts, a time when competing media would probably join the story, the press would broaden the inquiry with discussion and analysis of the causes of the migrant condition. Why this underclass exists is the question to be an-swered. Finally, by tapping into advocacy groups and reform-minded legislators, as well as by allowing opponents to argue against reform, the press would explore remedies and solutions. The process then would be one of discovery, reaction, discussion, and solution. Analysis of press coverage of the migrant plight indicates that only half of this suggested approach—exposé and follow-up—has been taken by the press. Therein lies a significant reason why efforts to eradicate migrant poverty have stalled and failed. Three factors that have prevented the press from doing more for migrant workers explain why press coverage has gone little beyond exposé: the restraints that are inherent in objectivity, the conflicting demands of commercialism, and the blinders and limits imposed by American culture.

Sociologist Gaye Tuchman notes that objectivity is a "strategic ritual" used by the press, at least in part, to defend itself against those who claim that it is biased.[99] This ritual, while it provides a defense, also acts as a remarkably restraining mechanism which limits the options of reporters. As an implicit form of advocacy, muckraking journalism stretches the boundaries of objectivity: if it needs exposing, it must be bad and it must need change, but who will decide on and propose the changes? In general, a reporter can advocate by exposé, but the line seems to be drawn at the point where certain questions need to be asked and answered. What are the causes and what are the solutions? These questions are difficult to answer under any circumstances, but especially so under the accepted rules of objective journalism. The press did not even attempt answers in the 1959–1961 period studied here, nor did it provide this kind of analysis in three nationally televised broadcast documentaries that appeared in a later period (a 1967 Public Broadcasting Service film, "What Harvest for the Reaper?" and the two NBC follow-ups already cited). The reason? Objectivity, which usually focuses on official events, pronouncements, or documents, leaves little room for interpretation, analysis, and perspective. In fact, "objective reporting discriminates against analysis in favor of exposition and against truth in favor of the facts," points out Lou Cannon, a reporter with the *Washington Post*. Moreover, it leaves little room for important historical connections to previous episodes, making news fragmented, not continuous. More than one observer has noted this tendency in the press. "News is normally defined in terms of discrete events . . . and the historical context of these events . . . is relegated to the ambiguous realm of analysis—and generally to the back pages," writes Daniel Hallin.[100] A history of the treatment of migrant workers, even a brief one, would have led to a key issue: the omission of farm workers from the protective labor legislation of the 1930s. Could it be, as Carey McWilliams charged in 1935, that migrants were left unprotected by this social legislation because of a deal between organized labor and farm groups? McWilliams wrote: "We, the farm representatives, will not object to this legislation, if you, the representatives of organized labor, will agree to exempt agricultural employees."[101]

An answer to the question of why migrant workers were and continue to be excluded is not possible from the media exposés because labor relations were simply not explored in any detail. The lack of a coherent national farm labor policy and the gross injustice of labor law exclusions for migrants have been, as a journalist would say, underplayed. Certainly, there were opportunities for such an analysis. In "Harvest of Shame," a poignant moment of worker solidarity was captured when workers gathered in California to protest wages and treatment. In PBS' "What Harvest for the Reaper?" producer Morton Silverstein exposed how the contract under which Long Island migrant farm workers toiled was violated consistently. In Martin Carr's 1970 NBC documentary "Migrants," the narrator pointed out that the migrants "don't have the rights guaranteed the rest of us"—no Social Security or unemployment insurance, no right to organize or strike, no workmen's compensation. But Carr, a fearless producer, steered clear of explaining why this was so. In Silverstein's 1980 NBC documentary, camera crews caught migrants in a job-action in an orchard, but the cameras shifted to the children who took the workers' places and ignored the worker grievances and the larger labor issues. One can only think that America's cultural ambivalence toward labor and unions as a threatening form of organization, with their implied threat of strikes and disruptions, has caused the press to avoid the labor relations issue. The American ideals of individualism and hard work, the spirit of capitalism, in essence, are contrary to the communal nature of unionization. Reporters, who probably share those values, avoided even a marketplace approach—classic objective balance—toward the question of farm worker organization. No union activists advocate worker solidarity; only aggrieved farmers yelp about what strikes at harvest time would do to the economy.[102]

Another explanation exists beside the cultural one. Had the press delved into the question of why farm workers do not have the same rights as other workers, journalists would have run smack into the powerful farmers' lobby. The secretary of labor told Murrow that in all his days in Washington, D.C., the farmers were the most powerful lobbying group he had ever encountered, a power that they carry with equal force into state capitols. To articulate an organization's desires and needs is perfectly legal and acceptable in American democracy, but the contrast between the ability of the farmers to influence legislators and the migrants' inability to make their own needs explicit is a telling and significant difference. The basic cause of the migrants' powerlessness—that they are no one's constituency and that they have no representatives—would have been evident. Perhaps the press avoided prying too far into the farmers' lobby because they feared retribution, but there is no direct evidence of this. However, the lesson of "Harvest of Shame" could not have been lost. In 1961, the farmers struck back with a vengeance. By the time Martin Carr brought his camera crews to Florida for a follow-up in 1969, the farmers were prepared: no one would cooperate. "I met with open and frightening hostility," Carr said. "Again and again, local growers told me that they wouldn't cooperate because, they said, I was going to tell only one side of the story—the migrant's side." Once, a farmer pointed a gun at Carr and chased him away from a migrant camp. Florida Governor Claude Kirk at first agreed to be interviewed by Chet Huntley, but then, apparently under pressure from the lobby, he refused. "We were not going to balance both sides of the story," Kirk's office told Carr.[103]

By attacking any stories that were not pro-farmer or even resembled having any sympathy for the farm worker, the farmers' lobby has played an intimidating role, limiting the reach and persistence of the press. Objectivity, a form of protection for the press against those who say it is biased, serves also as a protection for the attacked, a way to keep the press in line. "Unfortunately," Carr wrote, "intimidation too often works."[104] By forcing the press to remain in the narrow confines of objectivity, various alternatives and direct criticism of the growers could be avoided. The farmers do, invariably, emerge as the bad guys in news media accounts, but as long as the media stick to exposé of migrant conditions and avoid careful analysis of possible new labor relationships, the status quo will remain—farmers entrenched, migrants disempowered and poor.

The commercial contradictions of the press need to be coupled with the unavoidable cultural biases of reporters and the rituals of objectivity to explain the press' shortcomings in news coverage of migrants. Media in America are mostly commercial products. They package their news and editorial comment around merchandise, and the merchandising inevitably affects the news product. At times, commerce's intervention is blatant. On the day before Martin Carr's 1970 documentary appeared, representatives of Coca Cola asked NBC to tone down its criticism of the giant company. Coca Cola owned Florida orchards where it used migrant labor to harvest fruit for its Minute Maid brand of orange juice. Carr found that the company, like so many others, paid low wages and provided substandard housing, and his interviews with migrant workers living in Coca Cola-owned shacks made this clear. After a tense meeting between NBC executives and Coca Cola representatives, NBC deleted two damaging references to the beverage company and added one that could have been written by Coke's public relations staff. In the addition, Carr said Coca Cola was preparing a "major plan" to correct the deficiencies it had found. "The pressure from Coca Cola was enormous," Carr said.[105]

Such pressure is rare, however, and the effects of commercialism are usually more subtle. After "Harvest of Shame" appeared, there was talk of a follow-up broadcast. CBS officials asked David Lowe to collect more material and to include the angry responses of the farmers. The follow-up that appeared in January was a debate between a labor leader and a representative of the Farm Bureau. This was not a follow-up in the sense that it explored solutions or introduced new evidence; it merely expanded the debate about "Harvest's" fairness. Since "CBS Reports" was appearing infrequently, a logical follow-up could have come on the nightly news broadcast. But nightly news was only fifteen minutes in 1960; moreover, CBS was more committed to profitable television than to controversial, money-losing news and public affairs.[106] When James T. Aubrey, Jr., took over as the network's president in 1961, he viewed news as a money loser, and the network that was once home to Edward R. Murrow became home to Jed Clampett's "Beverly Hillbillies." This was a triumph of money over ideals. It took another network to follow up on the migrant story, and that came ten years later.[107] An equally subtle, but undeniably commercial decision affected the work of Dale Wright. When he completed his six months as a migrant laborer, he was forced to write hurriedly, and with little thoughtful analysis. Editors decided that, because of a fire in a Long Island migrant camp, Wright's series would have to begin the next day. The fear that other publications might "scoop" the *World-Telegram* forced him to write before he was ready. Better to be first in the market than to be best.

The work of producer Morton Silverstein provides a rare opportunity to contrast commercial and noncommercial models of journalistic inquiry. Silverstein produced PBS' "What Harvest for the Reaper?" (1967), which has rightfully been compared to "Harvest of Shame" and NBC's "The Migrants" (1980). In "What Harvest," Silverstein diligently followed a group of migrants from Arkansas to Long Island. His focus was the crew chief, a light-skinned, fast-talking black man who hustled workers off the streets and into Long Island's potato fields. Whereas the migrants earned a few thousand dollars a year, most of which they paid to the crew chief for food and liquor, the crew chief brought home $40,000. In a slow-paced, thoughtful, and clear manner, Silverstein documented the systematic bilking of the workers by the crew chief and the contempt in which the workers were held by the farm owners, an unsympathetic, tough-talking, crew-cut bunch. Although both the crew chief and the farmers were allowed to respond to this damning portrait near the end of the broadcast, there was a sense that they had already been convicted. When crew chief Andersen said, "I cares 'bout my fella man," his hypocrisy was obvious. The broadcast was a compelling, passionate, muckraking document that confirmed Silverstein's belief that "there are no two sides to economic repression, or to social injustice." Twelve years after "What Harvest" appeared, after working for ABC and CBS, Silverstein worked, again, on a migrant documentary, this time for NBC. His next product was much more in the entertainment mode than his PBS effort. Either Silverstein had mellowed or commercialism had intervened. In the same interview in which Silverstein said that the documentary must strive to confront social injustice, he conceded that it "must strive [also] to present information in an arresting, filmic, involving way." He added, "The documentary, too, is entertainment."[108] His 1980 version was as much entertainment as documentary— a series of dramatic confrontations, much like one would find in the highly rated "60 Minutes." The targets were a small-town sheriff, a part-time judge, an antipoverty agency official who was misusing money for migrant housing, and some farmers. This made for entertainment and some enlightenment, but the targets were small potatoes. Silverstein produced good, dramatic, commercial television, but not a social document which enabled the public to see solutions. To NBC's credit, it presented this broadcast at a time when the national mood was decidedly conservative and documentaries were rare. Nonetheless, the point is that commercial television—along with the culture and the routines of journalism—invariably works to neuter the final product, limiting what the audience gets to see and altering what it eventually will believe. "Migrants," 1980, exposed conditions again, but offered no way out.

The final segment of "Harvest of Shame," in which Edward R. Murrow implored the public to do something about the migrant plight, was not what he initially had envisioned. Murrow's original ending was longer, no less angry, but a bit more elegiac. Murrow said, "This is not the full story. One hour or one hundred hours is not enough time to document the plight of these people." Then, elegantly, Murrow retraced the migrant path up the East Coast, "the aching days and nights of travel . . . these cars, buses, and trucks and their tired cargo of human freight . . . the shacks and the straw of the halfway work shop." Just as he had ended the McCarthy broadcast by reciting a segment from a poem, he had wanted a similar finale for "Harvest." He wrote, "In this wealthiest of nations, an American poet asked this question, 'Who gave me this sweet/and gave me brother dust to eat/And when will his ship come in.' "[109] For some reason—perhaps because the tone was softer—the finale was cut out. But the words he never spoke are well remembered. The migrant farm worker's ship has still not come in. Journalism and journalists have for many years fought the good fight on behalf of migrant farm workers. Yet, muckraking exposé has not done the trick: many still suffer and many die young. The press is not the cause of this, certainly, and Howard Van Smith, David Lowe, and Dale Wright have all helped to bring some relief. The task ahead for future muckraking journalists is to find a way not just to expose, but to offer and to help implement solutions.

NOTES

1. On screen, Mrs. King said that she had fourteen children; seven of her children had died at birth. CBS' choice of Mrs. King as a key example became a center of controversy. The farmers contended that her husband also had an income, and that many of her medical expenses at Florida hospitals had been borne by taxpayers. See the letter of W. M. Anderson, Jr., an official of the Florida Fruit and Vegetable Association, to Senator George Smathers, January 24, 1961, in the Edward R. Murrow Papers, Fletcher School of Law and Diplomacy, Tufts University; Sanford, N.C.: Microfilming Corporation of America, reel 22.

2. The federal government defines migrant farm workers as those persons who leave their home county, stay overnight, and do farm work for cash wages or salary. Leslie W. Smith and Robert Coltrane, *Hired Farmworkers: Background and Trends for the Eighties* (Washington, D.C., 1981), 23.

3. Secretary of Labor James P. Mitchell made his comment in the broadcast of "Harvest of Shame." A transcript is available in the *Congressional Record—Senate*, January 23, 1961, 1145–50, and in the Murrow papers. New Jersey Senator Harrison Williams, foreword, Dale Wright, *They Harvest Despair* (Boston, 1965). "Misfortune's Children on the Move," *New York Times Magazine*, 6 August 1961, p. 8.

4. "Migrant: An NBC White Paper," broadcast, July 16, 1970.

5. "The Migrants: An NBC White Paper," broadcast August 15, 1980.

6. Louisa R. Shotwell, *The Harvesters: The Story of the Migrant People* (New York, 1979), 8. The history of migrant investigations can be found in *Migratory Labor in American Agriculture* (Washington, D.C., 1951); *Report to the President on Domestic Migratory Farm Labor* (Washington, D.C., 1960). A good bibliography on migrant farm workers is included in Truman Moore, *The Slaves We Rent* (New York, 1965), 161–66.

7. The current condition of migrant laborers is discussed in Diana Zimmerman, "America's Nomads," *Migration Today* 9 (1981): 24–32. Similar conclusions are reached by Donald J. Barr, Aurora Demarco, Carl Henry Fever, Robin Lee Whittlesey, *Liberalism to the Test: African-American Migrant Farmworkers and the State of New York*, (Ithaca, N.Y.: New York African-American Institute, 1988), 4. See also Robert Wasserstrom and Richard Wiles, *Field Duty: U.S. Farmworkers and Pesticide Safety* (Washington, D.C.: World Resources Institute, 1985). Ron D'Aloisio, director, Farmworker Justice Fund Incorporated, Washington D.C., concluded that conditions may be worse. Telephone interview, July 15, 1988.

8. "News' Pulitzer Winner Howard Van Smith Dies," *Miami News*, 16 August 1986, p. 4A. Interview with Howard Kleinberg, executive editor of the *News*, October 17, 1988. A description of Van Smith's work is included with his Pulitzer Prize nomination, School of Journalism, Columbia University, New York.

9. Howard Van Smith, "Immokalee up in Arms over Delay," January 25, 1958; "How Could They Allow Such Filth?" October 17; "Immokalee Migrant

Plight Called Worst Ever in State," January 14. Unless otherwise noted, all Van Smith's articles are from the *Miami News*, 1958.

10. Interview with William Van Smith, a sports writer at the *Miami Herald*, October 25, 1988.

11. I discussed Van Smith's work with several of his former colleagues, including Howard Kleinberg; Clarke Ash, editorial page editor, *Palm Beach Post*; Milt Sosin, a retired *News* reporter, on October 25, 1988; and Ken Heinrich, a former *News* city editor now working in public relations, on October 26, 1988. Ironically, it was not the *News* but a Miami area physician, Dr. George Karelas, who nominated Van Smith for the Pulitzer Prize. Letter from Karelas to John Hohenberg, Pulitzer Prize secretary, February 2, 1959. The committee gave Karelas time past its normal deadline to complete an official nomination and to ask the *News* to supply copies of Van Smith's articles to the Pulitzer committee. Letter to author from Bud Kliment, assistant administrator, the Pulitzer Prizes, November 9, 1988.

12. Van Smith, "Immokalee Tries to Feed and Shelter 2,000 Jobless," January 12, p. 1. Van Smith's former editors agreed that his writing needed much editing. The newsroom rumor was that Haines Colbert, a rewrite editor, was responsible for much of the writing of Van Smith's stories.

13. The second-day stories on January 14 are "Immokalee Plight," "Surplus Food Is Sought by S. Dade Migrants," and "U.S. Can Aid Immokalee—Smathers."

14. Van Smith, "U.S. Health Service to Aid Immokalee," January 17; "Food, Money Ease Immokalee Plight," January 19; and "U.S. Is Sending More Food to Aid Immokalee Migrants," January 23.

15. Van Smith, "Migrant Crisis End Is Denied by Immokalee," February 1; "Baby Food Firm Comes to the Aid of Immokalee," February 9; "Miami Kerosene Gift Eases Immokalee Woe," February 14; "Funds and Supplies for Migrants Now at $100,000," February 20; and "News Sends $708 Gift to Migrants," February 18.

16. In numerous stories Van Smith said that certain developments came about because of the *News'* stories. See "Doctors' Immokalee Study Based on Stories in *News*," April 18. Van Smith placed blame in "Food, Money Ease Immokalee Plight," January 19; "5,000 Jobless Migrants Fed at Homestead," January 25. "Collins Sees Immokalee, Calls Conditions Horrible," February 15. Van Smith's chasing of Governor Collins was recounted by his son, interview.

17. Van Smith, "Migrants Begin Shacks Cleanup," February 12; "Immokalee Leaders Want 'Shacktown' Blot Erased," February 13.

18. Van Smith, "Hovels Doomed at Immokalee," March 23; "Migrant Housing at Immokalee Probed," August 8; "Immokalee Farms Facing Loss of Crops over Hovels," August 10; " 'Shacktown' Must Be Cleaned up or State May Ban It to Migrants," August 11. "A Miracle Takes Place at Immokalee," December 26, pp. 1, 2.

19. Pulitzer Prize Awards, Columbia University.

20. Murrow's work and celebrity are detailed in two biographies: Alexander Kendrick, *Prime Time: The Life and Legend of Edward R. Murrow* (Boston, 1969) and A. M. Sperber, *Murrow: His Life and Times* (New York, 1986). On his work, see also, James L. Baughman, " 'See It Now' and Television's Golden Age, 1951–

58," *Journal of Popular Culture* 15 (Fall 1981): 106–15; Jeff Merron, "Murrow on TV: 'See It Now,' 'Person to Person,' and the Making of a 'Masscult Personality,' " *Journalism Monographs* 106 (July 1988).

21. A discussion of the McCarthy broadcast is found in Michael Murray, "SEE IT NOW vs. McCarthyism" (Ph.D. diss., University of Missouri-Columbia, 1974); Murray R. Yaeger, "An Analysis of Edward R. Murrow's 'See It Now' Program" (Ph.D. diss., State University of Iowa, 1956). On "See It Now's" replacement, see James L. Baughman, "The Strange Birth of 'CBS Reports' Revisited," *The Historical Journal of Film, Radio and TV* 2 (1982). Most scholarly attention has been centered on Murrow, while Friendly has been somewhat ignored. Friendly went on to become president of CBS News from 1964 to 1966, an author, and a professor of journalism at Columbia University.

22. Interview with Fred W. Friendly, November 30, 1988.

23. To piece together David Lowe's career, I interviewed various people, including John Schultz, April 23, 1988; Palmer Williams, May 26, 1988; Harriet Van Horne, June 3, 1988; David Lowe, Jr., August 30, 1988; Sue Davidson Lowe, August 18 and September 18, 1988; and Ellen Lowe, September 19, 1988. Sue Davidson Lowe had her own successes after her marriage to Lowe. See her book, *Stieglitz: A Memoir-Biography* (New York, 1983).

24. "The Excluded Americans," *Time* (December 5, 1960): 50.

25. Interviews with Harriet Van Horne, June 3, 1988; and Sue Davidson Lowe.

26. Interview with Sue Davidson Lowe, August 18, 1988.

27. Interview with David Lowe, Jr., August 30, 1988.

28. Fred Friendly, *Due to Circumstances Beyond Our Control*. (New York, 1967), 121; interview with Friendly.

29. Transcript, "Harvest of Shame." Subsequent quotations from the broadcast are also from the transcript.

30. Interview with Ellen Lowe, September 19, 1988.

31. A. H. Raskin, "For 500,000, Still Tobacco Road," *New York Times Magazine*, 24 April 1960, p. 14.

32. Interviews with John Schultz, April 23, 1988; Palmer Williams, May 26, 1988; and Lowe, Jr.

33. Interview with Williams.

34. Sperber, *Murrow*, 568. Interview with Schultz.

35. Sperber, *Murrow*. Schultz went on to teach film editing at the Columbia University Graduate School of Journalism in New York City.

36. An attorney for CBS, Thomas K. Fisher, described Lowe's research: "He visited a number of the States. He read numerous reports that have been issued on the migratory labor situation. He interviewed countless people. He visited many labor camps in the States in which he traveled." From CBS' response to criticism of the broadcast, January 23, 1961, reprinted in the *Congressional Record*, February 16, 1961, 2221.

37. Sperber and Friendly say that Murrow and Lowe went to Florida more than once; other participants recall only one visit. Interview with Friendly; Sperber, *Murrow*, 121. Williams, letter to author, October 7, 1988.

38. Sperber, *Murrow*, 595. Interview with Friendly.

39. Sperber, *Murrow*, 594.

40. Interview with Friendly; Sperber, *Murrow*, 604.

41. *Time*, "The Excluded Americans," 50.

42. Interview with Lowe, Jr.

43. Lewis Jacobs, "The Turn toward Conservatism," in *The Documentary Tradition*, ed. Lewis Jacobs (New York, 1974), 276. FBI investigations of Murrow began the day after the McCarthy broadcast. See Sperber, *Murrow*, 736, note 49.

44. Carey McWilliams, "The Continuing Tradition of Reform Journalism," in *Muckraking: Past, Present and Future*, ed. John M. Harrison and Harry Stein (University Park, Pa., 1973), 118–34. Muckraking fiction between the world wars is discussed by Jay Martin in "The Literature of Argument and the Arguments of Literature," *Muckraking*, eds. Harrison and Stein, 100–115. Louis Filler summarizes post–Progressive Era muckraking in *The Muckrakers* (University Park, Pa., 1976), 379–416. Carey McWilliams, *Ill Fares the Land: Migrants and Migratory Labor in the United States* (Boston, 1944).

45. Sperber, *Murrow*, 111. Kendrick, *Prime Time*, 285–86.

46. Murrow was particularly attacked on this question by television critic Gilbert Seldes. See Sperber, *Murrow*, 434.

47. Quoted in Yaeger, "An Analysis," 57.

48. *Edward R. Murrow Heritage: Challenge for the Future*, eds. Betty Houchins Winfield and Lois B. DeFleur (Ames, Iowa, 1986), 2. William S. Paley was furious after the Murrow speech: "... it was very much of a personal attack. Which I resented very deeply." Sperber, *Murrow*, 542. See also, Lewis J. Paper, *Empire: William S. Paley and the Making of CBS* (New York, 1986), 188–89.

49. Farmers made very similar comments in NBC's 1970 follow-up, "Migrant." One farmer called them "our darkies." Another, one of the largest farm owners in Florida, told producer Martin Carr, "The Negro are fine people but they have to respect you. If you want to get down to their level and get dirty or whatnot . . . they won't respect you." Chet Huntley concluded that racism was a key problem facing migrant laborers. This conclusion is echoed in Barr et al., *Liberalism to the Test*, 3.

50. Lowe wrote the script for "Harvest of Shame." According to John Schultz, the film editor, the analogies cited in this paragraph were written by Murrow, not Lowe.

51. Interview with Van Horne.

52. *Murrow Heritage*, eds. Winfield and DeFleur, 106.

53. Interview with Friendly; Friendly, *Due to Circumstances*, 121.

54. Jack Gould, "Harvest of Shame," *New York Times*, 26 November 1960, p. 62; *Time*, "The Excluded Americans." Other reviews were Ben Gross, "What's On," *New York News*, 26 November 1960, p. 20; Harriet Van Horne, "Churchill's V for Valiant," New York *World-Telegram and Sun*, 26 November 1960, p. 17.

55. By contrast, CBS' 1954 broadcast on Joseph McCarthy brought 4,000 telephone calls, 15,000 letters, and 4,000 telegrams. See William S. Paley, *As It Happened: A Memoir* (Garden City, N.Y., 1979), 284.

56. *Congressional Record—Senate*, January 23, 1961, 1145. Letter, Rosemary Mullen to Leslie Orear, December 23, 1960, Murrow papers.

57. Interviews Lowe, Jr. and Williams; Robert Louis Shayon, "The Fuse in the Documentary," *Saturday Review* 43 (December 17, 1960): 29.

58. From "Analysis of 'The Harvest of Shame' " by the American Farm

Bureau Federation. Reprinted in *Congressional Record—Senate*, February 16, 1961, 2216.

59. After "Harvest," David Lowe produced a number of critically acclaimed and controversial documentaries for "CBS Reports," including "Who Speaks for Birmingham?," "Abortion and the Law," "The Right to Bear Arms," and "The Ku Klux Klan: The Invisible Empire." William Leonard, former president of CBS news, said that Lowe was "perhaps the most successful in Friendly's original 'CBS Reports' stable . . . a suave and brave practitioner of the art," in *In the Storm of the Eye: A Lifetime at CBS* (New York, 1987). In 1965, two nights after a marathon session in the cutting room working on the Ku Klux Klan broadcast, Lowe died of a heart attack.

60. Murrow's eroding relationship with CBS is discussed by Kendrick, *Prime Time*, 384–460; and Sperber, *Murrow*, 529–622. Murrow was particularly angry at Frank Stanton for describing his "Person to Person" show as the equivalent of the quiz show frauds. See David Halberstam, *The Powers That Be* (New York, 1979), 124–25; Friendly, 108, and Kendrick, p. 434.

61. Friendly, *Due to Circumstances*, 125; and Halberstam, *The Powers That Be*, 147–51, 154–56.

62. *Congressional Record—House of Representatives*, February 2, 1961, 1609–10, 1612.

63. *Congressional Record—Senate*, February 6, 1961, 2216. The farmers' point of view can be seen amply in a special newspaper supplement, "Glades Side of the Story," *Palm Beach Post*, 8 February 1961.

64. From a report, "Action of Board of Directors of the American Farm Bureau Federation," January 4, 1961, *Congressional Record*, 2218.

65. Interview with Van Horne.

66. Letter to Charles B. Schuman, president, American Farm Bureau Federation, from Thomas K. Fisher, CBS vice president, January 23, 1961, *Congressional Record—Senate*, February 6, 1961, 2218.

67. Friendly, *Due to Circumstances*, 121; *Congressional Record*, 2220.

68. Friendly, *Due to Circumstances*, 92, 122.

69. Ibid.; interview with Friendly. Phillip Morris' representatives are quoted in the *Tampa Tribune* as found in the Murrow papers.

70. Spessard Holland's comment was made on the floor of the Senate, February 15, 1961, 2224. He added, "The name 'Harvest of Shame' is almost the ultimate insult to our fine people."

71. Letter from Murrow to David Sarnoff, March 23, 1961, Murrow papers.

72. *Edward R. Murrow Heritage*, 51. Murrow papers.

73. Murrow to Williams, March 10, 1961; Williams to Murrow, March 14, 1961. Murrow first learned of the broadcast in a memo from a U.S. Information Agency aide; Oren Stephens to Murrow, March 3, 1961. Murrow papers.

74. It is unclear whether the call was made before Murrow's confirmation to the USIA. He appeared before the U.S. Senate on March 15, and the broadcast was aired in Great Britain on March 30. The call may have been made in those two intervening weeks. Kendrick wrote that Murrow did receive pressure, from an unnamed Florida senator, probably Holland, and, according to Kennedy's press secretary, from the president. Kendrick, *Prime Time*, 458.

75. Sperber, *Murrow*, 630.

76. Letter from Patrick Malin to Murrow, March 23, 1961; Murrow papers. The editorial responses are cited in Sperber, *Murrow*, 630–31.

77. A transcript of Murrow's April 4, 1961, press conference is included in the Murrow papers.

78. Friendly, *Due to Circumstances*, 123; interview with Friendly. The quote from the Britisher is contained in a report made by the BBC after the broadcast appeared; Murrow papers. Paley's comment is recounted by Friendly in *Due to Circumstances*, p. 123.

79. Paley, *As It Happened*, 293.

80. Interview with Dale Wright, September 20, 1988.

81. Ibid.

82. Ibid.

83. Dale Wright, *They Harvest Despair*, 21, 23. After Wright's articles appeared in the *Telegram*, he wrote this book as an expanded version of the experience. Reviewer Robert Colet said the book was "in the finest muckraking tradition," in the *Herald Tribune*, 23 May 1965. Edward P. Morgan said on ABC Radio, 11 May 1965, that the book was "the sequel to Steinbeck's 'Grapes of Wrath.'" Wright wanted to write a fictional account of life as a migrant, but Beacon Press was not interested, according to the interview with Wright.

84. Dale Wright, "Migrant Pay $4.32 a Day in Florida Tomato Field," *World-Telegram and Sun*, 11 October 1961, pp. 1, 29. The *World-Telegram and Sun* is subsequently referred to as the *W-T&S*. Wright's articles were collected and reprinted by various agencies. See, for example, " 'The Forgotten People' . . . a Report on the Migrant Laborer" (Chicago: Bishops Committee for Migrant Workers, 1968).

85. Wright, "I Saw Human Shame. . . . ," *W-T&S*, 10 October 1961, pp. 1, 17. Wright detailed housing conditions in "Farm Camp Slum, Exposed 8 Years Ago, Is Still Hell," *W-T&S*, 18 October 1961, pp. 22, 42; and "Migrants Exist in Duck Sheds," *W-T&S*, 20 October 1961.

86. Wright, *W-T&S*, 10 October 1961, p. 17.

87. Tom Goldstein, *The News at Any Cost* (New York, 1986), 127–51. Wright, *They Harvest Despair*, 27–28.

88. Wright, *They Harvest Despair*, 53, 77.

89. Ibid., pp. 77, 29. Also interview with Wright.

90. Ibid., 62. See also, "Closeup: Dale Wright Faced Peril on Story Job," *W-T&S*, 19 October 1961, p. 13.

91. Wright, *They Harvest Despair*, 86, 107.

92. Interview with Wright.

93. Interview with Wright. Wright, "State Could Remedy Conditions for Migrant Labor," *W-T&S*, 21 October 1961, p. 3.

94. Harrison Williams, foreword, Wright, *They Harvest Despair*, no page number.

95. Telephone interview, July 15, 1988. The lawyer asked not to be identified, saying that the admission that the committee was doing nothing for migrant workers would anger advocates for the migrants.

96. Barr et al., *Liberalism to the Test*, p. 3–4.

97. Note 7 cites recent sources on the migrant condition. See also Peter T. Kilborn, "Drugs and Debt: Shackles of Migrant Worker," *New York Times*, Oc-

tober 31, 1989, pp. 1, D23; Loretta Schwartz, "The Plight of America's Five Million Migrants," *Ms.* (June 1978), 65–68; Alec Wilkinson, *Big Sugar: Seasons in the Cane Fields of Florida* (New York, 1989).

98. Clifford Christians, "Reporting and the Oppressed," in *Responsible Journalism*, ed. Deni Elliot (Beverly Hills, Calif., 1986), 110.

99. Gaye Tuchman, "Objectivity as Strategic Ritual: An Examination of Newspaperman's Notions of Objectivity," *American Journal of Sociology 77*, 4 (January 1972): 660–79.

100. Lou Cannon, *Reporting: An Inside View* (Sacramento; Calif., 1977), 45. Daniel Hallin, *The Uncensored War: The Media and Vietnam* (New York, 1986), 74. On the fragmented nature of news, see also, Herbert Schiller, *The Mind Managers* (Boston, 1974), 24–29.

101. McWilliams, *Ill Fares the Land*, 356.

102. The farmers made it clear that strikes were one of their biggest fears. For example, in "Harvest of Shame," the president of the American Farm Bureau said that no worker should be allowed to strike at harvest time. In "Migrants," the largest grower in Florida denounced unions, saying, "I don't believe they won't strike." American ambivalence toward labor is discussed by Varden Fuller, "Farm Manpower Policy," in *Farm Labor in the United States*, ed. C. E. Bishop (New York, 1967), 98–100. Michael Parenti criticizes the press' general coverage of labor in the chapter "Giving Labor the Business," in *Inventing Reality: The Politics of the Mass Media* (New York, 1986), 76–88.

103. Martin Carr recounts the problems in making "Migrant" in "Shame Is Still the Harvest," *New York Times*, 12 July 1970, p. 15, 2.

104. Ibid.

105. Quoted in Fred Ferretti, "Coca Cola Denies Link to Farm Ills," *New York Times*, 17 July 1970, p. 63. Coca-Cola subsequently mounted a major public relations campaign to showcase its new treatment of migrant workers. See "Coca Cola Will Improve Status of Its Migrant Farm Workers," *New York Times*, 25 July 1970, p. 23. Carr, who produced in 1971 the award-winning "Hunger in America," left NBC in 1973, accusing the network of mishandling and underplaying his documentaries.

106. In CBS' formal response to criticism of "Harvest," Thomas Fisher wrote that "CBS has been making arrangements for the broadcasting of another program sometime in February of this year in which varying points of view concerning legislative proposals" will be discussed, *Congressional Record-Senate*, February 16, 1961, 2222. Murrow also discussed a follow-up. "We hope to return one day to this subject," he wrote to Gerald F. Britt, on January 18, 1961; Murrow papers. Schultz said he wanted to do a follow-up while a free-lance in the early 1960s, but CBS refused his request; and Fred Friendly also wanted to do a second broadcast; Schultz and Friendly interviews.

107. James T. Aubrey, Jr.'s, disdain for news is cited by Friendly, *Due to Circumstances*, 195–96; Kendrick, who says Aubrey tried to "subvert CBS Reports," *Prime Time*, 452–53; and Halberstam, who calls Aubrey the "huckster's huckster . . . the greediest side of the network," *The Powers That Be*, 252–55.

108. Alan Rosenthal, *The Documentary Conscience: A Casebook in Film Making* (Berkeley, Calif., 1980), 108, 110.

109. Murrow papers.

5

Old People and Objectivity: The *Times* Crusades

In the summer of 1974, John L. Hess, a reporter with the *New York Times* for twenty years, was preparing to take a leave from the newspaper. Hess, who was fifty six years old, and his wife, Karen, were planning to write a book on dining out in America. Arthur Gelb, the metropolitan editor of the *Times*, approached Hess with a story proposal, and asked him to delay his long-planned leave.

Gelb's mother had recently visited a friend in a New York City nursing home, and she found the home gloomy and the conditions appalling. Gelb asked Hess to investigate the state's nursing-home industry, where $1 billion a year was being spent—most of it taxpayer money—to support 90,000 people in 650 nursing homes. Hess was reluctant to take the assignment. He had been the *Times'* Paris correspondent for a decade, a food critic, and a copy editor, but he had never written about health care. Moreover, he was anxious to get started on what would be his fourth book.[1] Nonetheless, Hess promised to search the *Times'* library for previous stories, to make a few calls to sources, and then to report to Gelb.

In the *Times'* morgue, Hess found scattered news stories over twenty years about the terrible living conditions in New York City nursing homes. Auditors and inspectors from New York State's Health Department—"the whistleblowers," Hess called them—confirmed for him the outline of a situation ripe for investigation. Hess was told of massive fraud, of a "syndicate" headed by a shrewd, politically connected rabbi, and of a giant Monopoly game that was taking place in which nursing homes were being traded back and forth by relatives, all to increase the money received from taxpayers. Hess knew, as a state prosecutor later declared, that he had discovered "squalid, sometimes inhuman conditions and sinister financial manipulations."[2]

"This is not a one-shot deal," Hess told Gelb. "This is a major story. Give me some kids and we can do something here." Gelb made no promises of "kids"—young reporters to help Hess—but Hess took the assignment anyway. His leave temporarily delayed, Hess, a small man with a trim white beard and piercing blue eyes, began work on what became a ten-month crusade that led to a nomination for the Pulitzer Prize in journalism. Hess' crusade enveloped New York City in a nursing-home scandal that for months dominated newspaper front pages and nightly television newscasts and became the most notorious scandal in the nation's history. By late spring of 1975, Hess' nearly 150 stories culminated in what he called "more than I could have ever imagined, but not all I would have hoped for."[3]

Hess' research began only a few blocks from his apartment on the West Side of Manhattan where he visited an infamous old hotel—the Towers. Here, he learned, residents often were left to sleep in urine and feces with vermin crawling about; in the winter months, the elderly shivered in cold unheated rooms; and health inspectors had long tried to close this fire-prone structure, to no avail, thanks to the mysterious political power of its owner. The owner, Bernard Bergman, had once charged taxpayers for a patient who had been dead for three years.

Bergman, a tall, heavy-set sixty-six-year-old man, had been born in Hungary and ordained a rabbi. He always wore black, donned a yarmulke, and had a wisp of white hair under his lip. In the early 1960s he established a network of perhaps as many as 100 nursing homes in New York City, developed extensive contacts in orthodox Jewish circles and in politics, and built a real estate empire that was worth at least $25 million. His nursing homes had hundreds of violations of the state health code; hospitals used the phrase "Bergman syndrome" as shorthand to describe a patient with infected bedsores, malnutrition, and dehydration. After months of scrutiny from legislative commissions and after he had filed a $1-million defamation lawsuit against Hess, Bergman was charged with stealing $2.5 million from Medicaid. Eventually he pleaded guilty to the charges, and he was forced out of the nursing-home industry, but not before his name and picture had appeared on newspaper front pages for months.[4]

Although he was the central figure in the investigation that ensued, Bergman was only part of what Hess uncovered. By the spring, Hess had revealed a scandal that brought the criminal indictment of 200 nursing-home owners for stealing millions of dollars and billing taxpayers for personal items that included a Renoir painting, trips to Europe, college tuition, servants, and interior decorating. Eventually, his work also prompted a nationwide inquiry into this $10-billion industry, bringing U.S. Senate investigators and federal prosecutors swarming into New York.[5] The political influence of Bergman, Hess found, implicated the vice-president, Nelson Rockefeller, and a score of high-ranking New York officials, some of whom were indicted.[6] In addition, Hess' work brought about the return to the public of millions of dollars that had been falsely charged to taxpayers; caused the revamping of New York's nursing-home reimbursement system, and forced the state to establish a permanent prosecutor to deal with nursing-home violations.[7]

When Hess began his research that summer, cries for reform of the nursing-home industry were stirring. Mary Mendlesohn's book, *Tender Loving Greed* and Donn Pearce's *Dying in the Sun*, neither of which Hess had seen, had appeared in the spring, detailing abuses in the nation's nursing homes.[8] A U.S. Senate committee on nursing care, which eventually became involved in the New York City scandal, had held some public hearings on the problems, but nursing homes remained largely out of the spotlight—the hidden repository for America's old people.

By late fall, however, the spotlight on nursing homes came into focus. When Hess' exposés began to appear regularly in the *Times*, both the electronic and print media jumped on the story, besieging prosecutors, regulators, and nursing-home owners and patients for interviews and information. The journalistic "pack" was never more evident. Microphones and notepads in hand, reporters surrounded suspects in investigations, barely allowing them to leave crowded courtroom steps after judicial hearings. Bergman compared the media coverage to a Joseph McCarthy witch-hunt.[9] The confluence of media coverage—from the weekly *Village Voice* to suburban Long Island's *Newsday* to the local nightly newscasts—made the pressure on government to act relentless. Hess began alone, but in the end there was a powerful press presence that made money for investigations and audits easy to obtain from a legislature under pressure. Thus, while a toddling reform movement was under way when Hess began, by the time he finished, every reform group from the Gray Panthers to the American Jewish Council, from the New York State legislature to the U.S. Senate, was calling for change. Even the future mayor of New York City, Edward I. Koch and the future governor, Mario Cuomo, became participants in the investigations.[10]

The plight of the elderly was a topic that the turn-of-the-century muckrakers had ignored, mostly because when people became old, their families had borne the burden of care. By the 1970s, family care had, to a great degree, broken down, and the government played a key role as a catalyst in that change. The nursing-home industry was relatively new in 1974. The construction of large facilities where the elderly were brought, ostensibly for rehabilitation after illness but in reality to spend their final days, was spurred by the passage in 1965 of federal legislation. Unknowingly, Congress had created an incentive for nursing homes when it created Medicaid (medical aid for the poor) and Medicare (government insurance for the elderly), including in its coverage reimbursement for long-term care of the sick and poor in privately run institutions. Nursing homes changed from family enterprises to big businesses. The resulting industry was almost entirely a creation of public policy. Seeing the chance for government-subsidized health care, hundreds of businessmen, most with no experience in health care, built nursing homes which they owned and sometimes ran. The chance for profit, as Hess would demonstrate, was tremendous.[11]

The government had no idea that it had opened a Pandora's box, and it took nearly a decade for reformers to see what had been created. Hess knew from the *Times'* previous stories that poor conditions had been exposed before. "I didn't want to write just about people lying in their piss, dying of malnutrition," Hess recalled. "The key question was: Why wasn't the state enforcing the laws? I had to look at the interface of money and government. There was money to be made, large amounts of money."[12]

The crusading that John Hess and the *Times* did on behalf of the old people of New York, the sordid characters he wrote about, and the stinking messes and Monopoly games that he uncovered were more inglorious than anything that could have come out of a fiction writer's mind. The retelling of what Hess found is less crucial in my account than the journalistic lesson it teaches. An examination of Hess' stories and of his reporting techniques—here traced from October 1974 to June 1975—provides a textbook look at how a modern muckraking reporter used the canons of objectivity to provide provocative, constructive, and progressive journalism. The episode reveals the far-reaching power of the press, as well as the clear limits to the change that a journalist can precipitate.

Hess' reporting represents two essential but contrasting strains in American journalism: "neutral" and "participant." Hess' shifting back and forth between objective detachment and subjective involvement, the dual approach that allowed him to play a creative role in the ongoing social process, made him both observer and participant.[13] This activism allowed him not only to find what the Hutchins Commission described many years ago as the "truth behind the facts," but also to become the key force in the policy-making process.[14] Hess did this not by advocating solutions, but by using the conventional techniques of objective journalism in a creative and socially responsible fashion.

This objective but activist approach found in the work of Hess raises troubling questions for journalists and the public, however. Hess' need to follow the rules of objectivity, especially at the tradition-bound *New York Times,* and yet still keep his crusade alive—to be both neutral and activist—led to questionable ethical behavior in his relationship with his principal source. Moreover, at a crucial juncture in the policy-making process, the limits of objectivity robbed the audience of learning, in a forthright manner, about the conclusions that Hess had drawn after months of reporting. Objectivity forced him to cloak his opinions behind official sources, when he could find them. When the audience—and the policymakers—would have benefited from Hess' opinions and advice, objectivity and the *Times* would not allow it.

No reporter, of course, ever expects to be objective in a definitional sense. Reporters undoubtedly have belief systems, social positions, workday routines, and professional obligations, and all of these affect their selection and presentation of facts. When they embrace the concept of objectivity, however, it means simply that they have adopted routines that allow them, as Mitchell Stephens points out, "to reach the end of their stories each day without the feeling of having sinned." [15] The word objectivity needs to be understood as sociologist Gaye Tuchman describes it: a "strategic ritual"—a set of routines and unwritten rules that determines what is acceptable in conventional reporting. These rules, which are discussed in more detail in chapter 1, include assuming the role of an adversary but one who is politically neutral; using standardized formats for packaging stories; balancing competing opinions or sides in a story; and focusing on officially sanctioned events.[16] To maintain objectivity, the reporter generally needs to follow those rules. For many, the rules can be a straitjacket; for Hess, they were a key to success, even as they limited his eventual options for influencing the outcome of a public policy dispute.

UNRAVELING A SCANDAL

Objectivity and investigative journalism were both flourishing when John Hess began researching nursing homes. It had not always been that way at the *Times.* Since the turn of the century, the newspaper had helped develop the ideal of objectivity, and, even though various movements had arisen in the 1960s to challenge objectivity, the *Times* and the conventional press had doggedly held on to objective journalism, even as it provided more interpretation and analysis.[17] Its managing editor, A. M. Rosenthal, fearful that leftist students would infiltrate the reporting ranks of the *Times* and destroy its devotion to objectivity, demanded dispassionate reporting especially during America's turbulent protest movements. By 1974, however, the *Times* had also hired Seymour Hersh and Denny Walsh, both noted investigative reporters.[18] Thus,

Hess was working in a climate that encouraged investigative reporting and in a newsroom that demanded objectivity.

Hess' coverage began in the *Times* on October 7, with a story on page one, placed in the top left-hand columns of a Monday edition. "Care of Aged Poor a Growing Scandal" is an understated story, not a hard-hitting blockbuster. The writing throughout has a background quality. "Since Medicaid opened the Treasury spigot in 1967," he wrote in his lead paragraph, "growing numbers of Americans have placed their aged parents in nursing homes. The result has been a national scandal." The scandal that Hess' story revealed had been known to investigators for years: exorbitant profits; fraud; illegal kickbacks; food that, a dietitian told Hess, "a cat could not eat"; shortages of nurses; the looting of patient money; high salaries for unqualified administrators; discrimination against the poor; and a shortage of auditors. In the coming months Hess would follow up on every problem, and discover more.[19]

On day two, Hess' series was moved to page 48 as he explored the "fiscal ruses" that operators used to increase their profits above the 10 percent allowed by law. Hess interviewed "scores of witnesses" and scanned "the records of a dozen government agencies" to find the ways in which nursing-home operators made earnings reach as high as 40 percent. "A perusal of files going back 20 years produces a dreary litany of scandals, denunciations and allegations, nearly all of which faded with little result," Hess wrote. Hess focused on Eugene Hollander, who became the second central figure in criminal probes. Hollander, a survivor of a Nazi concentration camp, owned two large nursing homes in Manhattan, was a spokesman for the nursing-home industry, and was a pillar of the religious community. Like Bergman, his homes had been cited for years for deficient levels of nursing care and for consistent overcharges for supplies. Hess was barred from one of Hollander's homes, but Hollander did consent to an interview in which he called his homes "the cleanest in town." At the interview, he rolled up his sleeves to show Hess the scars left from his imprisonment in a concentration camp. Months later, prosecutors charged Hollander with billing taxpayers for a Renoir painting, for the interior decorating of his apartment, for dental work and liquors—a total of $1.4 million in fraud. Hollander pleaded guilty and pledged never again to operate a nursing home. On October 8, however, Hess was content to sketch out previous problems Hollander had with regulators to show that the government "has only the sketchiest data" on the true operation of nursing homes.[20]

Day three offered the most dramatic of Hess' four parts. "[A] two-month study by The *New York Times* confirms that what nursing-home operators here call the 'Syndicate' is alive and thriving, in this city and across the country," Hess wrote. The leading figure in this syndicate was Bernard Bergman, "a large benign man, rather resembling Sydney

Greenstreet." Hess was modest in his description of Bergman's nursing-home interests: he linked Bergman to twenty-six health facilities in seven states, a figure which would quadruple, and he placed his income at $19 million, an amount Bergman attested to in a document Hess read. For his part, Bergman said in an interview, "I happen to be involved in a couple of operations." It was many months before Bergman allowed Hess to interview him again. In December, when legislative commissions were seeking to interrogate him, Bergman fled the country. All the while, by telephone, Hess was in hot pursuit.[21]

On the final day of the opening articles, Hess explored alternatives to nursing homes. In a theme that emerged in the next ten months, Hess asserted that philanthropic or nonprofit homes were providing better care than profit-making ones. He backed this up with inspectors' eyewitness reports and clinical studies by health specialists. He avoided impressionistic reporting, relying instead on experts and written reports. The lure of describing patients in drug stupors, watching television in confusion, must have been great since, by all accounts, that was what life in many nursing homes was like. Hess avoided the easy way out; he never used anecdotal or feature material to expose poor patient care. All charges of patient abuse, throughout his reporting, came from official records or testimony. Along with the need for more nonprofit homes, Hess indicated, was need for increased home care. "For decades," Hess wrote, "officials have defended their failure to close the worst nursing homes on the ground that there was no place to send their patients." Authorities agreed that nursing-home patients could be kept at home, if Medicaid would pay. He ended by paraphrasing reformers who said money could be saved with home care and that care would be improved. His closing was cool and understated, but the response of the public was soon white-hot with indignation.[22]

PURSUING TWO THEMES—POLITICS AND PROFITS

Although Hess was no student of public opinion, he was aware that for state agencies to make the changes they wanted, an aroused public would be necessary. "Momentum would be crucial" if reform was to occur, he said.[23] Responses by two public officials kept the story alive. The state's attorney general said that the *Times*'s articles prompted him to begin an investigation into an "interlocking syndicate of operators."[24] A young, maverick member of the state legislature, Andrew Stein, said he also would begin public hearings into industry practices. Stein was a twenty-eight-year-old Democrat from the East Side of Manhattan, a wealthy district. His father, Jerry Finkelstein, was a millionaire Republican, a long-time friend of Nelson Rockefeller. The Finkelstein money had gotten Andrew elected. Thanks in part to his father's relationship with Rockefeller, Stein had become chairman of a temporary commission to investigate rising living costs, a mandate that Stein stretched to include nursing homes. Stein, however, wanted independence—from his father and from the political establishment.

Stein, known in New York as publicity hungry and ambitious, was often accused of government-by-press-release. He was famous for holding press conferences in dramatic locations, knowing that the lure of a good photograph would attract the press. Soon after Hess' articles appeared, a Stein aide told Hess that Stein was interested in pursuing the story. Hess was glad, for he knew that Stein had a large staff who would be able to follow leads that he could not, and he knew that Stein would have subpoena power. Stein could keep the story alive. Hess gave him the names of potential witnesses, names of sources, and areas that needed to be researched, laying out a blueprint for investigating the scandal. The Hess-Stein collaboration, as much as anything else, made a crusade possible.[25]

Over ten months, Hess kept the scandal before the public by varying the mix of stories he wrote and by unfolding a drama. Especially important was his good use of the "events" that were produced as a result of his exposé— government hearings and the release of reports and audits, for example. To these he added revelations from his own research which usually appeared when there was a lull in the official investigations. Each time Hess exposed a new aspect of nursing home corruption, the need for regulatory reform and criminal prosecution became more evident.

Between October and January, Hess, often working twelve hours a day for seven days a week, wrote thirty-two stories on nursing homes. Of those, twenty-three can be traced to government investigations that began because of his exposés. In thirteen of those stories, Hess either prompted the story with an inquiry or discovery, or used a piece of evidence to get a public official to react. Nine other stories were completely the result of Hess' research, in which the reporter turned up new—often dramatic—information.[26]

Just as an earlier muckraker, Lincoln Steffens, focused on the "invisible government" in his work, Hess, too, showed how hidden forces aided nursing-home entrepreneurs, and he revealed a connection between politics and money.[27] Hess uncovered how elected officials from both political parties had inquired repeatedly about the problems of nursing-home owners. The same officials had received campaign contributions and payments for nonlegislative work from nursing-home owners; in return, the owners were aided by the officials. Hess' source: state documents on which notations were scribbled. The callers included the three most powerful elected legislators in the state and a confidante of Nelson Rockefeller.[28] In a humorous story, Hess chronicled how the state had wrested regulatory authority over nursing homes away from the city. "Nobody," Hess wrote, "cares to acknowledge paternity" of the relevant legislation. Enter the "invisible government" in the person of Charles Sigety, a nursing-home owner who was a former deputy attorney general and aide to U.S. Senator Jacob Javits. The legislation was Sigety's creation, a behind-the-scenes way to get city inspectors off his back.[29] Concerning money, Hess used public records to document that salaries for the owners were enormous ($158,000 for Hollander), that no-show jobs were rampant, and that taxpayers were systematically being billed for luxury items.[30]

Despite success in uncovering the scandal, Hess seemed to despair in early December. "A mood of helplessness and frustration pervades a corps of civil servants whose job is to assure decent care . . . and block looting of Medicaid funds," Hess wrote.[31] Part of Hess' despair came from his problems with the *Times'* city desk. He felt that the editors were blocking and underplaying his stories. Once, he had to threaten to resign if a story was not published. Fearing that the investigations would fail, Hess turned to another reporter, Jack Newfield, a well-known writer for the weekly *Village Voice*. Hess, according to Newfield, told him the following: "Those bastards at the *Times* are cutting my stories and burying them. . . . They've held up my last piece for a week. But, believe me, Bergman is the worst. And he's going to get away with everything, unless someone like you picks up the story." Newfield did; he wrote fifteen stories on nursing homes over the coming months, and he traded information and documents with Hess. "Our mutual objective," Newfield said, "was exposure and reform." If Newfield's account is to be believed, it would seem that he not only traded information with Hess, but that he also used some of the exact words that Hess was giving him. In a December 23 piece in the *Voice*, Newfield wrote, "Bernard Bergman . . . is the worst. He is the worst because he is the most respectable. And he has gotten away with it all." This might have been Newfield's writing, but the words were Hess'.[32]

By December, much of the New York City press corps was beginning to follow the nursing-home story. At some hearings and press conferences, as many as fifty reporters covered the events.[33] Bergman and Hess were the central players in the scandal—one in public and the other behind the scenes. In late November, the state ordered Bergman's Towers Nursing Home in Manhattan to close; three days later, Hess reported "no-show jobs" held by Bergman and his wife. The next day Bergman left the country when a summons to appear before investigators was tacked on the door of his Manhattan apartment. On December 5 a state audit (leaked to Hess) revealed that Bergman had charged taxpayers for a new car, parking tickets, and liquor. By telephone Hess followed Bergman as he traveled in the Mideast and Europe. A Bergman

lawyer quipped at a hearing that if investigators wanted to locate Bergman, they should read the *Times*.[34] By late December, demands were
mounting for an independent special prosecutor to take over for the
attorney general who, a confidential memorandum given to Hess
showed, had been urged by associates to go easy on Bergman. "All hell
may break loose" if Bergman is prosecuted, the memo said. Hess' activist
reporting had indicated that only an independent counsel could be
trusted. Hess, the objective journalist, could not reach such a conclusion
in print, however. Newfield at the *Village Voice* had no such limitation.
After writing a sensational story about Bergman's possible links to organized crime, Newfield concluded that "the only way to get to the
bottom of it is to appoint a Special Prosecutor."[35]

WATCHING THE REFORMERS

As 1975 began, New York State had to decide how to reform a publicly
funded health care system that was being bilked by private entrepreneurs. Hess was among those who wanted to see an end to profit making
in nursing-home care. It remained to be seen if his reporting of the reform
effort would lead to such a major restructuring. He knew, however, that
the rules of objectivity would not allow him to advocate such a position.

The *Times*' coverage of the scandal was extensive as it followed the
seventeen state and federal investigations. From January to July Hess
wrote nearly 100 stories. On some days the *Times* had four nursing
home–related stories. "I barely ever saw John in those days," recalled
Hess' wife, Karen.[36]

January was a dramatic month. First, on New Year's Day Hess revealed that in 1971 the state's attorney general and the two top leaders
of the state legislature had helped Bergman open a nursing home despite
the building's structural problems and Bergman's record of fraud. The
news came from a memorandum leaked to Hess from the files of a health
official.[37] Angered by the leak, the official released the entire contents
of his nursing-home files, a gold mine of memos which Hess began to
explore. The files revealed Bergman's meeting with Rockefeller's secretary and with Rockefeller's successor as governor.[38] The files provided
the smoking guns, documentary proof of what Hess had implied in his
October opening.

In his first official act as governor, Hugh Carey appointed a nursing-
home commission to devise legislative remedies and a special prosecutor. At this point, the U.S. Senate directed Bergman to testify about
his nursing homes. In an interview with a weekly newspaper, Bergman,
just returned from Europe, declared, "Only God in heaven knows that
I am not guilty." Before the hearing, Hess used material he had gathered
for months to write a profile of Bergman. He portrayed Bergman as

philanthropist and pillar of the religious community, but also as a deceitful, shrewd businessman.[39] Ten days before, Bergman had filed a $1-million defamation lawsuit against Hess and the *Times*.[40]

In dramatic testimony on January 22 in a crowded, ornate hearing room in lower Manhattan, Bergman said the charges were "baseless and false . . . all a big lie." He compared the hearing to a Joseph McCarthy witch-hunt and said that the nursing-home industry was not profitable. He named the *Times* and the *Voice* as publications that were concerned only with headlines and profit, not the truth. The audience laughed and hissed as Bergman's lawyers clashed with the committee's counsel. The story was placed on page one of all the city's newspapers.[41] In the next day's *Times*, Hess challenged Bergman's testimony; he quoted state documents that showed Bergman to be worth $24 million. "It was nothing personal. The guy just lied," Hess said many years later. "I had the facts and I knew the facts were different from Bergman's testimony."[42] Bergman refused on subsequent occasions to testify in public. The Senate hearing was a turning point in Hess' coverage. He stopped pursuing Bergman and turned, first, to a chronicle of the various hearings and pronouncements taking place and, second, to the matter of what type of reform should occur.

THE REPORTER'S TECHNIQUES

From the outset of his crusade, Hess was keenly aware that objectivity imposed limitations on a reporter. "Newfield at the *Village Voice* could get away with things I couldn't," Hess said, referring to the flexibility of the alternative weekly. If Hess had drawn any personal conclusions about Bergman, he "never said so in writing. Newfield, on the other hand, could write, "In my lifetime I have never encountered anyone as rotten as Bernard Bergman."[43] But since, as two former reporters have noted, "objectivity builds credibility, making it easier to get investigations past nervous editors," Hess knew also that the rules of objectivity were useful. One of those rules is an adherence to standardized news formats.[44] To mount his crusade, Hess wrote stories that met common journalism formulas but included the activist elements of interpretation, background, and analysis.

Hess' stories can be divided into seven different categories. First, he wrote ninety "breaking" news stories, including forty-four about events taking place—for example, government hearings, court cases, and visits to nursing homes by officials;[45] thirty-five stories based on statements from public officials or groups to form the basis for at least the lead of stories;[46] and eleven articles on official reports released by government agencies.[47] In a second category are Hess' investigative stories which often had no evident news peg. These twenty-five stories represent high-quality investigative journalism.[48] Third are the four follow-up or second-day stories in which Hess followed one day's story with related information. Fourth are the four advance stories that previewed a major upcoming event in the nursing-home probe.[49] Fifth are the four stories in which Hess used unidentified or anonymous sources to reveal new information. Sixth, three stories that the *Times* labeled "news analysis." Finally, two feature stories, both of which profiled nursing-home owners under investigation.[50]

Ostensibly, breaking stories are neutral, collected in whatever "news web" the press has developed. If, for example, a reporter covers a press conference, he reports what is announced. If he receives a government report, he writes about its contents. The bulk of Hess' work revolved around these kinds of events. If he was to show the relationship of these events to the facts he had uncovered in his investigation, however, Hess needed to go beyond being a mere purveyor of other people's findings. Thus, he often used an event he covered for his news peg, beginning with a summary of the event, but then he added perspective. Many of his "event" stories contained more of the facts Hess gathered than the facts put forth by those who initiated the event.

When Mayor Abraham Beame asked that New York City be given authority to inspect nursing homes, Hess used this as his lead three paragraphs. Hess then described in detail how the city had lost its authority and why, in the end, city inspection power would not change regulation. Beame's statement, which Hess prompted at an exclusive interview, provided a news peg for Hess to write the story, and a way for him to get his independent findings into the newspaper.[51]

When officials announced they were investigating Bergman's influence in New Jersey's nursing homes, Hess wrote a long story, based on his research into New Jersey health files, to show Bergman's political connections across the river from New York.[52] Again, the official comments provided the news peg. When state officials inspected a Bergman nursing home in 1975, Hess used the event to show how the home was originally built without proper approvals and how Bergman used political influence to get it opened. The background and detail in this story could have been provided only by a reporter with many months on a "beat"—and by one who was willing to look past official statements. Hess' events coverage shows an added dimension: event coverage plus independent research and background—the objective and activist reporter.[53]

Hess used events in other activist ways. He wrote stories before an event—"advance" stories—and soon after events—"follow-up" stories. In this way not only did he build drama, but he also focused the key questions and got his findings before the public and policymakers. An impressive advance story, for example, appeared the day before Bergman testified before the U.S. Senate. In a profile he had compiled since the summer, he traced Bergman's career via interviews and public documents. He showed how over two decades scandal had brushed Bergman as he built his profitable empire.[54] Hess' reporting of Bergman's public testimony, on the other hand, was the epitome of a "straight" news account—no activism, simply clear coverage of what Bergman said.[55]

Because Hess felt Bergman had been treated gently by the Senate questioners and that, in fact, he had lied under oath, Hess followed the hearing with a story that challenged Bergman's assertions. Hess combed state files to find Bergman statements on his net worth. He cited Bergman's public comments that he "was not a poor man, but not a millionaire," and then he recounted how he had filed documents putting his net worth at $24 million. Hess interviewed bankers who said they had stopped giving loans to Bergman because bank charters forbid loans to people with assets worth more than $48 million. Hess never had to say that Bergman's testimony was a lie; public documents and interviews showed it.[56] The coverage of the climactic Bergman testimony shows how Hess could be objective in the traditional sense, yet still effectively call Bergman a liar—a use of objectivity's rules to achieve an end.

Event stories may have dominated Hess' coverage, but his investigative stories called for the most skill. A simple formula produced them: he combined the reading of public documents, the bread and butter for a reporter, with his own interviews. This formula mirrors the conclusion reached by Mark Fishman when he investigated how reporters "manufacture the news." To construct a news account that is not likely to be challenged by editors or the public, Fishman found the journalist must rely, first, on documents in agency files and, second, on a competent source, usually a high-ranking bureaucrat.[57] This combination meets the criterion for objective reporting, yet, the result is a story that has been produced by various subjective judgments, an activism born of critical thinking and hard work.

In his story on how elected officials had helped nursing-home owners, for example, Hess read files to see which officials had called the health department on behalf of nursing-home owners; he then read public election reports to see if those officials had received contributions from nursing home owners; and finally he called the elected officials to get responses.[58] By using a strategic ritual of objectivity, the activist reporter pieced together the connection of money and politics. In a story on salaries received by nursing-home owners, Hess read public reports on ninety-two homes and interviewed owners and regulators. He showed that huge salaries were being doled out to entrepreneurs who often did not show up for work.[59] The same formula worked for Hess in a story on how Bergman made $150,000 by hiding his relationship with a business partner. Hess used U.S. Securities and Exchange Commission files to detail a Bergman partnership with a man he had told auditors he did not know. State files revealed to Hess that the same partner ran two Bergman-owned nursing homes. Even Bergman's lawyer, when confronted by Hess, said the relationship was different from what Bergman had said.[60]

Perhaps Hess' most dogged pursuit of a story dealt with one public document—a fifteen-year-old report—about which he wrote five stories. Issued in 1960 by the city's investigation commissioner, the report charged that nursing home owners in New York City had criminally defrauded taxpayers. The report was turned over to the Manhattan district attorney for criminal prosecution. No one was charged with crimes; no money was recovered; and the nursing-home owners, in fact, received raises in their rates. The Manhattan district attorney told Hess there was no record that the report was ever received.[61] Hess first referred to the report in his October articles. In December he finally got a copy of the report and wrote about how the owners accused in 1960 were still operating nursing homes. In January, two days before Bergman testified to the Senate, Hess wrote about the allegations made in the report in 1960 against Bergman. In February, a state commission held a hearing on the report, and Hess used this as his news peg to trace the report's path. Hess felt that someone had purposely misplaced the report, but he could not prove this, and he did not write it. What his activist use of one report did, however, was to raise a key question: would the owners accused fifteen years ago get away unscathed again?[62]

Hess' boldest investigative technique came late in the spring when the scandal was nearing its conclusion. Hess did his own "audit," inspecting ten nursing-home ledgers that were in public files. He found profits had increased by twenty percent. State officials vowed the next day to reclaim the excess profits. Hess had become so knowledgeable about the complex Medicaid system that the state's special prosecutor once referred a reporter's question to Hess at a press conference.[63]

Although Hess often combined activism and neutrality, at times he made judgments that stories had to be written "straight," in the traditional objective style. "The news tale shall be told plainly with no obvious straining for effects," wrote the author of a journalism textbook in 1940.[64] Hess did this effectively. When Bergman was formally charged after months of publicity, Hess wrote, "Bernard Bergman, the central figure in nursing home investigations since last October, was indicted by federal and state grand juries yesterday on charges of stealing $1.2 million from Medicaid."[65] No gloating, just crisp, clear sentences—textbook journalism. Similarly, in May the state decided that Eugene Hollander was unfit to run a nursing home. "Members of the state Public Health Council," Hess wrote, "read in silence yesterday a report on Eugene

Hollander's nursing homes, then unanimously recommended that he be put out of business."[66]

Seeking the other side in any story is basic in fair reporting and an important attribute of objective journalism. Hess was diligent but also activist in balancing his stories. Many of the people involved in the scandal tried to avoid him. Hollander barred Hess from his nursing home, and Hess printed it. When Bergman fled the country as the scandal's tempo quickened in early January, Hess pursued him by telephone. Once, Hess got Bergman, then in Jerusalem, to respond to charges, but subsequently Bergman's relatives refused to bring him to the telephone.[67]

On some occasions, when sources were unavailable, Hess went to the homes of people he wished to interview. Bergman's accountant could not be located by investigators, so Hess went to his Bronx home, where Hess had been told that the accountant had been regularly picking up mail. Daniel Chill, a lawyer for a top state official who was also a lawyer for Bergman, was said to be on vacation, but Hess wrote, "Chill was seen in Albany yesterday but could not be reached for comment." The inference was always clear: people were hiding from the reporter.[68] Not content with simply balancing sides, Hess at times got responses to responses. When Stein accused the state's most powerful Democrat, Stanley Steingut, of blocking his investigation, Steingut told Hess that the charge was "an insult to my integrity." Steingut denied the charge, and Hess went back to Stein who said, "Will he say that under oath?"[69] Even in being objective, Hess could be activist.

INFLUENCING THE OUTCOME

During the ten months that New York's nursing home scandal unfolded, there were two turning points. The first came after Hess wrote his opening series of articles. Hess knew that someone had to respond to his exposé to, first, investigate the illegalities and, second, to give him the news pegs around which to build a crusade. The most important response came from Andrew Stein, who is today the New York City Council president. In the ensuing months, Hess worked closely with Stein, quoting him often and feeding him information.

Some editors at the *Times* were unhappy at the reporter-source relationship that developed between Stein and Hess, and they questioned whether a reporter should have so much influence over events.[70] Years later, Hess scoffed at such an attitude, saying he fully encouraged Stein's investigation. The relationship between the two may be evident from Stein's first public comments on the scandal. On October 31, Hess wrote about the "giant Monopoly game" that was taking place in real estate transfers of nursing homes. Four days later, Stein was prominently quoted as denouncing "a vast Monopoly game" in the industry. Hess cannot recall if such similarities in language were a coincidence, but he concedes that at times he "set on Stein" to pursue certain leads.[71] At least once, however, his close relationship with Stein backfired.

Hess had told Stein's staff about a nursing-home owner who was willing to talk about how an association which represented nursing homes had covered up abuses. The owner had quit the association rather than cooperate. The night before the owner was to testify, a Stein aide leaked details of the testimony to a tabloid daily, the *New York Post*, which headlined it in its next day's edition. Hess had been scooped on his own story, which he said he didn't mind because headlines like those on the *Post* added to the momentum the crusade needed.[72]

The second turning point came in late January, soon after Bergman testified before a senate committee. A commission appointed by New York's governor was beginning to explore alternatives. A clue to the direction in which Hess wanted to see changes go can be seen in a January 12 story he wrote for the *Times'* "Week in Review," a section that recaps the week's events each Sunday. In it, the reporter usually has more room for interpretation, and Hess used that room: "Many in the industry believe that so long as it is operated for profit it will generate abuses and corruption. The problem is to replace a system that relegated the elderly to commercial depositories . . . with a system of dignified care."[73] In all likelihood, Hess' bias was coming through in this story. In his news stories, he was more careful and he allowed others to suggest changes. As a sociologist points out, the objective reporter "may remove his opinion from the story by getting others to say what he himself thinks."[74] Thus, Stein, who either agreed with Hess or was prodded into agreeing by Hess, was often quoted on the need to eliminate profit.

On February 26, in a *Times* story that Hess did not write, Stein declared, "Our elderly deserve institutions which seek to provide quality care, not which provide only profit for unscrupulous real estate investors." This was, in essence, the position of Hess. On nine occasions over the next four months, Stein and others urged that profit be eliminated. On March 7, in a Hess story, Stein said, "The system will have to change, because as long as there is profit in the system, the Bergmans et al will be able to beat it." A week later, Stein offered, "My feeling is that the only way to cut out fraud is to have a nonprofit system." Stein was not alone, of course, and Hess quoted Congressman Morris Udall who called for a gradual phaseout of profit-making homes.[75] Morris Abram, chairman of the special state investigating committee, said at a news conference that he hoped hearings would establish "whether or not there is a role for the profit motive."[76] The commission's hearings, although explosive, never took up the issue. In fact, two weeks after telling reporters that he would explore this key issue, Abram had already resolved it. In a letter to Governor Carey, Abram said there were no "simple panaceas," but it was clear, he wrote, that the voluntary sector could not take over the work of proprietary sector. Hess seized on this part of Abram's letter and led his story with it.[77]

Three days later, events gave Hess a chance to focus the debate further. A New York City senior citizens group declared that a nonprofit nursing-home system and expanded home support were needed; witnesses at a legislative hearing also called for expanded home care by nonprofit agencies; and Stein toured centers for the elderly campaigning for a phaseout of profit-making homes.[78] What was shaping up—partly by Hess' creation—was a battle between Stein and Abram. Stein criticized Abram's legislative proposals, saying they did not get to "the cause of the abuses, the profit motive." Two weeks later, Hess quoted Stein making the same point.[79] Stein got in one final criticism of Abram in his commission's final report which concluded that the proprietary nursing-home industry is "so riddled with corruption that it may not be capable of complete reform. . . . We cannot and must not continue to place the lives of the elderly under the domination of a proprietary system."[80] Abram had the final say. He imposed new regulations even while conceding that the rules could be circumvented. "It would not surprise me," Abram told Hess, "if we need another investigation in 10 or 15 years." Hess wrote a year later that "the structure of the industry remained what it was, and the cast of characters is only slightly different."[81] The profiteers stayed in control.

OBJECTIVITY'S DILEMMA

At the two key junctures in the nursing home saga, Hess attempted to influence the outcome by using Andrew Stein, a source over which he undoubtedly had some control. Was it ethical for a reporter to be so close to a source that he could influence what the source does and says, and then to turn around and report that source's deeds and words? There is a very fine line between a reporter's prompting a source to say what the reporter needs, and the source's initiating the news for a story. As Herbert Strentz points out, reporters often disclose their opinions, views, and expectations to sources and at times share information. Bruce Swain says the key to trading information, however, is to do so and yet not compromise independence.[82] This form of activist journalism does have dangerous possibilities, a danger created by the rules of objectivity. If the muckraker does not have a reform movement behind him, his reporting possibilities are limited. Reporters cannot say what they want to see happen; they are limited under the rules of objectivity to reporting what others want or say or do. Privately, Hess was supplying information to would-be reformers (or at the very least suggesting where that information could be found) and then publicly writing about what they found. He needed to do this to mount the crusade.

For example, on November 21, Stein, accompanied by Hess, visited a Bergman nursing home in Manhattan. Hess reported the visit and wrote that the facility had had the same violations of regulations for seventeen years, that its operator was drawing another salary at another Bergman home, and that it had been the subject of twenty-nine lease and mortgage transfers over those seventeen years. All these facts were available in public documents. Hess did not need Stein to write this seventeen-paragraph story which contained only five paragraphs attributed to Stein. The rest was based on Hess' research. The Stein visit, to a home that Hess said he had visited when he began his investigation, gave Hess a news peg. Without the Stein visit, the *Times'* city desk might have blocked or killed Hess' story since the visit came about the time that Hess told Newfield that the desk was blocking his crusade. Because of the rules of objectivity, Hess needed Stein just to get into the paper.[83]

Was it unethical for Hess to use Stein in this fashion? Only perhaps if there was a quid pro quo—if Hess promised Stein publicity if he visited the nursing home—or if the material eventually disclosed by the source was unreliable. Then certainly it should never have been used. But reporters always have the problem of trying to ascertain whether the information given by a source is credible. In the end, Hess' reporting of Stein's findings held up under close scrutiny. The indictments brought by a special prosecutor and the conclusions of the Abram Commission provided confirmation. Do the ends then justify the means? Not always, but in this case, with a careful veteran reporter whose stories had to be processed by a series of editors (albeit editors who were unaware of his relationship with Stein), there was no breach of journalistic ethics. Where the line between reporter and source should be drawn, however, remains problematic.

A more troubling aspect of this case was Hess' having to resort to using Stein to advocate the elmination of profit. Here was John L. Hess, a trustworthy and veteran reporter, who had reported the scandal for ten months. He had become an expert on the nursing-home industry. Yet, when the time came for a solution to be discussed, he was unable to either advocate or strongly urge a solution. Even the *Times'* "news analysis" format would not allow Hess to propose a solution. In that format he was still limited to balancing alternatives suggested by others. How could he objectively continue to report if he had taken a side? At least that is the thinking. So, Hess was limited to reporting what others said—Abram for reform; Stein for the elimination of profit—and the public would then have to pick a solution.

The rationale behind objectivity lies in the libertarian concept of a "marketplace of ideas," where rational individuals form their beliefs based on their access to ideas and information.[84] The marketplace concept is only a romantic notion when one considers that Hess' facts had been displayed over ten months. What is shown in November is largely forgotten in July. Objective reporting does not allow for a lengthy repetition of what was reported before; it is episodic and fragmented, and the necessary connections to previous episodes are often lost. In American journalism, James Carey wrote, "each story starts anew as if no one ever touched the subject before."[85] In the spring of 1975 the public needed more than stories that were the sum of opposing viewpoints. They needed to be told what one reporter had found over ten months of constant research and interviewing, research that showed a historical pattern and led to certain logical conclusions. The public needed Hess' conclusions, but objectivity—even as practiced by an activist reporter— would not allow reportorial conclusions. Hess did all he could but it was, as he said, not all he hoped for.

A NEED FOR MORE THAN FACTS

When John Hess began his investigation in 1974, the problems of old people in nursing homes were not on the public's agenda. By the time Hess finished exposing corruption in the spring of 1975, both the public and the government were clamoring for change. Hess was a catalyst, prompting reform to begin and then reporting on the efforts of the reformers. This marriage of reform and journalism occurred only because Hess used the credibility and rules of objectivity in an activist fashion to reveal corruption and to force a government response.

Journalistic objectivity and activism would seem to be at odds with each other. One implies a neutral stance—the reporter as an observer, not a participant, one who watches events and newsmakers but who does not consciously seek to influence or make the news. The activist, on the other hand, is involved in the social process, cajoling, prodding, and perhaps advocating. Hess had practiced objective journalism for many years with the Associated Press, United Press International, and the *Times*. Yet, he developed a great distaste for its limitations, calling objectivity "this subversive thing in American journalism." Nonetheless, he used objectivity to mount his crusade, but he was activist in ways that neutrality would normally forbid. His tactics, especially his close relationship with a key source, led to tension with the Times' city desk. Hess was able to continue his coverage only because—thanks in part to Hess' activism—competing media had begun to follow the controversy.[86] After the nursing–home scandal ended, Hess fought even more with his editors when he attempted to pursue corruption in other areas of city government. Eventually, embittered, he resigned from the *Times* and became a critic of the newspaper.[87]

Objectivity, as it is used today in American journalism, is not, as one author suggests, "obsolete."[88] Muckraking journalists like Hess know that it serves an important purpose, ensuring contrasting viewpoints and contributing to a wide open marketplace of ideas. The fact that objectivity forces reporters to maintain some measure of political neutrality ensures that the public receives reasonably unbiased news and information.[89] Objectivity, however, also has a stifling effect on the reporter's ability to show the truth behind the facts.

The most frustrating flaw in objectivity is its inflexibility concerning reporter opinion. When Hess was exploring reform solutions in 1975, he was unable to state his conclusions in a forthright manner. Louis Hawpe, managing editor of the *Louisville Courier-Journal*, says, "Too often, American journalism . . . relies too much on the facts provided by others and too little on the conclusions journalists should draw from them." What Hawpe calls "sterile, objective journalism" needs to give way to activist but responsible journalism. The journalist needs to be able to deliver conclusions drawn from what Hawpe calls "thorough, dispassionate, neutral inquiry."[90] Hess could not do that in the *New York Times* or, one suspects, in most American newspapers which practice objectivity. Perhaps editorial writers or columnists could, but they did not have Hess' insight.

At some point in the scandal—most likely in April, when solutions were being debated—Hess should have been able to deliver a commentary on what he had found and what he believed should happen next. This, of course, would have compromised his objectivity. The reality, however, was that his objectivity had already been compromised; only the appearance of objectivity remained. Hess should have been able to either remain on the story as a commentator or have been allowed to go back and forth between commentary and straight reporting. Could not a reporter schooled in the rules of objectivity do this? Hess could have. If the appearance of bias made such a tactic improper, then a new reporter could have written about subsequent developments, with Hess remaining an activist commentator-reporter. The press need not discard the rules of objectivity, but new ways must be found to allow reporters more flexibility and to give the audience a wider range of informed opinion.

NOTES

1. John Hess worked for the Associated Press and United Press International before coming to New York where he worked with the *Post* and the *News* before

joining the *Times*. After leaving the *Times* in 1976, he became a syndicated columnist and then a television commentator on WNEW in New York City.

His fourth book, written with his wife, Karen, was *The Taste of America* (New York, 1977). His other books are *The Case for DeGaulle: An American Viewpoint* (New York, 1968); *The Grand Acquisitors* (Boston, 1974); and *Vanishing France* (New York, 1975).

2. Charles J. Hynes, deputy attorney general, *Third Annual Report* (New York, 1978), prologue.

3. Interview with Hess, August 27, 1986, at his Manhattan apartment. Hess was nominated for the Pulitzer Prize in local special reporting. It was won instead by the *Indianapolis Star* for articles on police corruption. Historian Bruce Vladeck calls the New York City scandal the nation's worst; see *Unloving Care: The Nursing Home Tragedy* (New York, 1980), 4.

4. Bernard Bergman's political influence is detailed in a report by the Moreland Act Commission on Nursing Homes and Residential Facilities, *Political Influence and Political Accountability: One Foot in the Door* (New York, 1975). The charges against Bergman are detailed in Hess, "Bergman and Son Are Indicted Here in Medicaid Fraud," *New York Times*, 6 August 1975, pp. 1, 70. (Unless otherwise noted, all of Hess' cited articles were published in the *New York Times*.) The "Bergman syndrome" is discussed by Jack Newfield, "The Rabbi Exposed and Anti-Semitism," in *The Education of Jack Newfield* (New York, 1984).

5. Nationwide, 1.3 million people live in 23,000 nursing homes. The national scandal is discussed in Robert D. McFadden, "Nursing Home Abuses Spur Action Nationwide," *New York Times*, 31 March 1975, pp. 1, 19. This chapter is not about the effects of Hess' work; nevertheless, as one New York official said, "[T]he chance for adoption of reform was enhanced . . . by the *New York Times* investigation of the nursing home industry." Hess, "State Denounces Nursing Home Deals as Costing State Medicaid Millions," 31 October 1975, p. 45.

6. Nelson Rockefeller was exonerated, but he and other officials were harshly criticized, and some were charged with crimes. See Moreland Commission, *Political Influence*.

7. As of October 1986, the New York State Special Prosecutor for nursing homes had completed 192 cases involving nursing-home fraud and had convicted 163 persons. Eighteen cases were dismissed, and eleven persons were acquitted. Telephone interview, spokesman for the New York State deputy attorney general for nursing homes. There is no exact accounting of money recovered; however, one nursing-home owner alone, Bernard Bergman, repaid $2.5 million. It took New York years to recover the money. Former U.S. Attorney General Ramsay Clark was appointed to oversee Bergman's finances. Some defrauded money was not recoverable. See, for example, Hess, "Medicaid Funds Called Lost on Nursing Homes," 13 April 1975, p. 55; "Medicare Terms 988 Overpayments 'Bad Debts,' " 7 May 1975, p. 36; "Upstate Nursing Home Foiled Prosecution for Double Billing," 22 June 1975, p. 32.

Moreland Act Commission on Nursing Homes, *Regulating Nursing Home Care: The Paper Tigers* (New York, 1975); and *Reimbursement of Nursing Home Costs: Pruning the Money Tree* (New York 1976) detail the new regulations.

Fourteen years after the original scandal, the prosecutor was still active. His jurisdiction was expanded in 1977 to include possible fraud in hospitals.

8. Mary Mendelsohn, *Tender Loving Greed* (New York, 1974); and Donn Pearce, *Dying in the Sun* (New York, 1974).

9. Hess, "Bergman Labels All Allegations as False," 22 January 1975, pp. 1, 44.

10. Edward Koch, then a congressman, wanted a special prosecutor soon after the scandal emerged. Mario Cuomo, then lieutenant governor, advised Governor Hugh Carey to appoint a special prosecutor when the scandal widened in 1975. Hess, "18 State Congressmen Ask Carey to Start a Nursing Home Inquiry," 18 December 1975, pp. 1, 34.

11. Frank E. Moss and Val Halamandaris, *Too Old Too Sick Too Bad/Nursing Homes in America* (Germantown, Md., 1977), 6. For a history of public reimbursment to nursing homes, see Paul L. Grimaldi, *Medicaid Reimbursement of Nursing-Home Care* (Washington, D.C., 1982) and Robert Stevens and Rosemary Stevens, *Welfare Medicine in America: A Case Study of Medicaid* (New York, 1974). In New York 70 percent of the nursing homes are operated for profit. See Hess on nursing home profits, "Nursing Homes Use a Variety of Fiscal Ruses to Lift Profits above the 10% Allowed by Law," 8 October 1974, p. 48; "A Cabal of Real Estate Deals Adds to Nursing Home Profits, Stein Says," 5 November 1974, p. 39; "Big Profits Shown in Nursing Homes," 3 December 1974, p. 37; "Queens Nursing Home's Profit Studied," 6 December 1974, p. 43; "Bergman Aides Predicted High Nursing Home Profit," 6 February 1975, p. 30. The Moreland Commission found "extraordinary profits were reaped by nursing home entrepreneurs through misrepresenting costs," *Long Term Care Regulation: Past Lapses, Future Prospects, a Summary Report*. (New York, 1976), 6.

12. Interview with Hess.

13. The two strains in journalism are discussed in Bernard C. Cohen, "The Reporter's Conceptions of His Roles," in *The Press and Foreign Policy* (Princeton, N.J., 1963), 19–38. The debate over which strain is correct is noted in John W. C. Johnstone, Edward J. Slawski, and William W. Bowman, *The News People: A Sociological Portrait of American Journalists and Their Work* (Urbana, Ill., 1976), 114. Various authors point out that the public affairs reporter is often a participant. See Dan D. Nimmo, *Newsgathering in Washington* (New York, 1964); Delmar D. Dunn, *Public Officials and the Press* (Reading, Pa., 1969), 12–15; and Penn Kimball, "Journalism: Art, Craft, or Profession?" in *The Professions in America*, ed. Kenneth S. Lynn (Boston, 1965), 249.

14. Commission on Freedom of the Press as quoted in Fred S. Siebert, Theodore Peterson, and Wilbur Schramm, *Four Theories of the Press* (Urbana, Ill., 1956), 87.

15. Mitchell Stephens, *A History of News: From the Drum to the Satellite* (New York, 1988), 266.

16. Gaye Tuchman, "Objectivity as a Strategic Ritual: An Examination of a Newspaperman's Notion of Objectivity," *American Journal of Sociology* 77, 4 (January 1972): 660–79. This article was later expanded into Tuchman, *Making News: A Study in the Construction of Reality* (New York, 1978). See footnotes 33–37 in chapter 1 of this book.

17. The history of objectivity is traced in Michael Schudson, *Discovering the News* (New York, 1978). For further references, see footnotes 33–37 in chapter 1 of this book. Journalists today embrace both the "objective" and "participant" approaches to journalism, conclude Johnstone, Slawski, and Bowman, *The News People*, 114–20. Movements which challenged objectivity included the "new journalism" and "advocacy journalism." These are described in Everette E. Dennis and William L. Rivers, eds., *Other Voices: The New Journalism in America* (San Francisco, 1974); and Robert J. Glessing, *The Underground Press in America* (Bloomington, Ind., 1970). On the rise in interpretation, see Gerald Lanson and Mitchell Stephens, "Trust Me Journalism," *Washington Journalism Review* (November 1982): pp. 43–47.

18. Gay Talese, *The Kingdom and the Power* (New York, 1966), 60; and Meyer Berger, *The Story of the New York Times, 1861–1951* (New York, 1951), 107–8, 273. "The duty of every reporter and editor is to strive for as much objectivity as humanly possible," A. M. Rosenthal once said. See Joseph C. Goulden, *Fit to Print: A. M. Rosenthal and His Times* (Secaucus, N.J., 1988), 175–176. Leonard P. Downie, *The New Muckrakers* (Washington, D.C., 1976), 87–99, 259–61. On the *Times'* new-found zeal for investigation, see Robert B. Semple, Jr., "The Necessity of Conventional Journalism: A Blend of the Old and the New," in *Liberating the Media: The New Journalism*, ed. Charles C. Flippen (Washington, D.C., 1974), 89–90.

19. Hess, "Care of Aged Poor a Growing Scandal," 7 October 1974, pp. 1, 40.

20. Hess, "Nursing Homes Use a Variety of Fiscal Ruses to Lift Profits above the 10% Allowed by Law," 8 October 1974, p. 48. Hess, "Two Grand Juries Indict Hollander," 3 July 1975, pp. 1, 12.

21. Hess, "Nursing Homes Here Linked by Interlocking Leadership," 9 October 1974, p. 85. The charges against Bergman are detailed in Hess, "Bergman and Son Are Indicted Here in Medicaid Fraud," 6 August 1975, pp. 1, 70.

22. Hess, "Alternatives Seen to Nursing Homes for Aged Infirm," 10 October 1974, p. 42.

23. Interview with Hess.

24. Hess, "Two State Inquiries Ordered on Nursing Home Control," 17 October 1974, p. 45.

25. Interview with Hess and with two former aides to the legislator, Andrew Stein, who became president of the New York City Council.

26. In identifying Hess' stories by category, I will give only the date of publication. Full citations can be found in Robert Miraldi, "Muckraking and Objectivity: John L. Hess and the Nursing Home Scandal," *Journalism Monographs* 115 (August 1989). Government investigation stories: October 26, 31; November 5, 8, 14, 19, 22, 23, 25, 30; December 4, 5, 6, 7, 11, 13, 17, 18, 19, 21, 25, 27, 28. Hess' investigative stories: October 7, 8, 9, 21, 25; November 3, 12; December 2, 30.

27. Justin Kaplan, *Lincoln Steffens: A Biography* (New York, 1974), 103–79. Hess makes reference to the invisible government in "Honorable Mentions," *Columbia Journalism Review* (September-October 1978):57. Hess, "Little Noticed Law Curbs City's Nursing Home Role," 25 October 1974, p. 43 in which he shows the hidden role of a legislator-turned-nursing-home owner.

28. Hess, "Nursing Home Promoters Get Political Helping Hand," 21 October 1974, p. 23. Hess' findings are confirmed in Moreland Commission, *Political Influence*. Despite the Moreland Act Commission's attempt, the state legislature refused to approve legislation that would have barred legislators from appearing before state agencies on behalf of private clients. In 1987 such legislation was approved.

29. Hess, "Little Noticed Law Curbs City's Nursing Home Role," 25 October 1974, p. 43.

30. The importance of profit in health care was noted by Moss and Halamandaris, who said that some feel the nation's "supreme failure" is a "policy which emphasizes profit over people," *Too Old Too Sick Too Bad*, 138.

31. Hess, "Primary Result of Effort to Improve Nursing Homes Is Frustration," 12 December 1974, p. 94.

32. Hess' threat to resign, personal interview. The *Times* may have been reluctant to allow Hess to proceed because of charges being made that his articles were anti-Semitic. This is discussed in Pete Hamill, "Anti-Semitism and the Writer," *Village Voice*, 30 December 1974, pp. 12–13. Newfield, "The Rabbi Exposed and Anti-Semitism," in *The Education of Jack Newfield*, 11, 13, see note 4; and Newfield, "Is This the Meanest Man in New York?" *Village Voice*, 23 December 1974, p. 5.

33. At the time I was a reporter for the suburban daily newspaper, the *Staten Island Advance*. I covered the nursing-home scandal from October 1974 to the fall of 1975. In early November, my editor gave me a copy of a Hess story on a Staten Island nursing home which, in one year, had undergone seventeen changes of ownership, resulting in a huge increase in reimbursement. The editor told me to drop all other stories: "We've got to play catch up on nursing homes." For the next eight months, I wrote dozens of nursing-home stories. It was typical of what was happening in all the city's media.

34. Hess, "Towers Nursing Home, Scored as Unsafe, to Shut," 30 November 1974, p. 35; "Big Profits Shown in Nursing Homes," 3 December 1974, p. 37; "Reply Is Awaited on Nursing Homes," 4 December 1974, p. 17; "Towers Charged Medicaid for Liquors, Car, and Gifts," 5 December 1974, p. 51.

35. Hess, "State Aide Sought to Curb Home Inspections," 30 December 1974, pp. 1, 14. Newfield, "Is Bergman Laundering the Mob's Money?" *Village Voice*, 30 December 1974, p. 13.

36. The day after the appointment of a special prosecutor and an investigatory commission, the *Times* carried six stories related to the nursing-home scandal, including an editorial hailing the actions. On January 15, 1975, page 17 was filled with an entire page of nursing-home stories. On January 22, the day of Bergman's hearing before the U.S. Senate, the *Times* used Hess' hearing coverage on page 1, filled all of page 44 with stories on the hearing, and used a transcript of Bergman's statement on page 45. Hess' wife was present and participated when I interviewed him.

37. Hess," '71 Memo Reports 3 State Officials Backed Bergman," 1 January 1975, pp. 1, 75.

38. Two Hess stories resulted from the files. See "Lefkowitz Challenges Memo Linking Him to Bergman," 4 January 1975, p. 46; and "Files Detail Political Help in Bergman Medicaid Rise," 14 January 1975, p. 31.

39. Hess, "Opinions on Bergman as Diverse as His Background," 21 January 1975, p. 20.

40. The defamation lawsuit filed on January 10, 1975, charged that Hess, Assemblyman Stein, and an assistant state attorney general had conspired to deprive Bergman of his constitutional rights by an "unremitting barrage" of false reports to the public. The lawsuit was eventually dismissed by a federal judge as having no merit. Hess feared that if it went to trial he would be asked to reveal confidential sources of information.

41. See note 9.

42. Interview with Hess. Hess, "Bergman Certified Worth was Almost $24-million," 23 January 1975, pp. 1, 23.

43. Interview with Hess. Newfield, "Is This the Meanest Man in New York?" *Village Voice*, 23 December 1974, p. 5.

44. David A. Anderson and Peter Benjaminson, *Investigative Reporting* (Bloomington, Ind. 1976), 161. Lance Bennett, *News: The Politics of Illusion* (New York, 1983), 87; and Tuchman, "Objectivity as a Strategic Ritual," 669.

45. Full citations can be found in Miraldi, "Muckraking and Objectivity." See note 26. November 14, 22, 23, 25; December 13, 18, 21, 24, 1974; January 7, 10, 22; February 1, 5, 8, 14, 15, 16, 20; March 6, 13, 14, 19, 24, 26, 27, 29; April 12, 22, 25, 30; May 3, 8, 13, 15, 17, 31; June 3, 8, 17, 18, 24; July 3, 4; August 6, 1975.

46. October 17; November 8, 14, 19, 30; December 4, 17, 18, 19, 25, 28, 1974; January 3, 4, 5, 8, 13, 16; February 3, 4, 7, 12, 13, 19, 25, 28; March 4, 5, 7, 20, 21, 30; April 9; May 7; June 4, 11, 1975.

47. October 31; November 5; December 5, 6, 31, 1974; March 9, 28, 31; April 1, 13, 1975.

48. October 7, 8, 9, 10, 21, 25, 26: December 3, 20, 1974; January 6, 14, 15, 19, 21, 23; February 9, 10, 18, 21; April 14; May 23; June 22, 29; July 2, 10, 1975.

49. The follow-up stories appeared on October 17, December 7, 1974; January 23, May 24, 1975. The advance stories were published on December 24, 25, 27, 1974; June 13, 1975. Technically, advance stories do not constitute a story format.

50. The anonymous source stories were printed on December 30, 1974; January 1, 9; February 6, 1975. The analysis stories appeared on December 12, 1974; May 12, 1975; January 12, 1976; and the features, on January 21, February 9, 1975.

51. Hess, "City Urges the State to Return Control over Nursing Homes Here," 5 January 1975, p. 36.

52. Hess, "Jersey Votes for Inquiry on Nursing Home Industry," 7 January 1975, pp. 1, 23.

53. Hess, "Park Crescent Is Reinspected," 29 June 1975, p. 22.

54. Hess, "Opinions on Bergman as Diverse as His Background," 21 January 1975, p. 20; "Bergman Labels All Allegations as False," 22 January 1975, pp. 1, 14. A similar investigative profile is Hess, "Senate Traces Successful Career of Operator of Nursing Homes Here," 9 February 1975, p. 44.

55. Hess, "Bergman Labels All Allegations as Totally False," 22 January 1975, pp. 1, 44.

56. Hess, "Bergman Certified Worth Was Almost $24-million," 23 January 1975, pp. 1, 23.

57. Mark Fishman, *Manufacturing the News* (Austin, Tex. 1980), 85–100.

58. Hess, "Nursing Home Promoters Get Political Helping Hand," 21 October 1974, p. 23.

59. Hess, "Big Profits Shown in Nursing Homes," 3 December 1975, p. 37.

60. Hess, "Files Detail Political Help in Bergman Medicaid Rise," 14 January 1975, p. 31.

61. The Moreland Act Commission concluded that the Kaplan Report was delivered to the Manhattan district attorney who found that prosecutions were not possible because of weak regulations and poor bookkeeping. See commission report, *Political Influence*, 157.

62. The Kaplan Report stories include Hess, "Massive Nursing-Home Fraud Found Here in 1960," 19 January 1975, p. 38; "Stein to Question Wagner on '60 Report," 10 February 1975, pp. 1, 44; " '60 Nursing-Home Report Said to Cite Present Group," 21 February 1975, pp. 1, 36; "Wagner Defends Record on Homes," 6 March 1975, pp. 1, 53; "1962 Report Cited on Nursing Homes," 7 March 1975, pp. 1, 32. Hess' comment about the misplaced report, personal interview.

63. Hess, "Windfall Indicated for Nursing Homes," 23 May 1975, p. 1; "State Vows to Regain Nursing Home Excess Profits," 24 May 1975, p. 26. The author attended a press conference at the Manhattan office of Deputy Attorney General Charles J. Hynes when Hynes referred reporters to Hess for an answer.

64. George Fox Mott, ed., *Survey of Journalism* (New York, 1940), 49.

65. See note 19.

66. Hess, "Health Council Asks Ban on Hollander as the Operator of Any Nursing Home," 3 May 1975, p. 35.

67. Hess, "Nursing Homes Use a Variety of Fiscal Ruses to Lift Profits Above the 10% Allowed By Law," October 8, 1974, p. 48, and "Towers Charged Medicaid for Liquor, Car, and Gifts," December 5, 1974, p. 51.

68. Hess, "Towers Charged Medicaid for Liquor, Car and Gifts," 5 December 1974, p. 51.

69. See Francis X. Clines, "Stein-Steingut Clash Spurs Legislators to Study Rules," *New York Times*, 12 February 1974, p. 73.

70. Interview with two *Times* editors who requested anonymity.

71. Interview with Hess. Hess, "State Denounces Nursing-Home Deals as Costing State and Medicaid Millions," 31 October 1974, p. 45; and "A 'Cabal' of Real Estate Deals Adds to Nursing Home Profits," 5 November 1974, p. 39.

72. "Bergman May Refuse New Testimony," *New York Post*, 31 January 1975, p. 3; Hess, "Ex-Aide Says Association Hid Nursing Home Abuses," 1 February 1975, p. 16. The ex-aide, Nicholas Demisay, the operator of a nursing home on Staten Island, was later charged with Medicaid fraud.

73. Hess, "The Scandal of Care for the Old," January 12 1975, p. 6, sec. 4.

74. Tuchman, "Objectivity as a Strategic Ritual," 668.

75. The Stein comments appeared in Hess, "Stein for Phasing Out Profit-Making Nursing Homes," 26 February 1975, p. 22; "1962 Report Cited on Nursing Home," 7 March 1975, pp. 1, 32; and "State Will Begin Posting Nursing Home Deficiencies Monthly," 14 March 1975, p. 78. Udall's remarks: Hess, "Moreland Commission, in First Visit to Nursing Home, Finds Dingy Place," 19 March 1975, p. 94.

76. Hess, "Rockefeller Faces 2 State Inquiries," 24 March 1975, p. 32.

77. Hess, "Abram Denounces Failures on Aged," 9 April 1975, p. 30.

78. Hess, "Change Is Pressed on Nursing Homes," 12 April 1975, p. 31.

79. Hess, "Stein Criticizes Abram Unit Proposals," 4 May 1975, p. 39; "Reform Plans for Nursing Homes Scored," 17 May 1975, p. 31.

80. Hess, "Jury in Westchester Cites Nursing Home on Medicaid Fraud," 17 June 1975, pp. 1, 22.

81. Morris Abram of the Moreland Act Commission made this point to Hess in an interview, "Abram Denounces Failure on Aged," 9 April 1975, p. 30, and repeated it in a cover letter in Moreland Act Commission, *Long Term Care Regulation*. Hess, "Nursing Homes Show Progress," 12 January 1976, p. 27.

82. Herbert Strentz, *News Reporters and News Sources* (Ames, Iowa, 1978), 53. Bruce Swain, *Reporters' Ethics* (Ames, Iowa, 1978), 23–25.

83. Hess, "State Panel, in an Unannouced Visit to Nursing Home, Finds Violations," 22 November 1975, p. 78.

84. A good discussion of the "marketplace of ideas" concept is found in Thomas I. Emerson, *The System of Freedom of Expression* (New York, 1970). Theodore Peterson writes that objectivity makes it "easier for the rational reader to discover the truth." Fred S. Siebert, Theodore Peterson, and Wilbur Schramm, *Four Theories*, 88.

85. On news fragmentation, see Herbert Schiller, *The Mind Managers* (Boston, 1973), 24–29; and James Carey, "The Dark Continent of American Journalism," in *Reading the News*, eds. Robert Manoff and Michael Schudson (New York, 1986), 152.

86. In an interview, Hess said that some of the editors wanted him off the nursing-home story but that others felt he was needed to compete with the growing number of reporters who were following the story.

87. Hess was critical of the *Times* in Lanson and Stephens, "Trust Me Journalism," see note 22, and in "The Shame of the Urban Press," 273–76.

88. Anthony Smith, "Is Objectivity Obsolete?" *Columbia Journalism Review* (May/June 1980): 61–65.

89. Despite the merits of objectivity, it is under attack as conservative and reinforcing of the status quo. This view can be found in Tuchman, *Making News*; Bennett, *News*; and Todd Gitlin, *The Whole World Is Watching* (Berkeley, Calif., 1980).

90. Louis Hawpe, "Point-of-View Journalism," *Editor and Publisher* (September 8, 1984): 40.

6

Inching Society and Journalism Forward

The supermarket in the small Hudson Valley town of New Paltz was busy on this sunny morning in the summer of 1988. Saturday shoppers were loading their tidy, polished station wagons and vans with groceries. A large green bus, apparently an old school bus that had been spray-painted, stood out like a sore thumb as it made its way out of the parking lot toward a traffic light. Many of the bus' window were broken and covered with plywood. The rear of the bus sagged, dangerously so, it seemed. This bus was a jalopy.

The bus' occupants were women, children, and men, most of whom were black. It had carried migrant workers to the local department store to pick up some odds and ends. They were traveling in a bus that could have come straight out of "Harvest of Shame" and 1960. But this was 1988, ninety miles from New York City, in an affluent valley where farms and small towns nicely coexist and where families of farm laborers earn, on the average, $3,900 a year.

Not far from New Paltz is the Esopus Creek, a small body of water which is adjacent to a farm owned by a prominent Hudson Valley family. Each growing season, the family employs dozens of migrant workers to pick broccoli, asparagus, and corn. At lunchtime the workers huddle together on the flat land where the broccoli grows. On one weekday in July, after a morning of stooping, the workers took a lunch break on a small grassy knoll. They wore big floppy hats, and they ate what appeared to be sandwiches while a large container with some liquid in it was passed around.

No one smiled; no one talked. They sat silently; a few women wiped their brows. The image of Aileen King, standing in a Florida bean field in 1959, with her children remaining back at a run-down camp, was immediately conjured. Indeed, just a few miles from this pickin' field, at the camp where the laborers live during the growing season, their children were playing, unsupervised, in and around a gloomy, grey brick barracks. The children were alone, playing with empty cans that had recently been filled with poisonous pesticides. Despite what journalists and reformers had tried to do to change conditions, life for this underclass was still grim. The migrants receive the minimum wage of $3.35 an hour. They work sixty hours a week, but get paid no overtime. Families of four live in 10-by-15-foot rooms, and they share showers and toilets with other workers. "It's so hard that I really can't tell you," said Ollie Beamon, a thin woman who has worked on farms for forty years, and who, at sixty-one years of age, still packs 300 crates of corn a day.[1]

Although one is tempted to despair about the migrant condition, another image balances that perspective. Adjacent to a busy state highway near the State University of New York's campus at New Paltz, sits a small wooden sign: "Agricultural Child Care Center." Behind the sign is a comely little building, with blackboards, schoolrooms, books, and teachers. Outside are swings and slides and a wooden playground where children play on fall afternoons. This education center, an outgrowth of exposés by the press throughout the 1960s, funded mostly with federal money, is for the children of the migrant workers who come to the valley. I stopped there one afternoon and talked with the children who seemed no different from the ones who play at my daughter's school playground. Some of the children said they go to a few different schools during the year, but that this one in the Hudson Valley, with the big mountain in the background, was the nicest. In 1985 Matilda Cuomo, wife of the governor, came to visit the school, for it is a model apparently of what can be done for the migrant workers' children.[2] Score one for the forces of reform and activist journalism, cohorts—at least sometimes—in inching society forward.

"Policies change and broaden under pressure of conditions." So wrote Samuel Hopkins Adams in 1905.[3] He was referring to the changing position of the government, to Washington's new receptivity to the regulation of the patent medicine industry. As thousands of Americans choked down poisonous cures that they believed would restore their health, the government had done nothing but had allowed private profiteers to take home millions of dollars while people died. When Adams' exposés began to appear, not coincidentally before millions of citizens, the government finally moved, at least in part, toward eliminating dangerous ingredients and controlling frauds. The climate that created the "pressure of conditions" was caused by Adams' activism—his combination of digging out facts, exposing them in a readable fashion, and then suggesting, at times subtly and at other times directly, the kinds of reforms that would eliminate the problem. Adams' work, typical of so much of the best of muckraking, was, as Whitney Cross has observed, "a middle line between arid factuality on one side, and pure propaganda on the other."[4] Adams was not simply a passive observer of conditions; he was an active participant in the search for a solution. In fact, as historian Richard Hofstadter has noted, much of the success of reformers in the early part of the century was due to the carefully constructed and highly readable exposés of journalists. "To an extraordinary degree the work of the Progressive movement rested upon its journalism," said Hofstadter, who added that "the Progressive mind was characteristically a journalistic mind."[5]

To achieve his goal of cleaning up an industry, Adams, the journalist, needed to be more than a neutral technician. And why not? What is there in the definition of journalism that says a reporter cannot—no, should not—sort out the facts and not only say what they mean but what should be done about them? This is called, and condemned as, advocacy. One is not supposed to step over the boundary, even if the facts lead in that direction. To do so is to become propagandist . . . to make facts less credible . . . to commit, as Joseph Goulden says, the "cardinal sin by a reporter of any rank": to no longer be objective.[6] Reporters must, under these unwritten but closely followed rules, maintain objectivity and disguise their opinions. Or, perhaps, they do something that is even worse: pretend to be objective when underneath they have some leftist (or rightist) hidden agenda which they will push forward by duping editors and readers about their neutrality. This, for example, is what Kent McDougall, now a professor of journalism, said he did in his years as a reporter at the *Wall Street Journal* and the *Los Angeles Times*.[7] He had to, McDougall explained, because objectivity—which is, in essence, a political limitation imposed by the conventional press—prevented him from candidly expressing his opinions and from suggesting that the facts he had collected pointed to certain conclusions. Objective reporters—and that is still what most reporters in America strive to become—do not draw conclusions and give their opinions; they cannot because they must remain above partisanship.[8] But why should those who gather the news and process information always have to wear a guise of neutrality?

Let's go back, for a moment at least, to the theoretical underpinnings of objective journalism. Reporters, under a "classical" view of democracy, are supposed to be independent observers—beholden to no political party or private interest—who deliver the facts that make enlightened, rational citizens able to choose the direction and leadership of democracy; in short, participatory democracy depends on access to the information that the press provides. If, as some posit, the mainstream of the population is uninterested and uninvolved in public policy questions, then a second (and complementary) understanding of how journalism must—and does—work is needed. That view, as espoused once by Walter Lippmann, is that elite groups actually govern society, and that the public intervenes only occasionally to direct the elites. In that scenario, journalism sketches out for the public what its leaders—and real governors—are doing, but, more important, it holds those leaders directly accountable.[9] In either interpretation, journalism is a vital force in not only making the democracy function, but in edging the world along a bit toward a more rational social order. Certain public policies, as Adams aptly offered, may change only when the press applies corrective or catalytic pressure with either muckraking exposé or with simple straight news coverage of ongoing events. When exposé and event coverage are combined, as was done by John L. Hess, the resultant crusade can be powerful indeed.

In the movie *The Untouchables*, there is a scene that is analogous to journalism. The movie's hero, Elliot Ness, played by actor Kevin Costner, is planning to make a raid on a mob hideaway. He gets his troops together and, before they embark, he yells, "Let's do some good." This is not far afield from Lincoln Steffens who said that his muckraking reporting made him "feel good." Journalists, at their activist best, act with an evangelical fervor as do-gooders.[10] To do this, they need to act as both observers of events and active participants in the social process— as trustworthy, independent, credible, and objective sources of fact; and as muckraking, goading, purposeful gadflies, prodding lethargic government bureaucracies, giving voice to voiceless groups, and holding private corporations accountable to public standards of decency and quality. Social responsibility calls for both neutrality and activism.

Journalists need to get the voices of others and, at times, their own voices before the public and the policymakers. Diversity of opinion, after all, is at the heart of the purpose of the press which must continue to embrace the eighteenth-century notion that if we allow a free and unencumbered marketplace of ideas to flourish, truth will survive and a rational people will choose the right direction, the right policies, and the right leaders. Undoubtedly, there are problems inherent in such thinking: those with money will inevitably alter the direction of the marketplace; advertisers and slick public relations firms will clutter peoples' minds with commercial nonsense and obfuscate reality; the arbiters of truth themselves—the press—are cogs in a commercial entity that cannot be entrusted to safeguard democracy's perogatives; people these days are not very interested in democracy's business; and there is such a proliferation of media and messages that perhaps meaningful comprehension is no longer even possible.[11]

These are real issues and dilemmas, but they are not crippling ones that disable the marketplace from functioning—either for the ruling elites or the masses when they are roused, as at times they are, to participate. The real issue is how to halt the limiting mechanisms that discourage discussion—by the society and by journalists—of the widest range of possible policy options. A starting place is to recognize what are some of the social controls on the press and to work then to eliminate the limiting mechanisms.

The limiting factors, undoubtedly, are many. One limit comes in the public and professional confusion over who we in the press are and what we are expected and allowed to do. Such a confusion was evident in the turn-of-the-century muckraking reporters who tried to be so many things at once—documentarians, literary storytellers, objective reporters, and muckraking activists. It is a confusion that is still evident today. When a band of journalists, chafing at the constraints of objectivity, championed a 1960s literary style of writing that became known as "new journalism," they were quickly condemned and attacked by those who saw them as a threat to carefully developed limits of journalistic technique. Fight with a passion this "bastard form of journalism . . . this parajournalism," argued Dwight MacDonald in the *New Yorker*. When, also in the 1960s, the so-called underground press began to stress conclusions and advocacy over facts, and such style became attractive to younger journalists, the establishment press reacted with equal furor in attacking this trend. "Take out the goddamn editorializing," snarled the *New York Times*' managing editor A.M. Rosenthal when he felt that some of his younger reporters were adopting the less-than-objective standards of the alternative media.[12]

If the adoption of literary techniques inherent in the new journalism was unacceptable to the mainstream press and if the brand of advocacy that was emerging in the alternative media were equally objectionable, was there any innovation that journalism's powers-that-be would embrace? A fact-based and ostensibly objective investigative reporting, a modern revival of muckraking, seemed to be journalism's answer to its critics who argued that the media must join in the Vietnam Era–clamor for a new progressivism. Thus, the identity of the reporter was shaped anew—at least for a short while—by the creation of a new modern American hero: the investigative reporter, the Woodward-Bernstein, Hoffman-Redford, larger-than-life crusader. Throughout the 1970s, with investigative reporting teams being created on most major urban dailies, muckraking was in vogue. Then came the crash. By 1981, Pulitzer Prize–winning muckraker Bob Porterfield could declare: "A lot of newspapers don't want to put out money to cut reporters loose for in-depth stories.

The volume of hard investigative journalism has dropped off considerably."[13] Today, muckraking is not dead, but certainly it is not breathing very hard. Activism, along with much of reform, largely left the mainstream press during the Reagan years and returned again to the journalistic fringes.

Meanwhile, the debate over what journalism should be continues to be pressed. For example, when a 1988 book on corruption in New York City's government was published by reporter Jack Newfield, some complained that the veteran muckraker acts not only as a journalist, but also as a prosecuting attorney, judge, and jury. Newfield, a writer for many years with the left-of-center *Village Voice*, who went on to write a column for the *New York News*, is a valued adviser to government officials ranging from New York Governor Mario Cuomo, a Democrat, to controversial federal prosecutor Rudolph Giuliani, a Republican. Where does his role as journalist end and that of adviser begin? "In the best tradition of muckraking," asked the *New York Times* about Newfield, "has he privately promoted the populist causes he champions in print?"[14]

David Broder, a prominent and respected political writer for the *Washington Post*, bemoans the fact that the lines between journalist-observers and journalist-propagandists are being blurred. We need purity, says Broder, who undoubtedly would have disapproved of Will Irwin's doing public relations for America during World War I and Ray Stannard Baker's working as an aide to Woodrow Wilson or, for that matter, Charles Edward Russell's declaring his affection for socialism and then continuing to muckrake on issues that concerned him. Journalists, perhaps Broder feels, must be value-free technicians, untainted by opinion and, presumably, passionate concern about the issues on which they write.[15] On the contrary, what journalism needs from reporters is honesty, not purity; it needs passion and commitment, along with facts and technical skills. "When a reporter covers a war," John Hess says, "he needs to bleed with the victims. He needs to hurt and needs to bring that hurt back to his writing. Antiseptic journalism is not what we need."[16]

A crisis of identity, of course, was not what put the muckrakers out of business before World War I; other, more intimidating forces were at work. A major deterrent to exposé journalism was the law of libel, a powerful legal club that haunts the press still today. Simply defending a lawsuit, if one wins and there are no appeals, can cost a publication $20,000. The 35,000-circulation *Alton Telegraph* (Illinois) shut down its printing presses in 1982 when it lost a libel lawsuit because of a memorandum its reporters wrote to the government, the contents of which it never even printed.[17] *Look* magazine stopped publication, in part, because of the money needed to defend itself in a lawsuit brought by the former mayor of San Franciso. An editor who headed up the investigative reporting team put together by the *Sacramento Bee* said in the mid–1980s that his team was largely stymied and doing little reporting because "its members have become full-time litigants," testifying in court in various libel lawsuits.[18]

Indeed, as First Amendment lawyer Floyd Abrams has concluded, it is the wise publication that holds back on certain stories. When John Hess wrote his nursing home exposés, the immediate response of his target, Bernard Bergman, was to sue for defamation, but the *Times* has deep pockets and was able to beat the challenge. Others, such as the weekly *Nation* magazine, a persistent progressive, muckraking voice with a small circulation, cannot afford to be sued. At times, its editors concede, it must simply back away from important stories.[19] How many contemporary editors have done what Samuel McClure did in 1908, when he declared after losing a libel lawsuit that he was done with muckraking? The *Columbia Journalism Review* aptly portrayed the libel situation when, on its cover, it showed a white polar bear standing on snow and ice.[20] The "chilling effect" of libel is real and perilous, and it needs to be lifted.

Another factor which limits the kind and quality of discussion in America is the marketing mentality which has so seized and pervaded the press in the 1980s. Spurred by the success of *USA Today*, which polled potential readers to see what they wanted before it ever published an issue, the press has increasingly adopted a "soft" news and "happy talk" mentality. *USA Today* does little in the way of muckraking or investigative reporting; its audience prefers short, bright stories, and that leaves little room for the aching misery of the homeless or poor farm workers. While the press, of course, is not a monolithic institution— *USA Today* is not being instantly cloned all over America—the attractive graphic format and apparent financial success of *USA Today* make it likely to be copied in many respects.[21] Such commercialism is troubling but, again, not particularly novel. Orison Swett Marden transformed his magazine *Success* in 1918 from one of exposé to one of sunshine, looking up, not down, just as Teddy Roosevelt had suggested and just as Marden had felt his readers wanted. Inspired perhaps by the success of the genteel *Saturday Evening Post*, Marden made the shift from substance to fluff. He lost—his magazine failed—but so, too, did his readers who needed to hear, as Edward R. Murrow once commented, about "the hard, unyielding realities of the world in which we live."[22]

Commercialism in a much larger sense threatens muckraking journalism. Muckraking is not safe, it is not orthodox, and it is a threat to the comfortable corporate class which runs and owns the American mass media. When Crowell publications took over the *American* magazine in 1912, the muckrakers saw the subtle—and not-so-subtle changes—that

began to take place. Ray Stannard Baker's stories about worker grievances were watered down, and hard-nosed exposé took a back seat to
warm feature stories.[23] Can muckraking attacks on the business establishment be expected today when the media—newspapers, magazines,
radio, television, and book publishers—are controlled essentially by fifty
giant corporations? Fifteen companies own and operate two-thirds of
America's newspapers; six companies control nearly half the nation's
magazines; and the three television networks, despite loss of audience
to cable competitors, still control the news and entertainment programs
that 60 million people receive in their homes each evening.

"Today," writes Ben Bagdikian, "the chief executive officers of the
twenty-nine corporations that control most of what Americans read and
see can fit into an ordinary living room."[24] This concentration means,
simply, that very few people are controlling much of what Americans
read, hear, and, consequently, think. One can argue that because they
are such large and powerful commercial entities, the modern news con-
glomerates can fight off undue pressure from advertisers—better perhaps than could turn-of-the-century magazines. But the real issue is, if
their primary desire is to maximize profits, will they carry the kind of
content—muckraking, for example—that will offend advertisers. Furthermore, if they are so concerned about the demographics of their
audience, the upscale audience that advertisers so covet, will they bother
with the problems of the underclasses and the disempowered?

Then there are the limitations and problems posed by the modern
concept of objectivity. Imposed initially from within the profession as a
way to prove professionalism and to ward off propagandists, objectivity
has evolved over the decades into a straitjacket mentality. Although it
still is an important and useful regimen to maintain independence, objectivity serves also as a way of limiting the options of reporters—and
decreasing the true range of information and opinion that the public has
available. The rituals of objectivity stop reporters from providing conclusions and personal insights when they are appropriate and needed.
Instead, to get their views across, reporters must either load stories in
secretive ways or omit their views altogether. Objectivity and commercialism might allow for the telling of a good story, but they mitigate
against analysis, assessment, and audience comprehension. Objectivity
does not allow for the involvement of reporters in reaching conclusions,
making recommendations, or expressing opinions about the facts that
the reporter has gathered.

The case of John Hess is a good one. Hess had written, objectively,
about the nursing-home scandal in New York for nearly nine months.
He was an expert on the government's complex Medicaid regulations,
and he had provided prosecutors with much of the beginning information they then used to convict hundreds of nursing-home entrepre-

neurs. What he showed was not much different from what Samuel Hopkins Adams had shown seventy years earlier: profiteers, left on their own, unregulated, with only profit as their motive, would usually over- charge and defraud. Money, not people, would come first. Hess believed that regulations would help, but he was afraid that the same kinds of problems would surface again in a few years if the profit motive was not eliminated. In a profit-oriented, capitalist society, this is sinful think- ing, although it is more likely to be at least an option in health care than in other fields. Yet the rules of objectivity effectively forbade Hess from express his opinion in the *Times*. Would it not have been refreshingly honest if Hess could have written: "After nine months of observing the pattern of behavior of the profit-seeking businessmen who run the nurs- ing-home industry, it is my conclusion that profit must be eliminated so as to safeguard the lives of our elderly and to protect the taxpayers' money." Such a statement was highly unlikely to come form a news- paper that so personifies the core values of objective journalism.

Listen for a moment to A.M. Rosenthal, the *Times*' former managing editor who vowed in the turbulent early 1970s to keep the *Times* "straight" and out of the hands of the radical fringes. "Our business is facts," Rosenthal said in a memorandum to his staff. "[A]lthough total objectivity may be impossible because every story is written by a human being, the duty of every reporter and editor is to strive for as much objectivity as humanly possible." That means, he wrote, that "no matter how engaged the reporter is emotionally he tries as best he can to dis- engage himself when he sits down at the typewriter." Moreover, Ro- senthal added, "[E]xpression of personal opinion should be excluded from the news columns."[25] In other words, the candor and honesty that Hess might have liked to add to his crusade were impossible at the New York *Times* of A.M. Rosenthal. The result, perhaps, can best be seen in the fact that the special prosecutor whose job was created after Hess' exposés was still actively in business rooting out the looters fifteen years after his appointment. To wit, Sheldon Weinberg of Lawrence, Long Island, who along with two sons operated medical clinics in New York City, was convicted in 1988 of defrauding taxpayers of $16 million of Medicaid money.[26] This was the ghost of nursing-home badman Bernard Bergman, and the revenge perhaps of objective journalism.

Edward R. Murrow once commented that he felt that a muckraking form of journalism would always be needed. "Democracy's business," he said, "is always unfinished."[27] Implicit in that statement is that, as a nation, we are always progressing, moving forward toward a more just, humane, and caring society. To inch forward, Murrow felt, we would need constantly to scratch the underside of the world and to search out solutions to our myriad and increasing problems.

The formula for achieving progress? First, journalistic exposé which will lead to public indignation and heightened discussion and then, finally, to solution and reform. The issue is what role journalism should play in fostering and aiding the process of finding solutions and bringing about reform. The exposé function is easily understood and generally accepted, although undoubtedly it is often disliked by those who are embarrassed or accused and by those who are satisfied with the status quo. Exposé should be accompanied by documentary fact, and here objectivity's rituals are purposeful and necessary. However, in the next stage, public discussion, the waters muddy a bit. If there is reaction to the exposé and if reformers begin to act, then a reporter can, of course, report their statements and proposals and write about their activities. If reformers are nonexistent or stymied, then the reporter's options—under objectivity, at least—are limited. Reporters cannot advocate or even fully explore solutions on their own, and that is a limitation that is stifling. Exposure is only part of what the public needs from the press; solutions, which most of the turn-of-the-century muckrakers shunned, are necessary also. A blending of purposeful objectivity and careful but outright subjectivity should not only be allowed for reporters, but encouraged.

NOTES

1. Mary Beth Pfeiffer, "Migrants: Lives of Farm Workers Lack Roots and Hope," *Poughkeepsie Journal*, 8 September 1985, p. 1. On migrant conditions in the Hudson Valley, see also Pfeiffer, "The Life Is Short, the Work Is Hard," 9 September 1985; and "Advocates: Workers Treated Like Lower Class," 10 September 1985, both in the *Poughkeepsie Journal*.

2. On Mrs. Cuomo's visit, see "Mrs. Cuomo Visits Migrant Center," *Middletown Times-Herald-Record*, 10 September 1985, p. 4.

3. Samuel Hopkins Adams, *The Great American Fraud* (New York, 1906), 11.

4. Whitney Cross, "The Muckrakers Revisited: Purposeful Objectivity in Progressive Journalism," *Neiman Reports* 7 (July 1952): 10–15.

5. Richard Hofstadter, *The Age of Reform* (New York, 1955), 186.

6. Joseph C. Goulden, *Fit to Print: A.M. Rosenthal and his Times* (Secaucus, N.J., 1988), 144.

7. A. Kent MacDougall discusses his work in "Boring from within the Bourgeois Press," *Monthly Review* 40 (November 1988): 13–24; (December 1988): 10–21. See also, Alexander Cockburn, "Secret Life of Radical Journalist Pure Milquetoast," *Wall Street Journal*, 9 February 1989, p. 23.

8. John W. C. Johnstone, Edward K. Slawski, and William W. Bowman, *The News People: A Sociological Portrait of American Journalists and Their Work* (Urbana, Ill., 1976), 114–22.

9. A discussion of these dual functions of the press is contained in Michael Schudson, "Making Journalism Safe for Democracy," *The Quill* 72 (November 1984): 24–30.

10. Letter to Harlow Gale, January 1904, *The Letters of Lincoln Steffens* vol. 1, eds. Ella Winter and Granville Hicks (New York, 1938), 165.

11. These criticisms against the press can be seen in Michael Parenti, *Inventing Reality: The Politics of the Mass Media* (New York, 1986); David Potter, *People of Plenty* (New York, 1954); and Marie Blyskal and Jeffrey Blyskal, *PR: How the Public Relations Industry Writes the News* (New York, 1985).

12. MacDonald, "Parajournalism, or Tom Wolfe and His Magic Writing Machine," in *The Reporter as Artist*, ed. Ronald Weber (New York, 1974), 223. Rosenthal quoted in Goulden, *Fit to Print*, 170. For discussions of these movements, see Everette E. Dennis and William L. Rivers, eds., *Other Voices: The New Journalism in America* (San Francisco, 1974); and Robert J. Glessing, *The Underground Press in America* (Bloomington, Ind. 1970).

13. Bill Bellows, "Why Investigative Reporting Is Dying," *Editor & Publisher* (March 14, 1981): 60.

14. Sam Roberts, "When Journalists Telling the News Also Make It," *New York Times*, 12 December 1988, p. B1.

15. David Broder quoted in William Safire, "Color Me Tainted," *New York Times*, 12 December 1988, p. 19.

16. Lecture, State University of New York, College at New Paltz, April 14, 1987.

17. David A. Anderson, "Libel and Press Self-Censorship," *Texas Law Review*, 53 (1975), estimated the minimum cost of defending a libel suit in 1975, on p. 453. See also "Cost of Libel Suits Prompts Calls to Alter System," *New York Times*, 25 February 1985, p. 11. The *Alton-Telegraph* declared bankruptcy after it lost a $9.2-million libel suit. Lyle Denniston, "A Punishing Verdict in Illinois," *Washington Journalism Review* (March 1982): 52.

18. *Look* magazine went bankrupt after losing a 1977 libel decision (in its third trial) to Joseph Alioto, the former mayor of San Francisco. See Wallace Turner, "Alioto Is Awarded $350,000 in Libel by *Look* Magazine," *New York Times*, 4 May 1977, p. 16. Denny Walsh is quoted in Michael Massing, "The Libel Chill," *Columbia Journalism Review* (May/June 1985): 37.

19. Floyd Abrams is quoted in the *New York Times*, 17 February 1985, p. 72. Carey McWilliams, "The Continuing Tradition of Reform Journalism," in *Muckraking: Past, Present and Future*, eds. John M. Harrison and Harry Stein (University Park, Pa., 1973), 132.

20. See the cover of the *Columbia Journalism Review* of May/June 1985. The problem of libel is detailed further in Rodney Smolla, *Suing the Press* (New York: 1986) and Lois G. Forer, *A Chilling Effect* (New York, 1983).

21. The prepublication methods of *USA Today* are detailed in Peter Pritchard, *The Making of McPaper; The Inside Story of USA Today*. (Kansas City, Mo., 1987), and in Katherine Seelye, "Al Neuharth's Technicolor Baby," *Columbia Journalism Review* (March/April 1983): 27–37.

22. Murrow made this comment in a 1958 speech to radio and television news directors. Quoted in Betty Houchins Winfield and Lois B. Defleur, eds., *Edward R. Murrow Heritage: Challenge for the Future* (Ames, Iowa, 1986), 21. Marden described his magazine's transformation in "A Foreward," *New Success* (January 1918): 13.

23. The cuts to Baker's articles are discussed in note 29, Chapter 3.

24. Ben Bagdikian, *Media Monopoly* (Boston, 1987), 7.

25. Goulden quotes this memo at length, *Fit to Print*, 175. Others discuss Rosenthal's fear of radicalism at the *Times*. See Harrison Salisbury, *A Time for Change* (New York, 1988), 287–302.

26. Selwyn Raab, "Father Jumps Bail in Fraud on Medicaid," *New York Times*, 11 January 1989, p. B1.

27. Murrow made the comment at a press conference sponsored by The State Department, April 4, 1961. Edward R. Morrow Papers.

Epilogue: When to Cross the Line

Fred Friendly sat in a chair in his office near Columbia University's School of Journalism in New York City. He wore a blue pin-striped suit. His nose looked larger and his body seemed thinner than in pictures. He was also much calmer, almost soft spoken, than the man who had been described as voluble and excitable, pulsing always with ideas and energy. It had taken months to get an interview with him, and he was quite nostalgic on the day that we finally spoke.

At the age of seventy-three, despite his obvious fitness and continued professional activity, he seemed to be scanning back over his career ... especially the controversial and very successful years with CBS television when, behind the scenes, he was the guiding hand for so many of the famous Edward R. Murrow documentaries. "When I die," he said, "I want to be remembered for three things." The first would be—and this was no surprise—the documentary he had produced in 1954 on Joseph McCarthy, the one which many believe helped push McCarthy out of his ruthless power spot. Second, he mentioned the follow-up piece that showed how McCarthyism had so devastated the earnest Annie Lee Moss.

Finally, Friendly said, "I want to be remembered for 'Harvest of Shame.' That documentary is special, it's what documentary should be, it's about what journalism should do—or try to do."[1]

What "Harvest of Shame" tried to do was to show a nation that thousands of its citizens were overworked, underpaid, and oppressed and had little hope of salvation. It was, in short, an activist attempt to take the side of a disempowered group and advocate change. "What other side could one take?" Friendly asked. "Could you see Murrow taking the side of the farmer?" Nor could David Lowe, the film's producer, study the plight of the migrants for nine months and decide to do anything less than crusade on their behalf. "No," Friendly said, smiling and shaking his head, "David could never learn to be neutral," despite the fact that some at CBS would have preferred neutrality. Lowe, Friendly, and Ed Murrow gave voice to voiceless people that night, an enlightened and inspiring lesson on how journalism can be so effective. If the true test of journalism is, as Clifford Christians suggests, how it treats those on society's fringes—its elderly and poor, its handicapped and disabled, its AIDS victims and its homeless—then CBS passed the test, at least for this one evening in 1960.

Yet, in the final product, much of the documentary followed the rules of objectivity, the careful balancing and documenting of the issue. Only at a few points did the broadcast cross the line between neutrality and partisanship. Was Friendly aware back in 1960 that he was crossing the imaginary line that usually forbids journalist from taking stands on issues and doing something besides mirroring a perceived reality? "I think we knew," Friendly said. "Certainly in retrospect I know."[2]

How, Friendly was asked again, do you know when to cross the line from objectivity to activism? How did Murrow decide when he would enter a script? At what point should John Hess, if the *Times* had allowed him, given up on objectivity and embraced a more personal, opinion-based brand of reporting? Friendly handed me a small card that he said he used to give regularly to his journalism students at Columbia. On it were a few sentences from Ed Klauber, a former CBS newsman. They were, in essence, cliches about a journalist's role. For example, "[I]n a democracy it is important that people should not only know but should understand." The cliches did not answer the question. When does a journalist know that he or she should cross over and become more than a neutral technician? On which issues can he or she be sure, as Murrow once said, that there is only one side? When does one choose to muckrake? or to become personally involved in a story?

Those are the questions that began this book, back on the streets of Stapleton on Staten Island. On the day I was offered methadone by a young man with whom I had gone to school, the question was not in my mind. I knew who I was. I was a storyteller and a muckraker, an entertainer and a crusader. My doubts many years later about my self-confident choice to be the brash journalist eventually helped me to focus my thoughts for this book, but it also gave me especial pause—and regret—during my writing. In the spring of 1988 I attended the twentieth reunion of my high school graduating class. When I arrived, I received a bulletin with short biographies of many classmates. In the front of the bulletin was a list of eight people who had died since our graduation.

One name on the list was that of the man who had offered to sell me methadone. At age thirty-four, he had died of a drug overdose. I had nothing to do, at least directly, with his death—but my journalism had had nothing to do with his remaining alive either. My scoop and my muckraking may have helped the larger cause of public discussion, but the individual most affected—drug dependent and desperate—died six years after the story was written. And so the question of my purpose as a reporter—and person—remains with me . . . and with journalism. The question is not easily resolved, but, if we are to have a meaningful and progressive press, it must be continuously asked and confronted. What function do journalists have in a democracy and whose interests are they seeking to serve?

NOTES

1. Interview with Fred Friendly, November 30, 1988. The broadcast on Annie Lee Moss appeared on CBS, March 16, 1954. Friendly describes it in *Due To Circumstances beyond Our Control* (New York, 1967), 45–50.

2. Ibid.

Selected Bibliography

Adams, Samuel Hopkins. *The Great American Fraud*. New York, 1906.
———. *The Clarion*. New York, 1914.
Anderson, David A. "Libel and Press Self-Censorship." *Texas Law Review* 53 (1975):444–57.
Anderson, David A. and Peter Benjaminson. *Investigative Reporting*. Bloomington, Ind., 1976.
Anderson, Jack. *Confessions of a Muckraker*. New York, 1979.
Anderson, Oscar E. *The Health of a Nation: Harvey W. Wiley and the Fight for Pure Food*. New York, 1958.
Aronson, James. *The Press and the Cold War*. Boston, 1973.
Bagdikian, Ben. *Media Monopoly*. Boston, 1987.
Baker, Ray Stannard. *American Chronicle: The Autobiography of Ray Stannard Baker*. New York, 1945.
———. *Following the Color Line/American Negro Citizenship in the Progressive Era*. Dewey Grantham, Jr., introduction. New York, 1964.
Bannister, Robert C., Jr. *Ray Stannard Baker: The Mind and Thought of a Progressive*. New Haven, Conn., 1966.
Barr, Donald J., Aurora Demarco, Carl Henry Fever, and Robin Lee Whittlesey. *Liberalism to the Test: African-American Migrant Farmworkers and the State of New York*. Ithaca, N.Y.: New York African-American Institute, 1988.
Barry, Peter. "The Decline of Muckraking: A View from the Magazines." Ph.D. diss., Wayne State University, 1971.
Baughman, James L. " 'See It Now' and Television's Golden Age, 1951–58." *Journal of Popular Culture* 15 (Fall 1981):106–15.
———. "The Strange Birth of 'CBS Reports' Revisited." *The Historical Journal of Film, Radio and TV* 2 (1982):27–38.

Bayley, Edwin. *Joe McCarthy and the Press*. New York, 1982.

Bennett, Lance. *News: The Politics of Illusion*. New York, 1983.

Berger, Meyer. *The Story of the New York Times, 1861–1951*. New York, 1951.

Berthoff, Werner. *The Ferment of Realism: American Literature, 1884–1919*. New York, 1965.

Blyskal, Marie and Jeffrey Blyskal. *PR: How the Public Relations Industry Writes the News*. New York, 1985.

Bok, Edward. *The Americanization of Edward Bok*. New York, 1930.

Brady, Kathleen. *Ida Tarbell: Portrait of a Muckraker*. New York, 1984.

Bragaw, Donald. "Soldier for the Common Good: The Life and Career of Charles Edward Russell." Ph.D. diss., Syracuse University, 1970.

Bremer, Robert H. *From the Depths: The Discovery of Poverty in the United States*. New York, 1956.

Cady, Edwin. *The Realist at War: The Mature Years of William Dean Howells, 1837–1885*. Syracuse, N.Y., 1958.

Cannon, Lou. *Reporting: An Inside View*. Sacramento, Calif., 1977.

Carey, James. "The Dark Continent of American Journalism." In *Reading the News*. Edited by Robert Manoff and Michael Schudson. New York, 1986.

Carlson, Oliver. *Brisbane: A Candid Biography*. New York, 1937.

Cassedy, James H. "Muckraking and Medicine: Samuel Hopkins Adams." *American Quarterly* 16 (Spring 1964):85–99.

Chalmers, David Mark. "The Social and Political Philosophy of the Muckrakers." Ph.D. diss., University of Rochester, 1955.

———. *The Social and Political Ideas of the Muckrakers*. New York, 1964.

———, ed. *The Muckrake Years*. New York, 1974.

Chamberlain, John. *Farewell to Reform*. New York, 1932.

Christians, Clifford. "Reporting and the Oppressed." In *Responsible Journalism*. Edited by Deni Elliot. Beverly Hills, Calif., 1986.

Churchill, Allen. *Park Row*. New York, 1958.

Cohen, Bernard C. *The Press and Foreign Policy*. Princeton, N.J., 1963.

Commager, Henry Steele. *The American Mind*. New Haven, Conn., 1950.

Connolly, Margaret. *The Life Story of Orison Swett Marden: A Man Who Benefited Men*. New York, 1925.

Cook, Fred J. *Maverick: Fifty Years of Investigative Reporting*. New York, 1984.

Cross, Whitney. "The Muckrakers Revisited: Purposeful Objectivity in Progressive Journalism." *Neiman Reports* (July 1951):10–15.

Crunden, John. *Ministers of Reform: The Progressives' Achievement in American Civilization, 1889–1920*. New York, 1982.

Darnton, Robert. "Writing News and Telling Stories." *Daedalus* 104 (1975):175–94.

Dennis, Everette E., and William L. Rivers, eds. *Other Voices: The New Journalism in America*. San Francisco, 1974.

Downie, Leonard P. *The New Muckrakers*. Washington, D.C., 1976.

Dunn, Delmar D. *Public Officials and the Press*. Reading, Pa., 1969.

Eckley, Grace. *Finley Peter Dunne*. Boston, 1967.

Emerson, Thomas I. *The System of Freedom of Expression*. New York, 1970.

Emery, Edwin, and Michael Emery. *The Press and America*. Englewood Cliffs, N.J., 1984.

Evenson, Bruce J. "The Evangelical Origins of the Muckrakers." *American Journalism* 6 (1989):5–29.

Feldman, Abraham. "David Graham Phillips: His Works and His Critics." *Bulletin of Bibliography* 19 (May-August 1948):144–46; (September-December 1948):177–79.

Filler, Louis. "Murder in Grammercy Park." *Antioch Review* 11 (December 1946):495–508.

———. "The Muckrakers in Flower and Failure." In *Essays in American Historiography*, edited by Donald H. Sheehan. Westport, Ct., 1960.

———. *The Muckrakers*. University Park, Pa., 1976.

———. *Appointment at Armageddon: Muckraking and Progressivism in the American Tradition*. Westport, Conn., 1976.

———. *The Voice of Democracy: A Critical Biography of David Graham Phillips: Journalist, Novelist, Progressive*. University Park, Pa., 1978.

Fishkin, Shelly Fisher. *From Fact to Fiction*. New York, 1985.

Fishman, Mark. *Manufacturing the News*. Austin, Texas, 1980.

Forer, Lois G. *A Chilling Effect*. New York, 1983.

Francke, Warren T. "Investigative Exposure in the Nineteenth Century: The Journalistic Heritage of the Muckrakers." Ph.D. diss., University of Minnesota, 1974.

Friendly, Fred. *Due to Circumstances Beyond Our Control*. New York, 1967.

Fuller, Varden. "Farm Manpower Policy." In *Farm Labor in the United States*, edited by C. E. Bishop. New York, 1967.

Gerbner, George. "Ideological Perspectives and Political Tendencies in News Reporting." *Journalism Quarterly* 41 (Spring 1964):495, 508.

Gitlin, Todd. *The Whole World Is Watching*. Berkeley, Calif., 1980.

Glessing, Robert J. *The Underground Press in America*. Bloomington, Ind., 1970.

Goldman, Eric. *Rendezvous with Destiny*. New York, 1955.

Goldstein, Tom. *The News at Any Cost*. New York, 1986.

Good, Howard. *Acquainted with the Night: The Image of Journalists in American Fiction, 1890–1930*. Metuchen, N.J., 1986.

Goulden, Joseph C. *Fit to Print: A. M. Rosenthal and His Times*. Secaucus, N.J., 1988.

Gramling, Oliver. *AP: The Story of News*. Port Washington, N.Y., 1969.

Grenier, Judson A. "Muckrakers and Muckraking: An Historical Definition." *Journalism Quarterly* 37 (Autumn 1960):552–58.

———. "The Origins and Nature of Progressive Muckraking." Ph.D. diss., University of California, Los Angeles, 1965.

———. "Upton Sinclair and the Press: The Brass Check Reconsidered." *Journalism Quarterly* 49 (Autumn 1972):427–36.

Grimaldi, Paul L. *Medicaid Reimbursement of Nursing-Home Care*. Washington, D.C., 1982.

Halberstam, David. *The Powers That Be*. New York, 1979.

Hallin, Daniel. *The Uncensored War: The Media and Vietnam*. New York, 1986.

Hapgood, Norman. *The Changing Years: Reminiscences of Norman Hapgood*. New York, 1930.

Harrison, John M., and Harry H. Stein, eds. *Muckraking: Past, Present and Future*. University Park, Pa., 1973.

Hays, Samuel P. *The Response to Industrialism, 1865–1914*. Chicago, 1957.

Heaton, John L. *The Story of a Page: Thirty Years of Public Service and Public Discussion in the Editorial Columns of the New York World*. New York, 1913.

Hess, John L. *The Case for DeGaulle: An American Viewpoint*. New York, 1968.

————. *The Grand Acquisitors*. Boston, 1974.

————. *Vanishing France*. New York, 1975.

————. "The Shame of the Urban Press." *The Nation*. (September 27, 1986):273–76.

Hess, John L. and Karen Hess. *The Taste of America*. New York, 1977.

Hicks, Granville. "David Graham Phillips: Journalist." *Bookman* 73 (May 1931):257–66.

Hofstadter, Richard. *The Age of Reform*. New York, 1955.

————, ed. *The Progressive Movement, 1900–1917*. Englewood Cliffs, N.J., 1963.

Holbrook, Stewart. *The Golden Age of Quackery*. New York, 1959.

Hoopes, Roy. *Ralph Ingersoll: A Biography*. New York, 1985.

Hudson, Robert V. *The Writing Game: A Biography of Will Irwin*. Ames, Iowa, 1982.

Hughes, Helen MacGill. *News and the Human Interest Story*. New Brunswick, N.J., 1940.

Irwin, Will. *The Making of a Reporter*. New York, 1942.

————. *The American Newspaper*. Edited by Clifford F. Weigle and David G. Clark. Ames, Iowa, 1969.

Isaacs, Norman. *The Mismanaged Gates*. New York, 1988.

Jacobs, Lewis. "The Turn toward Conservatism." In *The Documentary Tradition*, edited by Lewis Jacobs. New York, 1974.

Jensen, Gordon M. "The National Civic Federation: American Business in an Age of Social Change and Social Reform, 1900–1910." Ph.D. diss., Princeton University, 1956.

Johnson, Walter., ed. *Selected Letters of William Allen White, 1899–1943*. New York, 1947.

Johnstone, John W. C., Edward K. Slawski, and William W. Bowman. *The News People: A Sociological Portrait of American Journalists and Their Work*. Urbana, Ill., 1976.

Juergens, George. *Joseph Pulitzer and the New York World*. Princeton, N.J., 1966.

————. *News from the White House: The Presidential Press Relationship in the Progressive Era*. Chicago, 1981.

Kaplan, Justin. *Lincoln Steffens: A Biography*. New York, 1974.

Kendrick, Alexander. *Prime Time: The Life and Legend of Edward R. Murrow*. Boston, 1969.

Kimball, Penn. "Journalism: Art, Craft, or Profession?" In *The Professions in America*, edited by Kenneth S. Lynn. Boston, 1965.

Kolko, Gabriel. *The Triumph of Conservatism*. Glencoe, Ill., 1963.

Lambeth, Edmund. *Committed Journalism: An Ethic for the Press*. Bloomington, Ind., 1986.

Lanson, Gerald, and Mitchell Stephens. "Trust Me Journalism." *Washington Journalism Review* (November 1982):43–47.

Lawson, Linda. "Advertisements Masquerading as News in Turn-of-the-Century American Periodicals." *American Journalism* 5, (1988):81–96.

Leonard, Thomas C. *The Power of the Press: The Birth of American Political Reporting.* New York: 1986.

Leonard, William. *In the Storm of the Eye: A Lifetime at CBS.* New York, 1987.

Link, Arthur S. "What Happened to the Progressive Movement in the 1920s?" *American Historical Review* 64 (July 1959):833–51.

Lippmann, Walter. *Drift and Mastery.* New York, 1914.

Lundberg, Edwin H. "The Decline of the American Muckrakers: A New Interpretation." Master's thesis, University of Vermont, 1966.

Lyon, Peter. *Success Story: The Life and Times of S. S. McClure.* New York, 1963.

MacDougall, A. Kent. "Boring from within the Bourgeois Press." *Monthly Review* 40 (November 1988):13–24; (December 1988):10–21.

———. "Memoirs of a Radical in the Mainstream Press." *Columbia Journalism Review* (March/April, 1989):36–41.

McWilliams, Carey. *Ill Fares the Land: Migrants and Migratory Labor in the United States.* Boston, 1944.

———. "The Continuing Tradition of Reform Journalsim." In *Muckraking: Past, Present and Future,* edited by John M. Harrison and Harry Stein. University Park, Pa., 1973.

Marcaccio, Michael D. "Did a Business Conspiracy End Muckraking? A Reexamination." *Historian* 47 (November 1984):58–71.

Marcossen, Isaac. *David Graham Phillips and His Times.* New York, 1932.

Martin, Jay. *Harvests of Change: American Literature, 1865–1914.* Englewood Cliffs, N.J., 1967.

Massing, Michael. "The Libel Chill." *Columbia Journalism Review* (May/June, 1985):31–43.

Maxwell, Robert S. "A Note on the Muckrakers." *Mid-America* 43 (January 1961):55–60.

May, Henry. *The End of American Innocence.* New York, 1959.

Mendelsohn, Mary. *Tender Loving Greed.* New York, 1974.

Merron, Jeff. "Murrow on TV: See It Now, Person to Person, and the Making of a 'Masscult Personality,' " *Journalism Monographs* 106 (1988).

Migratory Labor in American Agriculture. Washington, D.C.: U.S. Government Printing Office, 1951.

Miraldi, Robert. "The Journalism of David Graham Phillips." Ph.D. diss., New York University, 1985.

———. "Fictional Techniques in the Journalism of David Graham Phillips." *American Journalism* 4 (1987):181–90.

———. "The Journalism of David Graham Phillips." *Journalism Quarterly* 63 (Spring 1988):83–88.

———. "Muckraking and Objectivity: John L. Hess and the Nursing Home Scandal." *Journalism Monographs* 115 (August 1989).

Moore, Truman. *The Slaves We Rent.* New York, 1965.

Moreland Act Commission, *Political Influence and Political Accountability: One Foot in the Door.* New York, 1975.

Moreland Act Commission, *Regulating Nursing Home Care: The Paper Tigers and Reimbursement of Nursing Home Costs: Pruning the Money Tree.* New York, 1976.

Moreland Act Commission, *Long Term Care Regulation: Past Lapses, Future Prospects, A Summary Report*. New York, 1976.

Morrison, Elting S., ed. *Letters of Roosevelt*, Vol. 5. Cambridge, Mass., 1952.

Moss, Frank E., and Val Halamandaris. *Too Old Too Sick Too Bad/Nursing Homes in America*. Germantown, Md., 1977.

Mott, Frank Luther. *American Journalism*. New York, 1941.

Mott, Frank Luther. "The Magazine Called Success." *Journalism Quarterly* 34 (Winter 1957):49–53.

Mowry, George. *The Era of Theodore Roosevelt and the Birth of Modern America, 1900–1912*. New York, 1958.

Murray, Michael. "SEE IT NOW vs. McCarthyism." Ph.D. diss., University of Missouri-Columbia, 1974.

Myrdal, Gunnar. *An American Dilemma: The Negro Problem and American Democracy*. New York, 1944.

Newfield, Jack. *The Education of Jack Newfield*. New York, 1984.

Nimmo, Dan D. *Newsgathering in Washington*. New York, 1964.

Noble, David. *The Paradox of Progressive Thought*. Minneapolis, 1958.

Paley, William S. *As It Happened: A Memoir*. Garden City, N.Y., 1979.

Paper, Lewis J. *Empire: William S. Paley and the Making of CBS*. New York, 1986.

Parenti, Michael. *Inventing Reality: The Politics of the Mass Media*. New York, 1986.

Patterson, Margaret Jones, and Robert H. Russell. *Behind the Lines: Case Studies in Investigative Reporting*. New York, 1986.

Pearce, Donn. *Dying in the Sun*. New York, 1974.

Persico, Joseph E. *Edward R. Murrow: An American Original*. New York, 1988.

Peterson, Theodore. *Magazines in the Twentieth Century*. Urbana, Ill., 1964.

Phillips, David Graham. *The Master Rogue*. New York, 1903.

———. *The Deluge*. New York, 1905.

———. *The Plum Tree*. Indianapolis, Ind., 1905.

———. *The Light-Fingered Gentry*. New York, 1907.

———. *The Treason of the Senate*. Edited by George E. Mowry and Judson A. Grenier. Chicago, 1964.

Porter, William. *Assault on the Media*. Ann Arbor, Mich., 1976.

Potter, David. *People of Plenty*. New York, 1954.

Powers, Ron. *The Newscasters*. New York, 1977.

Pritchard, Peter. *The Making of McPaper: The Inside Story of USA Today*. Kansas City, Mo., 1987.

Raskin, A. H. "For 500,000, Still Tobacco Road." *New York Times Magazine* (April 24, 1960):14, 128–30.

Reaves, Sheila. "How Radical Were the Muckrakers? Socialist Press Views, 1902–1906." *Journalism Quarterly* 61 (Winter 1984):763–70.

Regier, C. C. *The Era of the Muckrakers*. Chapel Hill, N.C., 1932.

Report to the President on Domestic Migratory Farm Labor. Washington, D.C.: U.S. Government Printing Office, 1960.

Reynolds, Robert D., Jr. "The 1906 Campaign to Sway Muckraking Periodicals." *Journalism Quarterly* 56 (Autumn 1979):513–20, 589.

Rivera, Geraldo. *Willowbrook: A Report on How It Is and Why It Doesn't Have to Be That Way*. New York, 1972.

Rodgers, Paul C. "David Graham Phillips: A Critical Study." Ph.D. diss., Columbia University, 1955.

Rosenberg, Norman L. "The New Law of Political Libel: A Historical Perspective." *Rutgers Law Review* 28 (1982):1141–83.

―――. *Protecting the Best Men: An Interpretive History of the Law of Libel.* Chapel Hill, N.C., 1986.

Rosenthal, Alan. *The Documentary Conscience: A Casebook in Film Making.* Berkeley, Calif., 1980.

Rothman, David J., and Sheila M. Rothman. *The Willowbrook Wars.* New York, 1986.

Russell, Charles Edward. "Trinity: Church of Mystery." *The Broadway Magazine* (April; 1908):1–12.

―――. "A Burglar in the Making." *Everybody's* (June 1908):753–60.

―――. "The Tenements of Trinity Church." *Everybody's* (July 1908):47–57.

―――. "Trinity's Tenements—The Public's Business." *Everybody's* (February 1909):278–79.

―――. "The Associated Press and Calumet." *Pearson's* (January 1941):437–47.

―――. "The Magazine Soft Pedal." *Pearson's* (February 1914):179–89.

―――. "The Keeping of the Kept Press." *Pearson's* (May 1914):33–43.

―――. *Bare Hands and Stone Walls/Some Recollections of a Side-Line Reformer.* New York, 1933.

Salisbury, Harrison. "Mr. *New York Times.*" *Esquire* (January 1980):26–37.

―――. *A Time for Change.* New York, 1988.

Schiller, Dan. *Objectivity and the News.* Philadelphia, 1981.

Schiller, Herbert. *The Mind Managers.* Boston, 1973.

Schudson, Michael. *Discovering the News.* New York, 1978.

―――. "Making Journalism Safe for Democracy." *The Quill* (November 1984):24–30.

Semonche, John. "The American Magazine of 1906–15: Principle vs. Profit." *Journalism Quarterly* 40 (Winter 1963):39–40.

―――. "Theodore Roosevelt's 'Muckrake Speech': A Reassessment." *Mid-America* 46 (April 1964):114–25.

―――. *Ray Stannard Baker: A Quest for Democracy in Modern America, 1870–1918.* Chapel Hill, N.C., 1969.

Semple, Robert B., Jr. "The Necessity of Conventional Journalism: A Blend of the Old and the New." In *Liberating the Media: The New Journalism,* edited by Charles C. Flippen. Washington, D.C., 1974.

Shapiro, Herbert, ed. *The Muckrakers and American Society.* Boston, 1968.

Shotwell, Louisa R. *The Harvesters: The Story of the Migrant People.* New York, 1979.

Siebert, Fred S., Theodore Peterson, and Wilbur Schramm. *Four Theories of the Press.* Urbana, Ill., 1956.

Sinclair, Upton. *The Brass Check.* Pasadena, Calif., 1919.

―――. *The Jungle,* New York, 1981.

Sloan, William David. "Scurrility and the Party Press, 1789–1816." *American Journalism* 5 (1988):97–112.

Smith, Anthony. *Goodbye Gutenberg.* New York, 1980.

————. "Is Objectivity Obsolete?" *Columbia Journalism Review* (May/June 1980):61–65.

Smolla, Rodney. *Suing the Press.* New York, 1986.

Sperber, A. M. *Murrow: His Life and Times.* New York, 1986.

Stallings, Frank L. "David Graham Phillips: A Critical Bibliography of Secondary Comment." *American Literary Realism* 6 (Winter 1970):1–35.

Stallman, R. W. *Stephen Crane: A Biography.* New York, 1968.

Steffens, Lincoln. *The Struggle for Self Government.* New York, 1906.

————. "What the Matter Is in America and What to Do about It." *Everybody's* (June 1908):723–727.

————. *The Autobiography of Lincoln Steffens.* New York, 1931.

————. *The Shame of the Cities.* New York, 1957.

Stein, Harry H. "American Muckrakers and Muckraking: The 50-Year Scholarship." *Journalism Quarterly* 56 (Spring 1979):9–17.

Steinberg, Salme. *Reformer in the Marketplace: Edward W. Bok and the Ladies Home Journal.* Baton Rouge, La., 1979.

Stephens, Mitchell. *A History of News: From the Drum to the Satellite.* New York, 1988.

Stevens, Robert, and Rosemary Stevens. *Welfare Medicine in America: A Case Study of Medicaid.* New York, 1974.

Strentz, Herbert. *News Reporters and News Sources.* Ames, Iowa, 1978.

Sullivan, Mark. *The Education of an American.* New York, 1938.

Swados, Harvey, ed. *Years of Conscience: The Muckrakers.* New York, 1962.

Swain, Bruce M. *Reporters' Ethics.* Ames, Iowa, 1978.

Swanberg, W. A. *Citizen Hearst.* New York, 1961.

————. *Pulitzer.* New York, 1967.

Talese, Gay. *The Kingdom and the Power.* New York, 1966.

————. *Fame and Obscurity.* New York, 1970.

Tarbell, Ida. *The History of Standard Oil.* New York, 1904.

————. *All in a Day's Work.* New York, 1939.

Tebbel, John. *George Horace Lorimer and the Saturday Evening Post.* Garden City, N.Y., 1948.

————. *The Life and Good Times of William Randolph Hearst.* New York, 1952.

————. *The American Magazine: A Compact History.* New York, 1969.

Tompkins, Mary E. *Ida E. Tarbell.* Boston, 1974.

Tuchman, Gaye. "Objectivity as Strategic Ritual: An Examination of Newspaperman's Notions of Objectivity." *American Journal of Sociology* 77, 4 (January 1972):660–79.

————. *Making News: A Study in the Construction of Reality.* New York, 1978.

Turner, John Kibbee. *Barbarous Mexico.* Chicago, 1910.

Unger, Irwin, and Debi Unger. *The Vulnerable Years.* New York, 1978.

Victor, Daniel. "The Muckrakers and the Dandy: The Conflicting Personae of David Graham Phillips." Ph.D. diss., Claremont Graduate School, 1976.

Vladeck, Bruce. *Unloving Care: The Nursing Home Tragedy.* New York, 1980.

Wakefield, Dan. *Between the Lines: A Reporter's Personal Journey through Public Events.* Boston, 1956.

Wasserstrom, Robert, and Richard Wiles. *Field Duty: U.S. Farmworkers and Pesticide Safety*. Washington, D.C.: World Resources Institute, 1985.

Weber, Ronald, ed. *The Reporter as Artist*. New York, 1974.

Weinberg, Arthur, and Lila Weinberg., eds. *The Muckrakers*. New York, 1961.

Weinstein, James. *The Corporate Ideal in the Liberal State, 1900–1918*. Boston, 1968.

Whalen, Charles W. *Your Right to Know*. New York, 1973:

White, William Allen. *Autobiography*. New York, 1946.

Wiebe, Robert. *The Search for Order, 1877–1920*. New York, 1960.

Winfield, Betty Houchins and Lois B. DeFleur, eds. *Edward R. Murrow Heritage: Challenge for the Future*. Ames, Iowa, 1986.

Winter, Ella and Granville Hicks, eds. *The Letters of Lincoln Steffens V. 1*. Westport, Conn., 1974.

Wright, Dale. *They Harvest Despair*. Boston, 1965.

Yaeger, Murray R. "An Analysis of Edward R. Murrow's 'See It Now' Program." Ph.D. diss., State University of Iowa, 1956.

Yoder, Jon A. *Upton Sinclair*. New York, 1975.

Young, James H. *The Toadstool Millionaires*. Princeton, N.J., 1961.

Zimmerman, Diana. "America's Nomads." *Migration Today* 9 (1981):24–32.

Index

About the Author

ROBERT MIRALDI is Associate Professor of Journalism at SUNY, New Paltz, and a former reporter with the *Staten Island Advance*. His previously published articles include "Objectivity and the New Muckraking: John L. Hess and the Nursing Home Scandal," "Scaring Off the Muckrakers with the Threat of Libel," and "Fictional Techniques in the Journalism of David Graham Phillips."